BIG RON
A Different Ball Game

BIG RON
A Different Ball Game

A Football Memoir by Ron Atkinson

ANDRE DEUTSCH

First published in 1998 by
André Deutsch Limited
76 Dean Street
London WIV 5HA
www.vci.co.uk

André Deutsch is a VCI plc company

1 3 5 7 9 10 8 6 4 2

Jacket photographs from Empics
Jacket design by Rob Kelland
Plate section design by Design 23

Typeset by Derek Doyle & Associates
Mold, Flintshire
Printed and bound by Butler and Tanner Ltd,
Frome and London

A catalogue record for this book is available from the British Library

ISBN 0 233 99217 0

DEDICATION TO MY DAD

I have dedicated this book to a man who could walk into most high-profile football clubs with a nod and a wink. My dad, Fred. He died during my period at Coventry, following a short illness, on 22 May 1996. Almost to the end, even at eighty-two, he was football crazy. Without his generous advice – it was my old man who urged me into the management business at Kettering – and the support of my mother, Nancy, not a single page of my memoirs could have been written. Fred, an all-round sportsman himself, spent his working life as a toolmaker. But I always suspected that was his hobby. Football was his real business. He loved it with a passion and was welcomed with open arms at any Premiership club in the land. When they showed me the door at Aston Villa, Fred was still guaranteed his boardroom invite. 'Why shouldn't I go?' he asked. 'They sacked you, not me.' And, without batting an eyelid, he added: 'You shouldn't blame Brian Little and don't criticize him either. He deserves a fair crack to prove himself.' Now that's what I call family support!

Still, he was a marvellous chap, sadly missed about the scene, and mourned by the great and the good within our game.

ACKNOWLEDGEMENTS

I would like to acknowledge the help and collaboration of Peter Fitton, the *Sun*'s Chief Northern Sportswriter, in the drafting and writing of this book. I have known Peter for around twenty years. Outside business hours, he spends his time involved in his other great passions of cricket, golf and sailing.

CONTENTS

Chapter One   Inside The Red Empire   1

Chapter Two   Captain Marvel   19

Chapter Three   Having A Go   49

Chapter Four   The Three Degrees   59

Chapter Five   The Hell-For-Leather Glory Years   79

Chapter Six   The Menace Within   94

Chapter Seven   Mad Max   102

Chapter Eight   Wheeling And Dealing   118

Chapter Nine   The Dream Turns Deadly   137

Chapter Ten   The Money Men   167

Chapter Eleven   People I Wouldn't Go On

                       Holiday With   190

Chapter Twelve   Maestros, Mentors And Movers   200

Chapter Thirteen   Dream Team   225

Chapter Fourteen   Dream On   235

CHAPTER ONE

Inside The Red Empire

Manchester United has long filled our minds as the club of magic and make believe. Yes, the ultimate in football fantasy, we are led to believe, where both players and managers fulfil and realize their otherwise unreachable dreams. And it *can* be all of that. For me, though, it was different. Not for a single moment did I ever think of myself as a United manager destined to be in control for ten years, twenty years, or even for life. Nor did I ever want to. I had other plans, different ambitions. I was never cut out to be the dynasty-type of manager; an ambition that always seemed close to the heart of my successor, Alex Ferguson. That particular notion wasn't ever a consideration on my professional agenda. Not my style, to be completely honest. But the date my football life changed so instantly at Britain's most famously élite club will, all the same, never be removed from my memory: Thursday, 6 November 1986, at dead-on 10.09 a.m. It was the exact time my car phone rang out as I motored in for another day more involved in a sporting privilege than merely earning a living. On the line was Pauline Temple, secretary to Martin Edwards. 'Ron,' she said simply, 'could you pop in to the ground? The chairman wants to see you.' And then, more insistently, she added: 'Right away, please!' I swung over the wheel of the big Merc and, instead of nosing past the Cheetham Hill shopping precincts of Manchester, little more than a couple of miles from United's Cliff training ground, I headed through the city for Old Trafford. Already the brainwaves were crashing against my skull. I tried to figure why Martin should need to see me with such haste. Talk about being caught wrong-footed and on the blindside as well.

But while my mind was racing through all kinds of options, I ignored what should have been blindingly obvious. The combination of a world-famous face and two highly influential words suspiciously became linked to my sudden departure: Bobby Charlton. He was hardly a soulmate and was, most certainly, a relentless boardroom adversary in my final year at United. Sir Robert, as he is now, was, as far as I am concerned, an inevitable part of that sacking day, even though he was nowhere to be seen. I recalled too a grapevine whisper from football's always alert inner circle that had reached my ears some months earlier at the World Cup in Mexico. The warning couldn't have been plainer or more prophetic. Alex Ferguson, then in caretaker charge of Scotland and firmly in the manager's chair at Aberdeen, had already been tapped for my job. That information proved subsequently to be startlingly correct. You might say a clear case of red man's shoes! But more about the significant dabblings of soccer knight Bob and a very sheepish Fergie a little later in the discussions of how and why a totally unexpected P45 suddenly took priority over 4-4-2.

Back, for now, to the morning when most experts would consider I was dumped from the most enviable job in British football. It had, in fairness, been an immense and demandingly exciting experience for me, disturbed by just a few disjointed weeks of poor form, crucial injuries, and a less than impressive League position at the start of the 1986–87 season. Nothing, I felt at the time, that couldn't be swiftly countered by another move, like the season before, to the top of the table by Christmas. Until, just forty-eight hours before I entered the unemployment statistics, we got whupped 4–1, courtesy of a seventeen-year-old called Matthew Le Tissier I might add, in a League Cup replay against Southampton at the Dell. Even so, as I nursed the car on to the Old Trafford forecourt, it never entered my head that I might be in any sort of jeopardy. Not, that is, until out of the corner of my eye I spotted my No. 2, Mick Brown. 'What's going on, Ron? The chairman has just called me over to see him.' Mick was clearly very concerned. For the first time so was I. 'Tell you what, Mick, if those boots of mine aren't laid out ready for the five-a-side this morning, I can promise you one thing: we won't be getting those six-year contract extensions.' A touch of black humour maybe, but if the bossman has raised the fateful finger there is little you can do to avert the inevitable. Except square up to it.

In I went to see Martin. Alongside him was Maurice Watkins, the club's solicitor and a United director. Business was very brief in the execution chamber that morning, I can assure you. They told me my contract, which still had two years to run, was terminated immediately. They clearly begged a response. With their decision irrevocable, I merely explained that I would leave all the arguments on financial settlements to my my legal people. They nodded agreement. And then, as my last request, I asked: 'Okay is it, Chairman, if I still use the indoor gym on Friday nights? Get the old internationals in for the usual seven-a-side. That all right?' Martin could barely believe it. He seemed to be taken aback. Here was I, having just been sacked by the biggest club in the land, and all I wanted was free hire of their facilities for a kick-about team. I smiled when I made the request, but I was being serious. And fatalistic. If they had decided I was history, that was it. Nothing I could do to change fate at that stage. It wasn't meant to be flippant, or insulting, but just maybe my own self-protective reaction to a decision I had not seen looming around the corner. Hand on heart, it was all a total surprise. Two or three months of dodgy results, nothing more, and here I was out on the street.

There were genuine reasons for the minor crisis that, because of United's position under the unrelenting focus of the media, ended up being portrayed as a national fiasco. Five of my most productive, essential and senior players – Bryan Robson, Norman Whiteside, Arthur Albiston, Gary Bailey and Gordon Strachan – had returned from the World Cup to face operations. Hardly the most encouraging medical news before the launch of a new campaign to resolve, even remedy, the increasingly annoying failure of the season before. That had been, of course, when United had flexed their muscles and their flair and appeared to be on the championship march again only to be struck down by the old title curse. It had stretched across two decades and apparently wasn't going to be conquered too easily. Remember it? Ten points clear in the autumn of '85. On cruise control, they said. All over before Christmas, they chorused. Well, it wasn't. And I, for one, had never thought it would be. Towards the end of that forlorn and frustrating season, we slipped disastrously into fourth spot at the finishing post. Another dream destroyed.

Our last hope of revival was killed off, I remember, down at QPR as the run-in quickened and gained more drama. At Loftus Road, on that vital spring day, I did offer to pack my bags and go. Voluntarily. Maybe it was a personal decision stirred by little more than an emotional reaction, the basic instinct that if so little had been achieved after so much promise, possibly a sacrifice to the future must be made. And that was to be me. Within an hour of the defeat at Rangers, I turned to Martin Edwards and saw his

4

jaw drop as I said: 'I'm just wondering whether this might just be the time for me to stand down. To get out of town for everybody's sake.' Quietly we discussed the implications. It remained a secret between us. Just a nod and a wink, that we would wait until the summer was over and the troops were back in camp. It was a time for studious reflection, not quickfire reaction. And so the issue was shelved.

The question that occupied my mind in those closing months was a fairly obvious one: I had been at United for five years, mostly with the same players, skilled and well-equipped enough to be champions, and yet we had tripped up and failed yet again. Was it time to go? Was the target unreachable and inevitably beyond all of us ? No, the issue was never the notion of a collective complacency stifling the great challenge, but whether it needed a new driving force to add another dynamic. In truth, another manager. In the end, I reported back and told the chairman: 'I am ready to give it another crack. This is it. Let's have one more go.' Less than five months later, I was gone, a management statistic, much like a few others who had tried to inherit Sir Matt Busby's empire.

I can't even now, with the benefit of ten years' hindsight, decide whether I planted the seeds of my own downfall in that late-season confessional with Martin Edwards. The answer to that will probably lie for ever within United's inner sanctum. I can only supply my version of events and point out the personalities I will always believe had a decisive input in the twists and turns of my United career.

In that highly significant summer of 1986 I was able to fire the spirit and my own footballing ambitions in a different way. At the Mexico mundial in 1986, television commitments allowed me to download, temporarily at least, the personal pressures of my existence with United. Witnessing the achievements of the global greats was inspirational therapy. Club priorities could be shelved and confronted a little later, I thought. At least, I felt contented that way until Lawrie McMenemy, also on the World Cup beat as a TV pundit, revealed that he had heard that Alex Ferguson had already been tapped for my job. Alex was, of course, in Mexico with Scotland, following the tragic death of Jock Stein in the dugout as his nation qualified for the finals. Alex, also, I am not too niggardly to admit, was doing a more than useful job with Aberdeen. Certainly he was a handy candidate for any English club to have in the frame as a very well qualified replacement. Bobby Charlton was over in Mexico, both in his capacity as a United director and as a television commentator for the BBC. I had my suspicions then, and I have not had any reason to change my opinion, that the approach was made by him.

Back on the domestic beat, I headed across the border to see Celtic play the outstanding Dynamo Kiev, a team blessed with nine of the Soviet national side of the time. In Glasgow before the big game, I bumped into Alex Ferguson. Now, Alex and me had always been fairly close. We got on fine, always enjoyed a joke and a bit of banter, and regularly talked to each other on the telephone. If there was any manager in Scotland in that period I regarded as a pal, it was Fergie. But there, he could barely force himself to say hello. He was very sheepish, more distant than I had ever known him, and really didn't want to look me in the eye. Gordon Strachan was with me at the time and couldn't understand the stand-off I got from Fergie. I could. And I had a quiet chuckle at his obvious discomfort. Why was Fergie so uneasy? Let's say that he knew that I knew what we both knew was a pending item for the in-tray at Old Trafford. His arrival.

The warning signs had been there even earlier, at my first

United board meeting after Mexico. As soon as I broached the planned signing of England's centre-back Terry Butcher, who had been earmarked as our priority transfer target for months, Bobby put a fairly hefty boot solidly through the idea. When Mark Hughes had been reluctantly traded to Barcelona for £2 million, the understanding was that the money from the deal would be stashed to one side, primarily to secure the signing of Butcher and, we all hoped, the capture of Kerry Dixon as Sparky's quality replacement. Later we were priced out of that second objective. But, yes, Butcher was always cast as our No. 1 priority. So I was understandably staggered, bemused in fact, when press reports trickled out that United just hadn't the cash to afford him. I didn't pay the speculation too much attention. Already Butcher, also high on the list of priorities at Glasgow Rangers, where he eventually enjoyed a fine career, was well sounded out. We had spoken in Mexico and there was a loose agreement on what he wanted to do. The night before the board meeting when my strategy was shot down, Terry – rooming with Gordon Strachan – called me from Pasadena where he was involved with a World Eleven. At the time Rangers were pressing him to put pen to paper. He was buying time, holding out for the outcome he still wanted at that stage: to join us at Old Trafford. He told me he was 'desperate' for the move. My answer . . . 'No sweat, Terry, we'll sort it.'

I went to confront the directors on the subject . . . and the roof fell in. 'Gentlemen,' I said during the manager's report, 'let me raise the long-standing issue of the signing of Terry Butcher.' Immediately, before the final word had barely dropped from my lips, Bobby Charlton was in. He was a sharp mover on the park, but this time he was lightning. In fairly frank language, he voiced the opinion that Butcher was no better than the first-team defenders already within United's squad. I wasn't having that for a second. I replied: 'I don't care who you have as the manager of this football club, whether it's Terry Venables, Graham Taylor, Alex Ferguson or me, I don't think any of us would be too unhappy to have Butcher alongside Paul McGrath for the next five years at the heart of this defence.' I also added a rider: 'He might just have been good enough, Bobby, to have kept Preston up when you were briefly there as manager.' Maybe it wasn't the most diplomatic comment to make friends and influence people, but the nitpicking had got to me by then. The words ricocheted around the room like a sniper's bullet.

Martin Edwards very quickly stepped in to cool the discussion. 'There is no argument,' volunteered the chairman very sensibly, 'that Butcher is a good enough player for United. The fundamental problem is that we haven't got the money to buy him at this moment.' Naturally, I countered with the Hughes transfer fee which should have been set aside as the Butcher bankroll. Martin responded that the money had already been committed to the development of the club's newly planned soccer museum. Being cruel, you might suggest the nation's most powerful club was investing in the past, not the future. Actually, being serious, I see that museum now as part of the 'bigness' of United. But I still insist the financial constraints should not have blocked the Butcher transaction. He would have helped considerably, too, in seeing us safely through the team problems that very rapidly cost me my job.

In my judgement, United needed strengthening players in certain positions. Liverpool, arguably the finest club team I had ever applauded during the seventies and eighties, always rigidly maintained their policy for English supremacy: they invested in a steady flow of reinforcements when they were on top and were recognized as *the* footballing power in the land. It was the secret that kept them in control for so long. The counter charge was that, when United's highly gifted and successful sixties team started to break up, nothing happened. It led to a very dangerous downward spiral and I know that George Best, for one, has always subscribed to the view that United's failure to build on their period of strength was a fatal flaw that handicapped the club for many years. Butcher, I would submit, was part of that failure. At £750,000, at the time, he was admittedly an expensive acquisition, but also a very sound and proven investment. The irony is that close confidants at United have told me that, apparently, when Alex first took over my position, he said: 'I cannot believe a club of this stature allowed Terry Butcher to sign for Rangers.' And it was pointed out to Fergie, very quickly and from within his own new dressing room, that that costly decision was reached within the boardroom and not at management level.

I have never ceased to be surprised at Bobby Charlton's seemingly deliberate and obstructive stand. Long after our little boardroom spat, I have pondered whether it was made as a genuine football judgement, which is the entitlement of any individual, or whether there was an ulterior motive. One undeniable fact is that Bobby's position was a clear indication that his support for me as United's manager had gone. Two important manoeuvres by him, unquestionably pushed my situation at the club to the critical stage. One, of course, was the sounding out of Alex as my swiftly installed successor. The second, due partly to Bobby's less than sympathetic attitude, was that Butcher was removed from my list of significant player targets.

At the time of my appointment in the summer of 1981, Bobby was no longer a primary figure in the United scene, but I have to confess I was very excited at the prospect of working with a man who, as a player, had rightly earned himself global appreciation and respect. At the time, the only thing I really knew about Bobby was his on-field role as a truly magnificent performer. The first inkling that there was another side to one of the nation's greatest sporting heroes came when he turned up to play in an Old Trafford testimonial for Sammy McIlroy. One of Bobby's United contemporaries, a well known England international, tugged at my sleeve and muttered: 'Bloody hell, what have we done to deserve him around here . . . he's just a moaning, groaning so and so.' I was taken aback, yet, apparently, Bobby's reputation as a grizzlin' old misery was legendary. So much for the public image!

When Bobby first joined the board at United, by and large, our relationship was, well, okay. There wasn't any animosity between the pair of us, but let me just say I don't think we would have chosen to go on holiday together. Mind you, it's strange how many people who really know Bobby quite candidly feel the same way. I would much prefer to make any trip with his brother Jack, and I reckon it's safe to suggest that feeling is mutual. It's not exactly a secret within the game that Bobby and Jack don't get on either. That first dawned on me at the final of the '92 European Championships in Sweden.

I was on a TV assignment, up on the stadium gantry with a galaxy of football's famous names. Franz Beckenbauer, Karl-Heinz Rummenigge, Michel Platini and, of course, Bob and big Jack. At no time, even though they were merely feet apart, did the Charlton brothers acknowledge or even look at each other. I found it all a bit bizarre, so later I quizzed my favourite Charlton about the family silence. 'Don't worry,' Jack informed me, 'we just don't get on. Our kid was a much better player than me, but I am a much better bloke.' Let me raise my hand immediately to second that. It ain't even an argument.

Apart from the Butcher Affair though, I only ever had one

other real one-on-one confrontation with Bobby. It was again on what I considered a serious football matter. It revolved around Bobby's summer soccer school, which he ran during my time at United for kids from all over the country during their school holidays. The word came to me that Bobby seemed to be trying to promote his own coaches over my club staff who were also deeply involved in running United's school of excellence. My coaches got the impression that there was interference. That I wasn't prepared to tolerate and I made my view directly and very forcibly clear. Now whether that upset Bobby I don't know. It happened roughly twelve months before I finally went through the exit door out of United management.

I might, I now accept, have trodden on Bobby's toes when I made it transparently clear I didn't want his men around. I had Eric Harrison, now proven as arguably the most successful youth coach of all time with the development of Beckham, Butt, Scholes and the Nevilles, running that side of the show. I was very confident in Eric's ability to educate the kids in the craft of the game, and I didn't want him being bothered by a bunch of schoolteachers with big ideas, whether they were there under Bobby's patronage or not. It might, I accept, have been an issue that grew in the great man's mind. Better ask him, really. When I did have any meaningful conversation with Bobby, it was only to discover his unexpected philosophy on the game. I learned he enjoyed and admired the approach of Graham Taylor's Watford and Sheffield Wednesday, under the guidance of Howard Wilkinson at the time, both noted for their long-ball emphasis. Not quite what you would expect from a player of Charlton's calibre, who was always so comfortable an exponent of the passing game.

In reality, whether on the football side or socially, I did not have too much in common with Bobby. I didn't mix with him at all outside United. The senior players, too, were never all that close to him. At times, they were quite disparaging in the mickey-taking way that is the favourite pastime of most footballers. Coming back from a game at Wembley, I remember them taunting Bobby as he sat at the the front of the team bus with the other directors. 'Bobb-ee, Bobb-ee, give us a smile,' they sang out until it was almost embarrassing. No question, almost to a man they regarded him as a dour, very distant individual. For some reason this famous product of the Charlton sporting family has never been the most popular guy in the game.

It's strange how sometimes people have a certain image of a well-known public figure which changes dramatically when they finally get to see them in close-up. Bobby did disappoint me as a bloke, and not just because he was clearly not exactly in my corner at United. But that never stopped my professional admiration for him as a player. All the same, I don't think, in all honesty, he would be welcomed into too many Happy Hours. He would probably be on the very same invitation list as that other soul of wise-cracking fun and well-known jollity in our game, Ron Saunders.

Alex, on the other hand, was always Bobby's man and they seemed very close confederates, particularly during the early phase of Fergie's management. But I haven't lost any sleep about the shenanigans surrounding my premature departure. I don't blame Alex one little bit. It's all part of the management game. Somebody is inevitably waiting to nick your boots in this business, whether as a player or a manager. If I was ever chairman of a club, I, too, would operate by the same unwritten rule: always have a reserve in waiting to take over, just in case. And I'm not going to deceive the world that the tapping routine has not gone on in my case. I have taken several jobs during the last twenty-five years thanks to a similar er, shall we say, invitation. It happens, it's soccer's jungle law if you like.

Once my sacking was confirmed, it didn't take long for the back-up system to be put into operation. I'm told on very good authority that within an hour of Martin delivering the dreaded words, he and Maurice Watkins left in a private jet for Aberdeen and the formalities with Fergie and his Scottish employers. Even as I arrived back at the Cliff, to summon the senior players to my office and inform them of what had happened, United's negotiating contingent were in the air and laying preparations for the next boss. The following morning, Alex was squarely positioned in my barely vacant chair and meeting the media world. As for myself, it was a case of a bit of tidying up. I called the people who needed to know, family and close friends, fellow travellers in the game, shared a quiet drink with the United squad and then headed off home for what should have been a consolation gathering of old mates and odds and sods. Instead it turned into an all-night rave with more than a hundred people packed into the house. It lasted until about five o'clock the following morning. Just as dawn was breaking I got a panic call from Gordon Strachan. He had been at our place with his wife Leslie, but had left a couple of hours before. 'Ron,' he said urgently, 'I'm outside a football ground and don't know where I am. It could be Maine Road.' It turned out to be Elland Road, a prophetic destination when you remember where Strach finished up after being sold by Fergie. Apparently, the pair of them had taken the wrong carriageway on the motorway and finished up in Yorkshire instead of Cheshire where the Strachans lived at the time.

Quite a few of the United players were aggrieved and more than a little upset when I was handed my cards. Apart from Gordon, the skipper, Bryan Robson turned up with Norman Whiteside at my impromptu sacking party. But, even at this late stage, I would like to stress that it was never a case of Atkinson's

final revenge: an act of soccer sabotage with United's top rank-
ing players before the Saturday game. This big-time bunch were
all out of contention at the time, unable to turn out because of
injury. (Amazingly, in the middle of that crazy night when the
telephone never stopped ringing, I got a call from a middle-man
for Atletico Madrid. They wanted to know if I would be interested in taking over as coach at the end of that season. So, with
champagne glass in hand and within eighteen hours of getting
the boot, I was back in the job market. But more of that later.)

I have always held the conviction that if certain delicate
matters concerning my future had been left in the hands of
Martin Edwards, I would have been given more recovery time at
United. Even when he was saying farewell, the impression was
that he had been pressured into the decision to sack me by
boardroom arm-twisting. Certainly I harbour no bitterness
towards Martin. He has my utmost respect and even now I
wouldn't change my view that there is no better club chairman
in the game. He was always extremely supportive to me, an
outstanding professional colleague as well as a good friend.
Later, Martin was to prove outstandingly supportive to Alex.

Let's not mince words, old Fergie had a pretty torrid experience during the first four years of his United management. There
has always been speculation that Mark Robins' famous FA Cup
goal at Nottingham Forest in 1990 was the special finish that
saved his job. Whether that is true no one will ever know, but I
believe that if during Fergie's crisis a suitable replacement candidate had been around the board would have exerted pressure
again. It is to Martin's credit that he stood squarely behind the
manager at that time. What has subsequently happened, with
United now dominant in our domestic game and also a very
powerful force in Europe, has justified that act of faith. No question about it, Fergie's championship and cup achievements

throughout the last decade have been nothing short of phenomenal.

I have never felt, in all modesty, that my own record was too bad either. I had five years in charge, spent a few quid and did enough shrewd business to get most of it back, and left with the best United record, at that time, since the great Sir Matt Busby. We never finished below the top four in the First Division, won two FA Cups and lost in the League Cup Final. And, what's more, during that period United were invloved every year in European competition, something that had never been achieved since Sir Matt's days. In the early eighties, when Liverpool were blessed with the capacity to boss most teams around, we sorted them out more often than not. We also did it with a certain amount of football panache and style, living up to United's finest traditions. So it wasn't all so bad, was it?

In the managerial world, most would accept United as not only the major club but the biggest prize for any ambitious managerial candidate. The same informed opinion is also likely to emphasize that once you leave United, no matter the circumstances, you are going at least one rung down the ladder to a lesser existence. I have never once subscribed to that widely declared argument. In all honesty, I can affirm that it was in no way my wish to spend the rest of my management lifespan with United, for all their glamour, mystique and attraction. No, it was very definitely not for me having a commitment that I wanted to stretch to ten, fifteen or even twenty years. Sure, I can understand Alex being in there now, his tenth anniversary in control already celebrated, and to be talking of United as his football destiny; maybe even the creation of a dynasty where he develops and grooms the next man to take charge. And, in considering that as an option, I do concede that my ambitions might have been very different if I had arrived at Old Trafford a little later on in my own career curve. But, in those very enlightening learning years with United, I still cherished another dream: the long-needed fulfilment of running a high-profile club in foreign football.

The irony is that it might have been realized, at least eighteen months before I was dismissed by United, if Bobby Robson had not inadvertently put his foot in it. The deep conviction that I could do well abroad had always been part of my personal make-up and, long before the well-documented approach from Barcelona, other lesser-known outfits in various countries had made overtures. But the one from Spain clearly had to be the great temptation, no matter where you could earn your keep. The ball started to roll just before the climax to United's 83–84 season and shortly after we had knocked the fabulous Barça out of the European Cupwinners' Cup. Next up, at the semi-final stage, we went the same way courtesy of Juventus. And at that moment, I recall, the feelers first started to come my way. My answer, discreetly passed along the grapevine, was simple: 'Sure, I'm ready to talk; just name the place.' I met the Spanish delegation at a London hotel. I confirmed that if everything regarding my United contract could be resolved with them, of course, I would be very willing to move to Barcelona. To be frank, apart from the clearly exciting professional opportunity, it offered the perfect escape route from the domestic upheaval that was then brewing in my private life. I could have gone, closed a page, and been spared so much hassle from the news boys as my first marriage broke up and my second, with Maggie, started. Just let me make the career jump, I thought at the time, and let me get the hell out of it. Oh, by the way, there was also the small consideration that in Spain my United salary would just about have quadrupled.

During the initial discussion the only stumbling point was that Barça wanted me to join them on a two-year contract, which is the usual practice abroad; I countered that proposal with a demand for an extra year. We broke up without any agreement, but I've always felt it was a negotiating point that could easily have been resolved. Then, without my knowledge, and as I awaited more talks, events took another twist. Bobby Robson, a long-standing friend of the most influential men within the Barcelona hierarchy, was asked for his opinion about my appointment. Apparently, without any malicious motive and with the best possible intentions, he told the Spaniards something along the lines: 'I don't think Ron would ever want to leave United. I suspect he is using this to secure his position in Manchester and maybe wants it as a lever for a new contract.' At the time, I was mystified why the contact with Spain suddenly petered out. The next I knew of the whole affair was when Terry Venables landed the job, ironically enough recommended by my old mate Robbo, when the Spaniards asked him to suss out another candidate if I wasn't available.

Hey, look, I have always totally accepted there was nothing devious intended by the England manager when he was consulted. His had been a completely frank and honest assessment. What he wasn't to know was my long-held desire to manage abroad and also the complicated domestic problems that made it even more urgent that I should get out of England. Not many months later, once again during the Mexico World Cup and after my marriage was officially confirmed as finished, Robbo quietly confided in a mutual friend: 'Bloody hell, I see now that Ron did want to get out of United. I think I made a mistake, didn't I?' But I have no grievance whatsover. He was asked a pointed question and delivered a reply he considered honest.

Roughly around the same period I was also under serious consideration at Spurs. Irving Scholar, then the chairman at Tottenham, wanted me to replace Keith Burkinshaw at White Hart Lane. Funnily enough, Spurs have always been the one London club that I hankered to have a go at managing. If Irving had known that I was unsettled at United, and maybe available too, he would have made an offer. But this was another opportunity that took weeks to surface and, by the time it did, it was too late.

So, with the benefit of hindsight, the wiser course in the climactic weeks of the 84–85 season, with so much uncertainty filling my mind, would have been to have walked out on United before they showed me the door. My indecision cost me two of football's biggest jobs – and also a few more months awaiting the eventual invitation to move abroad.

CHAPTER TWO

Captain Marvel

If the end of my United era was largely unexpected, at least by me, then the beginning was truly bizarre. Shortly after entering my new football domain in Manchester, I became entangled, and that's the best way to describe it, with that highly complex character, Mr Brian Clough. Old Barmpot himself. It happened within days of placing my feet beneath that challenging desk at Old Trafford in June 1981. Naturally enough there was an urgent task to perform: the sussing out of prospective targets with the United board, establishing the financial clout at my disposal and then, of course, the swift move to make signings for the new season. One of the first was a speculative double deal, built around the departure of goalkeeper Gary Bailey and striker Garry Birtles to Nottingham Forest in exchange for the England pair, Peter Shilton and Trevor Francis, bolstered by a cash adjustment. The four-part swop had already been aired when, along with Dennis Roach, the agent for a couple of the players, I was lured into one of the most peculiar, nay, off-the-wall meetings I have ever experienced in what has always been a lunatic game.

The rendezvous was set for the Midland Hotel, Derby, in mid-summer of 1981. I showed early, so did Roach, and we ended up locked in small talk and hanging around in the foyer, waiting for the odd couple to turn up. Out of the corner of my eye, I spotted a car roll up with the pair of them inside. Only Peter Taylor, Cloughie's right hand man, clambered out, skipped up the steps towards us in open-neck shirt and nonchalant as you like, to ask: 'Have you seen my mate around here?' Fortunately, because of having worked in the Midlands area soccer scene for quite a while, I was fully aware of the methods of operation mastered by the deadly duo from Nottingham. So I buttoned the lip and waited. Five minutes later, Brian came bounding in to the foyer. Picture the scene: usual green casual sweater, shorts naturally, and covered squash racket strapped to his back. The Cloughie uniform in fact. He completely ignored my presence, Roach's as well, and headed straight for Taylor without a nod, never mind a word. Then he delivered his famous monologue: 'How are you, old son? Where've you been? What kind of summer have you had?' I thought to myself, 'He must think we are both crackers; I've just seen them in the same car together.' It was Cloughie's attempt at being smart, exploiting his strange notion of some off-putting mind games.

Next a conference was arranged, and dear old Brian waited until everyone was scattered around in various positions before he grabbed the loftiest seat in the place. Then, in the belief he had established the position of power, Clough tried to bully the whole transaction through in his particularly idiosyncratic way. By that stage Bailey was out of the equation. I had worked with him for a few days at United, and rapidly my long-distance assessment had changed. He could do a job for me at Old Trafford, no question whatsoever. Gary was undoubtedly a better performer than I had previously thought. So the deal on the table was a two-way swap: Francis to us, Birtles back to Forest, plus a cash adjustment for the benefit of the men in Nottingham. Because of certain circumstances, the finances couldn't be agreed between us, but during the stalemate, Cloughie still couldn't resist relishing the role of bully. At one moment, he accused me of leaking the potential transfer business to the press – something, I hasten to add, of which I was certainly not the guilty party. I leapt to my feet, loomed over Cloughie, jabbed my finger repeatedly in his chest, and bawled: 'Brian, don't ever accuse me, don't come the old soldier with me, we all know who let that one out of the bag.' Immediately, I lowered my eyes in the direction of Taylor, and amiable old Pete was just lounging back on the settee, chewing on some gum and quietly smiling to himself. Clough backed off and shrugged: 'You're right, old son.' It was my first important battle with Clough and it was one I had to win. It was necessary to establish some sort of pecking order, particularly as I was now manager of United, to demonstrate to one of football's most infamous bullies that we wouldn't be intimidated and pushed around. Eventually, though, the Francis initiative fell by the wayside as the details of the deal became ever more difficult. I did, in fact, have to wait ten more years to recruit one of England's most talented, postwar players. It didn't happen until after I had moved on to Sheffield Wednesday in the early nineties.

In that summer a decade earlier, I considered I didn't have too much chance of landing the highly prized job at United either. Speculation was flying around, of course, following the dismissal of Dave Sexton, but the general understanding was that Lawrie McMenemy was very much the leading runner, to such an extent that he was almost past the post. I actually believed that as well until Frank Worthington, by that time playing for Tampa Bay in the North American League, came up to me in a Florida bar while I was on tour with West Brom. In that typical, Elvis-style drawl, Frank leaned over my shoulder and said: 'I know who is going to get the Manchester United job.' 'Don't we all,' I replied, 'No big secret in that – it's Lawrie.' Frank, who had played a season or two under Mac at Southampton, was blessed with better and more up-to-date info than me: he knew Lawrie had already turned down United. We continued the chat, had a drink or two, he filled me in a bit more, and, naturally, I picked up the waiter's tab!

Shortly afterwards I flew back to England, stayed a couple of nights at home in the Midlands, before I jumped on another plane for Paris to watch Liverpool against Real Madrid in the final of the European Cup. While I was over there, a contact phoned to ask: 'Would you be interested in the United job?' Answer: 'Leave the jokes to Tarbuck, please.' But he was serious and the pay-off line was a definite arrangement for me to make a detour on my journey home for a meeting with Martin Edwards. It took place at the house of an intermediary in Cheshire. Martin tried to interview me, but it quickly turned into a different kind of conversation with me asking most of the questions. Quite early in the meeting, it was apparent the pair of us could get on very well together. I realized we could work together, too. One of the first admissions Martin made was that, as chief executive, he would be at the ground on a daily basis. For me, that was a totally new concept. I didn't want him breathing down my neck all the time and I told him so. Martin never blinked: 'If you don't want to see me, you never will.' And that, with a three-year contract rapidly agreed, was the job done. Apart, of course, from the club car. Martin pointed out that my predecessor, Dave Sexton, had a Rover. 'Well, I've got a dog called Charlie, Mr Chairman, but I thought we were talking cars.' On the spot, he agreed to replace the car I already had, a Mercedes coupé, for a bang, smack, up-to-date model. Mr Bojangles, as they say, was on the road and ready to motor.

With everything seemingly cut and dried, my old club West Brom decided to make a song and dance about my departure. They rattled on about me being tied to them by a four-year contract. What they failed to explain was something even more fundamental. I had only six weeks left to run on that agreement. Furthermore, to quell their public squealing, United agreed to pay compensation of £75,000 to calm the storm. These days that may not sound like heavy loot, but back then it was probably the highest 'bounty' ever handed over in a change of manager. It was hardly an era in which money dominated and fees for the likes of me were a very rare event.

To be honest, my own priority was to focus on the reconstruction of the United team and how much hard cash would be available to help me do it. I was fully aware of the real value of United's first-team squad. Sure, in the closing weeks of the previous season, they had gallantly rallied to the Sexton cause with seven straight wins. But it was all an illusion, camouflage for serious underlying defects. Their influential stars, like Martin Buchan and Lou Macari, were reaching the end of their United careers. To a lesser extent so was Gordon McQueen. And on the day I walked in, Joe Jordan was walking the other way. Off to join AC Milan, after the Scot had opted for contract freedom to test his muscle and method with the best in Italy. The true state of Sexton's side in that period was underlined by the use of Kevin Moran as the supposed ballwinner in the midfield. Now Kevin was never less than a cracking centre-back, a great Gaelic footballer, a top-quality bloke for company, but, do me a favour, midfield ballwinner he wasn't. It was clearly a case of restorative surgery being needed without too much delay, so I was determined to be the personification of action man.

Okay, I might have promised a solid, potentially successful team maybe two years down the line, but, at United of all places,

23

the insistent demand from their supporters is for instant rewards. That shaped my strategy. I drafted a blueprint, examined it with the board, and argued why we had to go in wholesale, aiming for the top players we needed, rather than recruiting them in dribs and drabs. That was agreed. The spending budget was around £3 million, about the price of your average First Division player in these inflated times. And there was a condition. More than half of it had to be dragged back within a limited period. Still, it was a starting point and I knew what I wanted. The first player I actually spoke to officially was Glenn Hoddle. He was out of contract at Tottenham and I came within a whisker of signing him. Eventually England's current manager told me if he didn't get an offer to take his talents abroad, he would be staying with Spurs. He felt that was the right thing to do.

Things started to roll very rapidly in other important directions. Within five minutes of occupying the management chair at United, I had my first caller. It was Mickey Thomas and that, I can vouch for, was a weird, weird experience. I had never noticed before, for a start, that he was such a small guy. Then he started twitching. He was just hyper, crossing his legs, scratching his nose, and fidgeting like a five-year-old. 'Mick, for chrissakes, sit still – you are wearing me out just watching you. And, anyway, what can I do for you?' He blubbered: 'I want a move.' Shake of the head, then the only possible reply: 'Thanks, Mick, I have only been in the building a matter of minutes and you want out. That's really giving me a chance.' He looked back at me: 'I've got to go, boss, I need the money.' Gambling too much, trouble with the missus? 'No, boss, I just spend more than I earn.' I cracked up. 'That, Mick, is as good a way as I know of ending up skint.' Many years would go by before Micky Thomas started making big money. From what I hear it was about half an inch too big and landed him in jail on counterfeit charges!

We managed to get him his move, anyway. I knew Howard Kendall, who had just taken over at Everton, wanted the Welsh international as his wide player. I, on the other hand, thought their fullback, John Gidman, could be useful at United. We decided on the exchange, pending agreement with the players. When I met Gidman I nearly had second thoughts. He was almost as agitated as 'mental' Mickey and, as he kept shooting off to the bathroom, his wife repeatedly explained: 'He hasn't slept all night; he is so nervous about moving to United.' Marvellous! Here was I, swopping one nerve-riddled twitcher for another, when United was the one club in Britain where an even temperament and the ability to withstand immense pressure have always been essential. Still, the deal went ahead and eventually Gidman did a more than useful job for us.

Next, but not in any order of priority, was Frank Stapleton. As I mentioned, I lost Jordan almost in mid-sentence of accepting the United job. I was lucky that in Stapleton, an internationally proven striker, there appeared an equally forceful replacement. His contract with Arsenal had just finished. Another fortunate twist around the bargaining table was that Frank's wife, Chris, happened to be a Lancashire lass. The meeting was fixed for the Haydock Park Hotel, where I spent a few weeks before setting up house initially in Cheshire. Frank arrived with Michael Kennedy, a lawyer and well-recognized adviser for most of football's Irish contingent. We parked ourselves in a hotel room and settled down to the nitty-gritty of personal terms. All of a sudden, there was a knock on the door. Totally unexpected, I have to say, because I believed our meeting to be a complete secret. There, in the doorway, stood Remi Moses, an outstanding young player for me at West Brom. Needless to say his contract had also run out. Gathering my senses in a hurry, and naturally not wanting Stapleton or Kennedy to see who had called, I made my excuses and briefly left them to it. I ushered Remi out of the way, and pressed him: 'What the hell are you doing here?' As I shoved him into my own room, he explained: 'I want to sign for you at Man U.' I told him to watch telly for a couple of hours, keep himself to himself, and I would see about that attractive proposition a little later. (He did, in fact, sign for United in the early weeks of my first season.) Back with Stapleton, matters progressed until we had the outline of a five-year contract roughly in place. Then Michael Kennedy, a shrewd negotiator with a solicitor's mind for detail and an understandable instinct for his client's best interests, stood up. 'Yes, we are very interested, and like what you have offered Frank, but now we must move down the road to meet Peter Robinson at Liverpool.' That was the moment I opted for a calculated gamble. 'That's fine,' I said. 'But if you want talks with Liverpool now, forget about United. Do that and there is no deal in place.' They asked for time to consider and adjourned to their own room. I took the precaution of ordering Mick Brown, my assistant manager, to take up a sentry's position outside their door. 'And don't let either of them leave there tonight.' I was aware of Liverpool's late-entry negotiating manoeuvres. We had lost Mark Lawrenson in a blind-side run by the Mersey club in a very similar set-up during that hectic August of 1981. Once bitten, twice shy, and I could be just as crafty as Bob Paisley and his allies if I had to be. I didn't want to take any risk of Stapleton and his adviser sneaking away to agree a transfer to Anfield. It worked. Frank did sign and was enlisted as a very effective centre-forward for, say, a couple of years.

Another player on my target list at that time was David Armstrong, then of Middlesbrough and later to be such a successful ammunition provider at Southampton. But Boro ended up demanding a slighly higher price than I could afford from my summer budget, because I didn't want to lash out too much of the cash I had earmarked for the big one – the capture of Bryan Robson. But that's a story in itself with so many twists and turns it's better related later . . .

In the event Mark Lawrenson, then a Brighton player, looked a more realistic objective. His club had already declared an interest in two United players, Jimmy Nicholl and Ashley Grimes. The wheeling and dealing, which is a part of the game I have always revelled in, was in full swing. For Lawrenson there was money involved, plus the two players, and it all added up to around £900,000, but more important, it wasn't siphoning off too much of my available hard cash. Also Lawro, a very gifted performer, wouldn't look all that bad, I figured, as I reshaped the back four. In the opening talks with Brighton's manager, Mike Bailey, I was led to understand that Liverpool were also sniffing around. Their negotiators, Paisley, Robinson and the late chairman John Smith, were granted the first crack, with the assurance that nothing conclusive would be agreed until I talked to Lawrenson. Then Bailey called. He wanted to know if Nicholl and Grimes were still available. I smelled a rat and demanded: 'Fine, but when do I get to see Lawro?' There was a hush before he explained that the deal was already done and dusted for Liverpool. I exploded and slammed the phone down with such disgust it must have been heard on the south coast.

So I never did get to Lawrenson. Which, in a peculiar way, was to prove that sometimes fate plays just the right part in anybody's planning. Of course, I was very annoyed at the collapse of the transaction, particularly as during that period the Robson move appeared a complete non-starter. My successor at the Hawthorns, Ronnie Allen, seemed keener on hurling cheap insults in my direction than anything else. He should have been eternally grateful, given the powerful side he inherited from my time at the club, and simply got on with his job. But, no, he kept rattling on about interference in Robson's career. One of the fundamental reasons I was so deflated by the Lawrenson fiasco was that, hand on heart, I did not believe I would sign Robbo either at that stage. Yet, ironically, if I had taken Lawrenson to Old Trafford, the main man probably would not have arrived a few weeks later. The cash might not have been available to cover Robbo's purchase. And, in the final twist, Robson would almost certainly have been destined for Liverpool. While we were pursuing him with great vigour, so were Paisley and company.

So, occasionally, if one door slams you in the face, another has a resplendently uniformed greeter waiting with the nicest welcome of all. That was the Robson deal. And if there is a sporting god, he had to be taking a benevolent look at United's long-term interests during that crucial phase of the club's development. I consider Robbo's acquisition only one way. Sure, in half a lifetime in the game, I have been a fortunate manager to work alongside some exceptionally gifted footballers, many of them magical, world-class talents. Quite a few could well have been a first pick in any team on earth. But Robbo, it goes without saying, is the finest, the greatest, the most rounded and accomplished footballer I have ever been blessed to work with. He was a magnificent technician, superbly aware team player, not a great captain but a good one, and a tremendous driving force in any famous shirt he wore. There has never been a better player with such a combination of ability and heart in the history of our business.

If you are looking for the ultimate tribute to Robbo, there can, to my mind, be no better than the one that came after one of his earliest United matches. It was at Liverpool and he was the formidable spirit that led us to a 2–1 victory. Afterwards I talked to a couple of very wise, if wizened, old soccer characters whom I respect greatly, Frank McLintock and Jimmy Armfield. Both, unequivocally, vowed that Robson had already proved himself to them a better player than the legendary Dave Mackay. I'm not, even now, bold enough to enter that argument, but I do know that Mackay is among the greatest footballers ever to lace boots in Britain. And the very fact that two of his contemporaries, men who actually faced and played with him, were convinced Robson was even better, is a career epitaph not to be eclipsed. That shows the calibre of the man I chased with a greater conviction than any other.

Let me go back to the beginning with Robson. When I first clapped eyes on him at West Brom in 1977, it was with hardly a buzz of excitement. To be precise, I didn't think too much of him. He was just a frizzy-headed Kevin Keegan look-alike, only not as good. The Afro-cut, such a footballing fashion statement of the time, was all they had in common. He wasn't even in the West Brom side. In his early years, they needed to shovel a diet of Guinness and hefty steaks down his throat because they suspected he wasn't big enough to make a real pro. And during my first sightings of Robson in action, I reached the opinion he was quite ordinary. Just as bad, he might have a problem with pace at the very top level of the game. Consequently, he didn't play much in the first team. Then, ironically against Manchester United in an FA Cup replay, I stuck him in at centre-half. He obliterated Joe Jordan – and he was only nineteen. Robson was nothing less than magnificent, a brain-rocking revelation. Personally, I don't think he ever got any better. Don't misunderstand me. That is a compliment, not a niggardly insult. The truth is he reached such a high plane as an immature, inexperienced player and never descended from it. He simply achieved his largely unchallenged status of greatness at a very young age.

Immediately, the Midlands press brigade launched a fervent campaign for Robson's inclusion in England's planning. Ron Greenwood, then the man in charge, scarcely granted him a second look, and that was a surprise to me. As a kid, even in his first season, Robbo was good enough for his country. When you now realize that he collected ninety-odd caps anyway, what might his personal tally have reached had he not been mysteriously ignored at first and then missed something like two and a half years of international football through injury? If you take all that into account, Robson might easily have played for his country at least 150 times.

We were both at West Brom when the first signal that Robson might eventually evolve into one of the massive contributors in United's post-Busby era came, after an early appearance for England. Robbo returned, a matter of a few days spent with the big boys clearly turning his thoughts to greater things, and asked for a transfer. I just burst out laughing. 'Right, who's tapped you? Come clean, Robbo.' Eventually, I prised it out of him that United wanted him. Apparently, he had been having a few discreet words with their players inside the international camp. 'There is only one way, Robbo, you are going there,' I promised him, 'and that's if I am there as the manager. Got it?' Immediately I was appointed manager at Old Trafford I suspected what might happen. I wasn't wrong. The morning the news broke, Robbo was on the blower. He was away on duty with England at the time, preparing for a World Cup qualifier in Hungary. It didn't stop him. 'Remember what you said, boss. If you are definitely going to quit and go there, just keep that promise.' I reassured Robson, of course, that if the move was at all possible, no sweat, he would be at United with me.

He was never anything less, for all the other initial signings, than my number one priority in my early planning of July 1981.

Subsequently, I made the inquiry for him, knowing full well that West Brom would knock me back. They did, time and time again. Mostly the message carrier was their manager, that man Ronnie Allen. I saw a chink in the armour of official resistance, though, despite all the bluster, when he came out with something of an unwise statement. It said, almost word for word I recollect: 'Bryan leaves this club over my dead body – unless the money is right.' Talk about a get-out clause – that had to be the best in football history! In effect, the hidden message, at last, was that Robson could be bought. I kept chipping away.

Suddenly, when it was least expected, we got a call from the Hawthorns. They were involved in Europe, up against Swiss side Zurich Grasshoppers, and the first-leg result left them on the very brink of survival. If they ducked in the return, came the unspoken but subtly transmitted message, we could have Robson next morning. The same night we faced Leeds United at Old Trafford. We won 1–0 but I must concede my train of thought was very much focused on events in the Midlands, rather than what I could watch from our dugout. Within hours, the deal I had waited weeks to complete just took off. Robson and his adviser arrived at the ground early doors. A fee was agreed, covering two players not just one. Remi Moses, of course, was already with us but his valuation was pending, about to be determined by a transfer tribunal. To expedite matters, the clubs agreed on an overall package of £2 million for the pair. Break it down, at £1.5 for Robson and £500,000 for the impressive youngster Moses, and either way it makes very good business. I have always maintained that, barring Moses's desperately unlucky injury record, he would have been a clear favourite to replace Robson at the very heart of the England team. Whatever the truth of that speculation, there was no issue that United now had the fearsome ball-winning ability so necessary for any successfully dominant side. Before they arrived, we had what I always described as a colander midfield – everything went through us. With the pairing of Robson and Moses we possessed an aggressive, solid barrier to match one of the best in that particular art, Graeme Souness at Liverpool.

Robson's acquisition marked the first of the high-finance signings that came to be commonplace in the nineties, the deal done by the men in grey suits. And a full squad of them at that. They huddled in corners, muttering figures and inventing protective clauses on both sides. Robbo and me just scarpered for a beer and a bite of lunch to let them get on with it. When we got back, everything was in place. I grabbed Martin Edwards by the arm, knowing he had just committed himself to the British record signing fee, and said: 'Don't worry a second about this one, Chairman, this one is solid gold.' Quite often in the buying and selling game, you do invest in a risk, never quite certain the way the chips might fall. But Robson was always a better bet than the Co-op dividend. When we lashed out so much for Robson, there were the inevitable headlines screaming outrage at a 'crazy deal'. You know the stuff – that it would lead to football's certain ruin. (Three years later, I recall, when the Italians declared an interest in him – at twice the price I might emphasize – the very same critics wrung their hands claiming it would be a soccer death-wish to sell him.) So much hollering that was mostly hot air.

But one highly respected, nay, totally revered, man made his own protest with dignity, a few quiet words, and an action of honour. Sir Matt Busby, without any public fuss or posturing, resigned over the Robson deal. I have to say that this great figure in United's history was never less than helpful in my time at the club. But over Robbo's arrival he felt it his duty to relinquish his seat on the board. Not, I might hurriedly confirm, because he believed Robson to be an inferior player, or unnecessary in United's planning. Matt's objection, based on his very strong principles, was over the cost. He just couldn't accept the explosion in fees. Remember, this is a manager who had handled the greats like Duncan Edwards, Eddie Coleman, Tommy Taylor, Roger Byrne, apart from the legendary trinity of Law, Best and Charlton. He didn't, for a single moment, question Robson's talent or value as a player of importance in the club's future. The two of them did develop into quite firm friends, the elder statesman and the vibrant young skipper were often seen in close conversations around the ground. What Matt did was what he believed was right. He refused to bow the knee to something he felt was inherently wrong and bad for the future wellbeing of the game. In his eyes, paying a million or more for a footballer, no matter how gifted or renowned, was nothing less than madness. He wasn't having a tantrum, just telling the world in a statement of principle that football might turn out to be the lasting loser if transfers were allowed to spiral out of control. Quite easily, he could have conveniently turned a blind eye to the whole affair and stayed as a United director. Nobody, let's be honest, more deserved to be in that room of executive power. But, no, Matt decided if the game was destined to travel what he regarded as the route to lunacy, it was time for him to bail out. And he did just that, to the consternation of the rest of us I must confess, but in a gesture we all respected.

Which is more than can be said of certain other individuals who occupied the management chair Matt made so important. Or one, to be precise. Tommy Docherty. I well recall when Robson and Moses were signed for the all-in £2 million, the Doc, in his best loud-mouthed and ill-conceived fashion, sneered that I could have bought the whole West Brom outfit for that kind of cash. Little more than two years later, tittle-tattle Tommy was renta-mouthing it again with another radio campaign. This time it was another cheap tirade that Robson should not be traded to Italy – it was more than United's life was worth to even contemplate the dreadful deed. Despite the fact that we had been offered double what we had paid for Robson less than three years earlier. The plain and simple facts were that Juventus made the running in 1984, bidding for Robson very quickly after they had eliminated us from Europe in the Cup Winners' Cup semi-final. At the same time, Sampdoria, their Italian rivals, attempted to trump that move. And that, to be candid, was the only possible deal that appealed to me. We tried to broker a transaction that involved Liam Brady and Trevor Francis, plus £2 million in hard cash, from Sampdoria with Robbo travelling in the opposite direction. I then had in mind to buy John Wark from Ipswich for £40,000, as Robson's direct midfield replacement, with money in the bank into the bargain. That proposal, swopping a great player for two other outstanding players and still ending up with a significant profit, was the only one that made sense in my judgement. Robson, understandably at that preliminary stage, had his heart set on a season or two in Serie A. There was the prestige of competing against the finest players in the world. And then there was the mind-boggling rewards as well. His focus was fixed on Juventus and, quite clearly, they had approach him indirectly in advance to pave the way for a record-busting transfer. For him, it meant bundles as they threw telephone number financial incentives at him. Their offer to United was for £3 million, a staggering valuation at the time, and, don't forget, a transfer figure not equalled in England for another eight years until Alan Shearer's signing for Blackburn Rovers.

I called Robbo in for talks. They followed very closely the earlier agenda we had at West Brom when I told him, very firmly, it was something I would stubbornly resist. Sure, I had to bear in mind that Robson was being granted the opportunity to make himself secure for life. But also I reaffirmed that, A, any transfer must be for the benefit of the club, and, B, for the benefit of the player. The Sampdoria initiative could certainly have been for United's benefit. The initial thrust from Juventus, I deemed, just wasn't. So Robson was persuaded, by financial arm-twisting and a bit of ego-polishing, to stay. That happened because United put together a personal package for him never offered before – and ever likely to be a rare event – of an extra seven years on his contract. It was big money, but it also took Robson to the guaranteed testimonial, and it could have been bettered only in the tax-free world of Italian perks. Thankfully, Robbo, shelving his ambitions for football abroad, decided it was attractive enough. And the heroics that followed surely made every invested penny extremely worthwhile for both parties.

He was such a precious commodity, a player without a peer in his era. During the eighties, Robson claimed the stage as the greatest English player of that period. Only Kenny Dalglish and Ian Rush, the legends of Scotland and Wales, might have matched Robson in the estimation of certain critics. For me he was the untouchable. Everybody now talks about Eric Cantona being the catalyst of United's latter-day glories. But without Robson, I maintain, United might not have had the same stature when Eric first arrived. To coin a phrase, they might not have got where they are today without Captain Marvel. During his time, he epitomized the team; Robson was the essence of United. That's why, barring a few matches at Middlesbrough as player-manager, he virtually completed his playing career in football's most famous red shirt. He had everything going for him, and was a top-class performer in any number of roles. You could employ him as the out-and-out attacking midfield player with a capability of notching twelve or fourteen goals a season. Or drop him back as the anchor man, where he could tackle, defend and read a game like a natural centre-back, another role he was able to fill very comfortably. If I harbour one regret about Red Robbo it's probably that I didn't have enough faith to play him at centre-forward. He could have made it there as well. I opted for the experiment once in a pre-season friendly in Scotland. He wasn't, it's true, exactly a threat to Alan Shearer on that occasion, but if I had persevered I have a hunch he might have been.

Down the years, I am delighted to admit I have had a close relationship with Robson, both professionally and privately. But that didn't protect the pair of us from quite a few heated bust-ups and harsh words. He was that sort of personality. You had to challenge Robbo, goad him in the right way, jab him with the spearpoint when you felt it necessary. I remember on one occasion we played Watford, during the couple of seasons when Graham Taylor forged them into a side that were always very difficult opponents. It was a game at Old Trafford and they were giving us a chasing. At half-time, grateful for the contest to be goalless despite the humiliating lesson we were being taught, I just laced into Robson. To a lesser degree, his partner, Ray Wilkins, also took an ear-bashing. 'You're a joke. Watford have two kids in with you in Kenny Jackett and that ginger-haired lad (Les Taylor) and they're just murdering you. It's embarrassing. If you don't get a grip, and win us this game, you want locking up, the pair of you.' Razor's response was typical: 'Know what you're saying, gaffer. Okay.' Robbo was something else. He barked back at me, accused me of being off my head. When he went back out, he was incensed, very much at boiling point. He had been affronted; even worse, his ability and pride had been questioned. I nudged Mick Brown: 'Just watch this. A volcano's about to erupt. Heaven help the Watford lads.'

Second half we screamed it; Wilko was special, but Robbo was nothing less than majestic. I had insulted him and he had shown me in return what he was all about. He guarded that global reputation of his very jealously. Like all great players, he believed nobody had the right to question him. Or else. In that vengeful mood, Robson was more lethal than a wounded lion. And, psychologically, I used the trick to wind him up. Friends, yes, but deliberate enemies when it suited me. In the five-a-sides he refused most times to play in my team – he wanted to kick lumps out of me with the opposition instead.

There was the camaraderie, too. Like the time in Hong Kong when I planned to give him hell over a disciplinary matter and ended up half-cut with him on champagne. It happened on an end-of-season trip. It was 1984, we had just lost to Juventus in Europe, and grovelled to just two points out of a possible twelve in the title chase. Liverpool, stumbling over the line, pipped us by four points and, in my estimation, we had blown our best chance of being champions during my reign with United. Given just average form during that run-in we would have been champs, no bother. Anyway, that was history and we were now in Hong Kong.

On arrival, I gave the players a free day, but warned them to be sharp at half-ten next morning for training, before we played a Select XI on the Monday afternoon. Anybody dodging the curfew or showing up late was in for a serious wage deduction. Next day, a sultry Sunday, everybody is gathered for the work-out. But there's no show from the skipper. Wilko was his room-mate and he was dispatched to find Robbo. Not in the hotel, came the reply. Off we go to training, badgered by the press corp on Robbo's whereabouts, me saying he was injured and, comically, Mick telling others that Robbo was jetlagged. Gordon McQueen even joked that England's premier footballer might be floating by now in the historic Victoria Harbour. Off the bus we piled with a further instruction to the players from me: dinner, dead on 7.30, don't be a second late or else.

About three in the afternoon, there was a knock on the door. A very conciliatory Robson waited for me to answer. 'Boss, you have always said whatever we do in the free time, there must be professionalism with the football. I'm out of order.' He apologized and explained that he had been at the races with Don Shanks and Malcolm Allison's son. Apparently, Razor had covered up for him at the morning call. He was, in fact, very much in his bed, but zonked and hardly fit for a Weetabix never mind a workout. By coincidence, a pal of mine, not directly involved in football, had just left our hotel hours before we arrived. His parting gift, left with a note in my room, was a crate of best-listed champagne. It was stuck in a corner when Robbo entered and the words started to fly. It all got very heated between us. I accused him of taking his foot off the pedal and letting us down in a couple of matches towards the end of the title chase. Robbo explained: 'Once I saw we couldn't win it, second or third didn't seem all that much of a prize.' I didn't agree with that and the jousting continued. About four hours later, we realized we had polished off at least half a dozen bottles of the bubbly and, more dramatically, it was by now 8.30 – an hour past my dinner deadline.

It wasn't quite a Freddy Frinton drunk scene, but it was for certain two emotional-as-a-rat people who entered the players' dining room that night. I just urged Robbo: 'Walk straight, keep the smile off your face, and give the impression that I've just given you a right dressing down.' The burst of laughter from the first-team lads, only a second or two after we reached our seats, told me it was just as well that we worked at Old Trafford rather than the Old Vic. It was in that afternoon session, too, that I discovered why Robson, once fed a diet of Guinness and steak to beef him up during his youth, in later years gave up the steak.

As I am only too ready to repeat, Robson remains the greatest player I have ever had under my control. He, conversely, believes that long-time clubmate Paul McGrath is the finest foot-baller, as a fair but powerful opponent, he has regularly faced. And I can qualify that mutual appreciation even further. Because Macca, from the first day I clapped eyes on him, when he was wearing a single earring long before it became a fashion state-ment for men, is the greatest buy I made in twenty-five years of management. At £35,000 he was an absolute steal. But McGrath, his exploits both on the field and off, is worthy of a story in himself and I'll be relating much more detail about this extremely likeable Irishman a little later in my reminiscences.

There are others, though, who were not far behind Robson in my estimation of outstanding signings, such as Gordon Strachan, Arnie Muhren and, yes, old misery himself, Frank Stapleton, as well as two flamboyant characters I should have enlisted. Kevin Keegan, for one, and Frank Worthington for another, both of whom came close to being United players. The offer to buy Kevin for £100,000, before his renaissance move to Newcastle in the early part of the eighties, was, in hindsight, a chance I allowed to go begging. He was with Southampton at the time when I spoke to his agent, Harry Swales – also the adviser for Robson – as well as Lawrie McMenemy. Kevin, I recollect, was somewhere around the thirty mark, certainly not too old for a footballer of his expertise and energy. They both told me at Old Trafford he would fill the stadium: not a tempt-ing negotiating card for me because the place was already full to bursting with season-ticket holders. But King Keegan would have been a knockout purchase anyway for, say, a couple of years at least. Just the right kind of dynamic performer, too, for the United terraces. They would have loved him. As for the team? Well, now, I can sit back and recognize a born winner of Kevin's calibre just might have brought that elusive title home long before Fergie's team managed to lift the curse. A mistake, on reflection, I can't ignore.

A different sort of operator was big Worthy. In his pomp, with all those flicks, tricks, shimmies and over the shoulder extravagances, he would have rivalled any of United's ball-juggling showmen. Yeah, too right, even Besty and Michael Knighton! But when the opportunity came for us to grab Frank he was still loaded with talent, but stepping towards the twilight years in the early eighties. Under Jim Smith, at Birmingham, he still possessed much of his match-winning verve and skills. Then Ron 'Ironsides' Saunders arrived. I knew for Frank that was the death knell. All he needed to do, I urged, was to sit back and be patient. Ron would have him hurtling through the door on a free transfer within a week. What did Worthy do? Well, he panicked and beat a hasty retreat to Leeds for a fee. My plan was to land him for nothing and turn him into a star (!) – a promise we still laugh about to this day. In all seriousness, Worthington had the charisma and the class to succeed at United even at that stage of his career. He would also have been a very useful tutor for the likes of Norman Whiteside and Mark Hughes, then developing as the team's youthful strike force.

They were the big two who got away and, in Keegan's case at least, an important influence on my decision-making was the arrival of Arnold Muhren. I was unsure about taking both players, as they approached the veteran stage, at the same time. It didn't seem the shrewdest strategy. And I plumped for the Dutchman because he was blessed with a well-proven creative ability and played wide on the left. It was a position I had always found hard to solve. I tried for a while to persuade

Sammy McIlroy to go for it. He, I believed, could do that linking, setting-up job from the flank that John Robertson performed so well at Forest. Sammy, though, could never be tempted. He preferred to play central midfield and there he had to take on the in-club competition of Robson, Moses and Wilkins which struck me as not the smartest move. So I took on Muhren. He was heaven sent and came cheap – the Dutchman didn't cost me a bent guilder. His free transfer from Ipswich, the summer after their UEFA Cup triumph, deposited a magnificent player on my doorstep.

Somehow, I don't think Arnold ever collected the credit he deserved from United's followers. Yet he was a superb technician, a player who with countryman Frans Thyssen, made a revolutionary impact on our game with his total-football education. He helped Robson no end in the art of passing, as he matured. Arnie didn't have to pass to feet, not when he could cause more destruction by passing into space. Robbo, at one stage, was just the opposite and that was the particular craft Muhren passed on to the England and United captain. People used to have an image of Arnie as a laid-back, maybe even lazy, strolling type of player. Far from it. He was a highly competitive trainer, a complete football nut, and never out of the top three in any of our training runs. When he left, I wanted him to stay another couple of years. But Johann Cruyff, his own hero, lured him to Ajax. His quality was underlined when Muhren, apart from his impact back in Dutch club football, also aided his country's European championship victory in the eighties when he was close to thirty-seven.

Arnie was a guy I liked, on or off the pitch. Frank Stapleton, I'm afraid, didn't fit into both categories. He was a great centre-forward, in my judgement, but I could never take to Frank as a person. As a manager, concerned primarily with the club's winning interests, the second factor should never be allowed to cloud your ideas. It never did. But, away from match build-up, Frank was always a complete pain in the backside. In the sad art of grumbling he was world class. Nothing, no matter how meticulous or prepared, was ever right for him. Gordon McQueen made the crack: 'Frank smiles in the mirror every morning and says, "Thank Christ I have got that over with for another day." '

Frank always seemed to be nitpicking about every conceivable thing. In Majorca, with the players on a three-day break before an FA Cup Final, I made small talk about the hotel, complimenting the standard of the place. 'It's okay,' muttered Frank, 'but not somewhere to bring the family.' Two years later he went back with his wife and kids. Puzzling, or just a moan for the sake of it?

One incident involving Frank is imprinted on my mind for life, and it is something for which I will never forgive him. Apart from being a class act up front, Frank was more than useful as a centre-back. At corners, he could read the danger and mop it up better than a lot of full-time defenders. I always felt he could be a fine centre-back when his attacking days finished. That was in my mind as United approached a very important game against Everton towards the end of the '85 season. We were neck and neck with them and a victory would have left us two points clear at the top. Trouble loomed, though, with a bout of injuries that left us down to McGrath as our only fit central defender. Mark Higgins was recovering from a broken arm, Graeme Hogg was also out of action, and even Robson was hurt and unable to stand in. I pulled Frank. 'Do me a favour against Everton, will you, and play at centre-half?' The answer was a glare and a point-blank no. I even gave Frank the guarantee that if, defensively, it turned into a disaster I would carry the blame. 'Frank, I'll go out and tell the press it was my fault. You have a nightmare and I'll take the rap. But you won't – you're too good in that position for it to happen.' Still the glare – and the NO! In the end, frustrated, I told Mick Brown to take the three players involved out of the room and only to return when we had a centre back. He did and Higgins, with a broken arm only slowly on the mend, volunteered.

We drew the game, our great championship chance, and Frank sat in the dugout as a sub. He always knew he wasn't going to play up front that day, but still chose not to play at all. I found his stubbornness a total betrayal of my management and apart from feeling that it was unprofessional, he had done something to me and his team-mates that I just couldn't stomach. That was the day, in fact, when any kind of football relationship between Frank and me came to an end. I lost faith in him and I also lost the respect I had for him as his manager. Yet, no matter my strong personal feelings, I still regard him as a truly special player for most of his time at United. Towards the end, the striker known to his team-mates as Grumpy, tended to play away from the box too often for my liking. He was such a good header of the ball, even then, but we needed to curse and cajole him to get in there and mix it. I appreciate he could be a feedman as well, able to direct headers perfectly to the feet of supporting attackers, but I picked him as a striker and that was his fundamental responsibility. His days, following the Everton affair, were inevitably numbered.

Gordon Strachan, another one high on a list of footballing favourites, also had management troubles. Not with me, but with Fergie. He arrived at United, a Scot known for his quick tongue and even quicker feet. Initially, he dropped in to play in a testimonial game for Martin Buchan. It was then I got the vibes he might be on his way out of Aberdeen. You could detect the friction, even at long range, between little Strach and Fergie. He, apparently, believed that, although Gordon was only twenty-seven, he had been flying down the wing on just one trip too many. He considered him burned out with nothing left in the legs. It was a suspiciously similar script when Fergie shipped him off to Leeds United, when I believed I had Strachan signed up for a second time during my spell at Sheffield Wednesday. Yet he went on to play for another ten years and, in my opinion, called it quits too early as a player with Coventry City. But that's what this job is all about – a matter of opinion and decision-making which can just as easily portray you as a mug or as a master.

My judgement was that Strachan was worth signing for United at a price of £500,000. There was just one snag – he had already taken it upon himself to sign for what appeared to be half the other clubs in Europe as well! To name but two: Cologne of Germany and the football gentlemen of Verona were very much in the frame. Eventually, we paid the German club around £70,000 to free Strach from a pre-contract agreement that carried his name. So, for two transfer fees, he was ours. Maybe he, too, was never lauded the way he should have been at United, but I considered him a very special package.

In his first season, Strachan notched close on twenty goals, a phenomenal return for a wide midfield player. Sure, a fair share were penalties, but then he won plenty of them as well. He got so overexposed in TV playbacks that revealed his technique, it blew little Gordy's mind and he started missing them. He had, it's true, earned himself a reputation as a ragdoll merchant. The diver stood accused. I remember the match-saver he pulled off against PSV Eindhoven in a very tight second-leg UEFA Cup game at Old Trafford. Very late in the game we won a corner on the left. Gordon read the script, delivered the signal, and collected the short one. He spun inside, threw a dummy, and

Ernie Brandts, the big Dutch defender, hung a leg out. Gordon knocked the ball behind him and went over. Penalty. The wee feller picked himself up, dusted himself down, and had the bottle to finish the job with a shot that saved United's then unbeaten home record in Europe.

So was he a diver? All I can say is he made the most of his attacking opportunities. The counter-argument, one fairer to Gordon, was always that if a forward was bold enough to go in the box, hold the ball, and show the courage of a dribbler, there could be the reward of a penalty. It was the bonus for all the times you tried the same manoeuvre, ended up being brutalized, and got nothing. In that way, Strach would maintain that any dodgy eyebrow-raisers were justified. When that now famously recorded ten-point lead went down the pan it was tied to a dislocated shoulder injury suffered by Strachan when he collided with a post at West Brom. In roughly three years at United, he was a player who always looked to be in the very place he was born to play. With his technical assets, he was bred for that red shirt, no question at all.

I didn't need a playback, naturally, when the indication came that Fergie was about to unload his wee star once more. I swiftly made an offer on Wednesday's behalf and even traded Mark Proctor to finance the package. Strachan was promised more in wages than the Sheffield club had ever paid in their history. He had, though, to talk to Leeds first. Before he headed to Elland Road for the meeting with Howard Wilkinson, we had talked. It seemed a formality: his trip across the Pennines had one destina- tion – Hillsborough. When, three or four hours elapsed after the time fixed for our appointment, I wasn't too worried. Strachan was never the most punctual timekeeper. Finally, he did turn up: 'Boss, don't even start talking terms because it's a waste of words.' I told him that I had drafted a smashing financial package for him. Like he said, though, he had been made an offer he couldn't refuse. Not even for a mate like me.

His arrival at United, all those years earlier, had been thanks to the departure of another footballer I rated highly – despite the popular theories that have been put about – in Ray Wilkins. He left for AC Milan – a spin-off from the aborted Robson move to Italy – and that supplemented the transfer budget enough to finance the recruiting of Strachan. Earlier that season, there had been a lot of transfer speculation around Wilkins. But the truth is we only ever had one offer. It came from Arsenal, a mid-winter bid of no more than £400,000. Then Milan made their move. Originally, Robson was the target. No deal. The next name they mentioned was Wilko. Less of a problem for me, obviously, because United then had a fair number of central midfield players. Ray, in a special system where he was our sweeper and cleaner, had just played his best ever season for the club and was headline material. I told Milan we couldn't allow him to leave for less than £1.5 million. Cheeky, considering the money so far on the table from Highbury, but worth the try.

The negotiation was fixed for a Saturday night meet at a Manchester hotel. I told the chairman I was prepared to be a bit bolshie and show them a lorry-driver's aggression if they stalled. Repeatedly, I kept hearing the figure £750,000. It then transpired that the middle-man had sounded out various managers in England about their valuation of Wilkins. He then fed the numbers to the men in Milan. Seven-fifty was the deal. I blew my top. Later they upped it to a million and, by this stage, Martin Edwards seemed ready to grab the money and run. He was really straining at the leash. I persuaded him to sit tight. Ten days later, they came up with the million and a half and everything went sweetly. Razor headed off to develop into a much better player in Italy and we got our wide midfield man for a third of the price. There has been a lot of unfounded tittle-tattle spread ever since that I didn't rate Wilkins. Mostly it was because I called him the Crab, and to that charge I can only plead guilty. But, in reality, it was only a quip, a bit of banter in the dressing room that I always enjoyed with Ray. Before one game I tried to wind him up: 'Right, Ray, what we going to see today – the Wilkins who can spray it about for England, or the Crab?' He laughed as much as me at the jibe because I never stopped rattling on in those days about his insistence on delivering the over-square pass. Unfortunately, on this occasion, my wise-crack was leaked to the press and it became an established fact that I thought Wilkins very much a wally as a player. Far from it.

At the time Ray left United, I felt his particular type of player we could cope without. We had two hard-drivers in there, Robson and Moses, with Muhren's steadiness and craft to balance the system. We needed a wide man on the other side, and that turned out to be Strachan. But that should never have been misinterpreted as a lack of admiration for Wilkins. He was blessed with as much bulldog character as any footballer I have ever known and two examples of that spirit will never leave my mind. The first was in my début game for United when Ray, bless him, had a game that was more like a holocaust. He couldn't put a pass, or a foot, right all afternoon. Yet not once did he flinch or evade his team responsibility. He was never to be cast as a shirker, a footballer hiding in the shadows. He just demanded the ball even more and buckled down to his job. That was his first major plus for me. Next, in a European game against Dukla Prague, Wilkins once again showed his mettle and the measure of the man. We didn't play well and it looked as if the Czechs would claim the title of first foreign winners on our home territory. Then, last kick of the match, we were awarded a penalty. Ray was not the designated kicker, I have got to say, and it was a very tense, critical situation for everybody. He just picked up the ball, brushed the rest aside, and planted a perfect strike in the net to preserve our unbeaten record. Guts and style, in equal measure. That, another act of sporting courage, placed him very high in my regard as a first-class bloke.

And that's why his name ran instantly through my mind when Andy Gray quit as my assistant at Aston Villa to move into television. Ray had returned from Italy a much improved performer, with a greater variety in his play, and I knew his character couldn't be faulted. He seemed the ideal candidate to replace Andy as first-team coach but, unfortunately, he went ahead and joined Crystal Palace as a player before I was able to put my plan into operation on a formal level.

Ray, the unsurpassable Robbo and the rest I have mentioned in these dispatches are all strong contenders for a place in my Best-Ever Team. I must ponder a little more before completing the selection process by the end of this book. But I think, mischievously, I'm tempted with just a little hint to force one final moan from Frank Stapleton. You're in, Frank me boy, if you will play centre-back. Otherwise it's the bench that's waiting – yet again.

CHAPTER THREE

Having A Go

It was a vastly different kind of football world that I walked into in 1971, urged on by nine vital and telling words from my late father. 'You will never know,' said Fred, 'unless you have a go.' Fred died, still a committed and regular watcher of the game, while I was in charge at Coventry. But, without his sound advice, I might now still be involved in the building game, rather than the real ball game. And I would just as surely have missed out on so many rich and unforgettable experiences. Like swopping one player for a lawnmower, selling another for a crate of champagne and getting a call from another star telling me he couldn't play that night – because he was stuck in jail! Oh, yes, and there was also the time when a now-famous footballing name got the bullet, on the spot, in my own boardroom after we gave his team a right hiding.

The old man, to return to the original point, whispered in my ear while I was playing for Oxford and being sounded out by several clubs, offering various opportunities for my continued connection with football. There was just one very important consideration to delay the big jump. I already had a well-paid, very promising job outside football. For about five years I had been working as a representative for one of the major construction companies in the south. It was training in the morning, then the rest of the day dealing in everything including the kitchen sink; in fact, kitting out house interiors with heating equipment, plumbing and all that stuff. Very shortly, the company promised, I would be made sales manager and, candidly, at that stage I had no real firmly established ambition to stay in football. It was enjoyable, of course it was. Playing under Gerry Summers' management at Oxford as skipper and *centro campista* (midfield to you, mate), I was being awarded nine out of ten and man-of-the-match every week until they figured my name was Asterisk!

In all seriousness, it was a good period of my life, full of fun and with enough money coming in from my two jobs to cushion the Atkinson household fairly comfortably. Then the tapping started. Reading offered me the player-manager's post; John Bond, with sleepy Bournemouth suddenly on a roll, gave me a nudge about being a player-coach; Crewe had something similar in mind. Then came Kettering Town, non-League but definitely wanting to be somebody in the big league, with a telephone call. In truth, it was the offer that initially had least appeal. But their chairman, John Nash, a local entrepreneur, wealthy businessman and real soccer enthusiast, changed all that. He won me over in one conversation. All it needed was my dad to chip in his few words and I was on the management ladder to meet more oddballs, have more laughs – and win a few tidy matches along the way – than I ever thought possible. The money wasn't too bad either. Old Nashy paid me £100 a week all those years ago – more than almost any manager outside the top division of the Football League. It was a salary that fully compensated me for anything I was set to leave behind. From house construction to team builder, with good dosh thrown in, seemed a pretty useful transfer deal to me. And with the unspoken bonus of the kind of football camaraderie –

the best of my life, I have to concede – that money just can't buy. I was in my element.

Experience in the building game had prepared me well to understand the business world and how to deal with people on various levels. But my first day at Kettering in December 1971, was something of a shock. The chairman slung me the keys and said: 'There's my football club. Now go and manage it.' A week before I had faced World Cup skipper Bobby Moore, Geoff Hirst and Martin Peters at West Ham. Now, here was I, taking on Bletchley (later Milton Keynes) in the Second Division of the Southern League. Let me tell you, it was easier against the Hammers. I don't mind confessing that at the back of my mind was the notion that if football management proved the wrong business for me, I could always opt for bricks and mortar again. But, with one or two patch-up buys, we climbed from half-way and went up as champions. Next season, we topped Division One, and just missed elevation into the League. In those days, it was a voting system – suspected by some to be based on who, rather than what, you knew – and we fell one vote short. But at least I had gained admission to the learning curve. I broke the non-league transfer record in signing Roy Clayton, a very good craftsman at that level, from Oxford for £6,000. I almost got Phil Neal for the same amount. Yes, the same Phil Neal later to be big licks with Liverpool and England. He was with Northampton, then having a torrid time and close to a merger with Kettering until Mr Nash stood on his principles and pulled out. Phil played all over the place back then, midfield, defence, even centre-forward, and I had in fact recommended him to Oxford as my replacement. (Later, maybe he became a little disillusioned because I discovered he had ideas of playing part-time while doing a teacher-training course at Loughborough.) He was only around the twenty mark and I offered six grand. Phil was keen,

Northampton less so, and the deal fell through. A year later, Phil went to Anfield and I have since spent half a lifetime telling him exactly what he missed. Just think of it, he could have had two Southern League championship medals, and he would have been on twenty quid a week as well with me. Fool!

It was, even a quarter of a century ago and outside the full-time pro scene, very much a taste of the sporting good life with Kettering. Pretty cushy, too. We were the first non-league outfit to have our own luxury coach. You know the type, with the tables and fancy lights and TVs thrown in. We stayed overnight at the best hotels, copied the big boys with pre-match meals, wore the fancy, upmarket team blazers, and were very much the Manchester United of our particular football environment. There were no fish-and-chip stopovers for my lads on the way back from matches. Not a bit of it. We were the people, to use a modern tag-line. At the end of the season, we always had a fully paid-up trip to Majorca for the whole team to wind down. Plenty of laughs, not much sleep, and a severe case of mass bacardi poisoning after about five days.

The vast majority of the players were ex-league, probably the best known being Joe Kiernan. His name might not twang too many memories in the nineties, but he was a first-class bloke who went all the way from Division Four to Division One with Northampton Town, turned at the terminal and then went all the way back down again. But he was a very useful asset to us, signed, I still recall, at roughly four in the morning at his house, with his wife, Pat, dishing up egg, sausage and bacon to celebrate. And they have the brass neck to call me Flash Ron. Dave Bowen, his boss at the Town, warned me to stay clear, describing him as a 'barrack room lawyer'. All I could say was that it had taken him quite a while to reach that conclusion after nine years at Northampton.

My first captain at Kettering was a great lad named Trevor Peck. Muck and nettles centre-back and as good as gold. One of the real characters of that era. The first night I was in charge, he helped heroically to win my début game. I gave him a tug, shoved a tenner into his hand, and told him to buy the rest of the lads a beer to toast victory. Next morning when I bumped into Pecky, he didn't look so happy. 'Got a problem, gaffer,' he said, looking very furtive about it. 'I had that drink with the lads, as you suggested, but then I got stopped by the law for drink-driving.' He had been nicked leaving the boozer an hour or three after the game. But even that temporary upset didn't stop me instituting a team ritual at Kettering. Every away victory meant I stopped the bus, packed everybody into a convenient pub and stood a round of drinks. One other condition was also enforced – I lashed out for a box of cigars, Hamlet or whatever, and it was a club rule that every player must smoke one. Unconventional, for sure.

The chairman was just as unorthdox. He cooked up a transfer deal with Chelmsford, our closest rivals, with whom we shared the reputation as the best non-league sides of that time. The motive was to get the greatest tax benefits out of the available budget, and old Nashy told me to pick the best player I could – and pay £34,000 for him. Now, back then and considering it was non-league, that was like close to a £3 million transfer present day. Anyway, I chose Eddie Dillsworth, a massive black lad, who played on the wing for Chelmsford. He was a tidy player who could easily have made his mark in the League. So, under this bogus arrangement, I went down to meet their manager, Dave Bumstead, with the thirty-four grand cheque tucked neatly in the briefcase. When I handed it over, we both burst out laughing at the farce of it all. The true value was approximately £3,000 and, a year later, the agreement was for Kettering to get their money back, minus the real valuation.

Anyway, for the time being, we had big Eddie on our books. Very valuable asset he was, too, as a winger able to terrorise most defences. Until early one afternoon, roughly three hours before we kicked off against Bedford Town, Eddie called me. 'Bad news, boss,' he says. 'I won't be playing tonight – just impossible for me to make it over there.' Why? 'I've got a problem – I'm in jail.' Now, if you're looking for a *bona fide* excuse to duck a game, that's about as good as I have ever heard. As I told him, from time to time you might get lucky and beat Liverpool, Man U or even Juventus, but one opponent gives you no chance – and that's the long arm of the law. Eddie was inside over various fraud allegations, a matter which was eventually resolved in his favour. But he was never the same player again. Perhaps it was the prison food.

Skipper Peck was a bit of a case, too. He had always sworn to me he was only thirty-one. Then, one day, a letter addressed to Trev arrived in my office mail while he was working away. He expected it to be another summons from Lancaster Gate – Pecky was always in disciplinary hot water – so he told me to open it. I did and it was an official notice of his Provident Fund money payments. Strange, I figured, you have to be at least thirty-five to qualify for that.

Frank Large was another who got muddled over his age. Phil played all over the planet, a powerful, raw-boned missile of a man in the air and as rough as you like, but he always seemed to return to Northampton. That's where I found him. He worked on the building sites and smoked like a trooper. My brother Graham came to a general agreement on the team bus travelling to away matches: the smokers would only be allowed a fag every hour on the hour. It was pathetic to see them with a Bensons drooping from their bottom lips, ready to light up, as they waited for the appointed hour. Frank volunteered to play without a toecap in his boot after dropping a full hod of bricks on his big toe. He eventually quit, telling me he had a big construction job waiting in London, but he would give football another crack in about three years' time. Ambitious that, Frank, I thought at the time – he was already coming up thirty-eight.

One of the weirdest transfer deals I struck down at Kettering was when I flogged one of our reserves – for a lawnmower. Even now, so long after the event, I might be wise to keep the identity of this poor, unfortunate footballer strictly secret. But the trade did happen, between myself and the then Stevenage manager, Bill Coldwell. He had been on about this player for a while, and finally asked me for a price. 'Easy, Bill, you know that fine old lawnmower you have got down there, I'll have that as a swopsy.' He went quiet on the other end of the phone. He just couldn't believe my side of the bargain. But I had been down to watch his team a few times on scouting missions and, in all honesty, the best thing I ever saw on show was that lawnmower. It was a better runner, and far more industrious and useful, than the player I flogged to get it. Last I heard it had made 335 consecutive appearances for Kettering and was due a testimonial.

I spent three enjoyable years at Kettering, building up the club's ambitions and creating what these days I am sure would have been recognized as both a team and stadium fit for the Football League. That target was not, unfortunately, achieved despite the committed support of the board and my own efforts. When I finally departed, though, there was a little acrimony. I was around thirty-five at the time, still with eighteen months on my playing contract. Kettering couldn't stop me moving to Cambridge as a manager, but they could, and did, thwart any chance of my being a player there by holding on to my registration.

A close challenger for top spot in my bizarre collection of football's strangest transfers was the Möet and Chandon exchange I agreed with Barry Fry. By that time I had moved on to Cambridge, having taken over from Bill Leivers around Christmas 1974. The deal involved a left fullback called Billy Baldry, who was shipped out from my club to Barry at Dunstable Town. I have got to admit the arrangement emerged from my own mischievous sense of humour and an element of tit-for-tat conflict with my chairman, David Rushton. He was an accountant, a bit of a stickler who always wore a pinstripe suit, and forever reminded me of Freddie Frinton, the famous stage drunk of the time, or an early Les Patterson – though, of course, that doesn't mean he had any problem with the bottle himself. Whenever I spotted chairman Rushton, he always had a burning fag jammed in the corner of his mouth, with roughly two inches of ash hanging perilously over his waistcoat, a destination it inevitably found given time.

Back to the scene though where I am in my office, on top of the Third Division after beating close challengers Bury 3–0. Little more than eighteen months earlier, when I had taken the job, Cambridge had virtually taken root at the foot of Division Four. So it was an occasion, I rightly judged, for a little celebration. Among certain football friends over for the night, I had been joined by John Bond and Kenny Brown from Norwich City. We were drinking, of all things, asti spumante and the total bill was all of fifty quid. In comes the chairman, clearly with a bee in his bonnet, and spouting nonsense about the huge cost of entertaining at Cambridge. It had to stop, he blustered. I was blazing. He was out of order considering what had been achieved at a little-known club in a very short period of team transition. 'Okay, chairman, don't bother in future – I'll sort my own drinks from now on.' And I did. Next morning I called up Barry Fry about the fullback he had always wanted. 'If you still fancy Baldy, get over here with a crate of Moët sharpish and the deal is done.' Barry couldn't have arrived faster by Concorde and the transaction was smoothed through.

Come Saturday, we beat Lincoln City 5–0 and this was the moment to literally drown the chairman's midweek protests. The rest of the directors, of course, were in on the secret. I broke open the bubbly and we drank the lot. Everybody got a glass except, you've guessed exactly right, old Fagash Rushton. He did have a friend or two, mind. The board meeting at Cambridge used to last longer than your average Test Match. It was like something between the Tory Party conference and the Lord Mayor's banquet with equal amounts of fancy words and even fancier food. You wouldn't believe it, really. Among the directors at the time was a smashing old guy called Paddy Harris. I had re-christened him the Colonel because of his impressive bearing and manner. At one meeting a big argument raged as opposite camps with conflicting opinions openly went to war. The row centred on dear Mr Rushton and Reg Smart, the subsequently long-reigning chairman at the club. Suddenly, old Paddy flung his chair back, rose to his feet and started to thump the very imposing, polished mahogany boardroom table with his hefty walking stick. In the space between each director, he repeated the threatening gesture as he bellowed: 'Nobody should insult my chairman – and think they can get away with it.' For a few minutes it was like a madhouse. 'Hey, Colonel, ' I shouted above the racket in an attempt to get some peace, 'go put the kettle on and make us all a brew.' And he did. That was the amazing, crazy but enjoyable world of the lower leagues. And I loved it.

One now well-recognized contemporary of mine might, I submit, have a very different view. His name is David Pleat, arguably the person I have known longest in the management business. We go right back to non-league days. Time has healed the wounds and now I can tease David about the night we put four past the side he managed – and dumped him in the dole queue. I played sweeper in the Kettering team and, without wishing to be too arrogant about it, I could have taken on Pleaty's Nuneaton Borough in a bowtie and puffing on a cigar. That night they were blitzed, beaten out of sight. Later, when I entered the boardroom, one of our directors pulled me into a corner and discreetly said: 'Grab David and take him out of here for a drink. There's been a row between him and his chairman. It wasn't very pleasant.' Worse than that, he had been dismissed on the spot. I grabbed him and ushered him away for a consoling drink. He was upset and understandably so. But, within a matter of minutes, David shelved his personal troubles and started arguing with me about the game. He believed Nuneaton could actually have won it and had already convinced himself they had been robbed. That was simply barmy: I had played in the game and Nuneaton, to my knowledge, had never crossed the half-way line. I was angry: 'David, if you sincerely believe all that claptrap, then you deserve to be sacked. Good night.' It was my first, but certainly not the last, glimpse into the unorthodox world of David Pleat. He's a nice feller, good knowledge of the game as well, but sometimes he is on a different wavelength to many within the management brotherhood.

CHAPTER FOUR

The Three Degrees

From non-league to the lower reaches of the Football League at Cambridge United can be measured as a relatively small step, but it placed me very swiftly in a quite different environment. It transported me for the first time into a world of racial tension, even open conflict on the football field. I had never experienced such ugly bigotry before; not between two rival footballers anyway. But it flared up in my first game in charge at Cambridge and involved Brendan Batson, now very much an eminent and successful ambassador for his own race and the game in general as an executive with the players' union. Since this largely unreported incident in the late seventies, the race card has, in my view, been dealt too often on the sporting table. It is an issue that should be approached with mellowed understanding and humour, not political correctness and the prejudice of personal agendas. And I believe that the vast majority of black players would subscribe to that philosophy.

But, first, let's return to the case of Brendan, who at the time was learning his trade and developing as a very useful defender, when he unfortunately crossed the path of Tony Coleman. He, you might recall, had played at Manchester City as a star of the Malcolm Allison era. By this time, though, the downward spiral had claimed him and he was on Stockport County's payroll. For some reason, lost from my memory, he got involved in a bit of aggro with Batson that prompted the referee's intervention. As the official attempted to restore order, behind his back Coleman was winding things up by making monkey-like gestures at Brendan. Something had to give. It did. Brendan suddenly uncoiled a fairly hefty haymaker, guided around the ref's left lughole, and clocked Coleman with a beauty. Brendan had to go but, unless I am very much mistaken, the provocateur survived. Maybe that fact fuelled the sense of injustice, certainly of prejudice, that was already part of Brendan's nature. A few months later, in the return League game, they were kicking sizeable lumps off each other again and once more Brendan saw the red card. Just born unlucky, Bren!

He certainly felt so when, in that very same season, his racial anger and maybe a bit of youthful insecurity led to a collision with me. When he arrived, it seemed to me that he had a chip on his shoulder, and I thought he possibly felt the reason Arsenal had sold him was because of a reluctance to play coloured players. This problem reared its head very shortly after I joined the club, during a training-ground altercation with me. My grievance was straightforward. I felt Brendan's commitment was questionable, he wasn't focused and the effort wasn't there. His attitude, boiled down to the basics, was that I was having a go because he was black. In that period of his life, Brendan could be bolshie and a bit of a jack-the-lad character. I had been tipped off that he was boasting to the other players that I wouldn't touch him; maybe that I daren't because of the race question. So when he was summoned to see me, the script was probably more predictable than *EastEnders*. 'Well, boss,' said Brendan, 'you don't know my problem.' Easy answer: 'If you think it's a problem being black, it's one you have got for life. So you had better get on with it and get it sorted.' And Brendan was right – I didn't touch him any more. I just dropped him from the team. Yet, within weeks of our little confrontation, he became my club captain and, following my subsequent move to West Bromwich Albion, my first signing for the Midlands club.

Back then, though, he was a very sensitive even sullen individual, carrying a chip on his shoulder and for ever smouldering about the colour question. He was, it's true, one of the early ground breakers for his race in the British game. As a result he may have suffered more distasteful abuse and bigotry than you can expect anyone to take. But, as a committed champion of black footballers, I felt banter and humour were the weapons to fight back with. Aggro causes lasting grief all round; it is not the formula for understanding or reaching common agreement.

Eventually, it seemed that Brendan adopted a similar view. He then countered much of the naked racism in our society with his own smartly effective one-liners. I well recall, not that long after our bust-up, standing with a group of journalists in the lobby of a London hotel waiting for the start of the Footballer of the Year awards. In strolled Brendan, immaculate as ever in the old tuxedo and bowtie. Tugging at his cuff-linked sleeves, he smiled: 'Gentlemen, is there room at your table for a well-dressed and friendly black man?' Only it wasn't black man that he called himself. I fully understand such frankness, particularly now, is not considered politically correct, but humour, in my estimation, is the one guaranteed route through the racial barriers. A snarl gets you nowhere, but a smile has a chance. I am a preacher of the basic belief that people are people and I treat them with respect if they deserve it whatever the colour of their skin. And I think that if Brendan, who clearly recognized his earlier attitude might have been suspect and counterproductive, hadn't got his head around the race question, he would probably never have made the career progress he has. That incident with me at Cambridge might just have been the crucial turning point. He learned from it, matured, and became an accomplished footballer who genuinely deserved one more reward: the England cap that never came. Still, as No. 2 in the hierarchy at the PFA, he now has an influence on the game that has been broadening for the last ten years. He has earned it.

At West Brom, of course, he was an integral part of what famously became known as soccer's very own Three Degrees. The other two members were Cyrille Regis and the late Laurie Cunningham, who played their own constructive role in combating the racists. Cyrille was always a big, open lad. He had worked in London as an electrician until he was nineteen before turning to football. It meant a life mixing with all sorts and so he never had a problem. Laurie, on the other hand, was very different. He had a much deeper, introspective personality and, like Brendan, was to some extent hostile to the wider outside world. I know he used to receive a lot of hate mail and, despite being in the game with white footballers from a very early age, that must have influenced his outlook. Even he, though, would share a belly laugh about one pathetic letterwriter who always drivelled on with the same message. He clearly supported a club in the north west, on Merseyside to be exact, but not Liverpool, and the litany of infantile hatred never changed: 'Atkinson, are you bringing those monkeys to play against us again? We don't want them here – they should be sent back to the jungle.' Deliberately, I used to call Cyrille, Laurie and Brendan across to read it. They treated it as a joke but, amazingly, we usually finished up with very good results on our trips to Goodison Park. Wonder why? I didn't need to motivate anybody.

In that era of what can only be described as widespread racial ignorance, there was even an element of prejudice in our own dressing room. Some players, senior pros mostly, were quite anti the Three Degrees. I haven't forgotten the names even now but I'll protect their anonymity, even though they may not have earned or deserved it. But at the time I urgently made moves to stamp out this undesirable threat to team harmony before it could undermine the club. It was a barrier I swiftly had to break down. Then the imperative was to re-educate the minority to make sure any ill-feeling didn't get out of control. The beef of the misguided few – the familiar one, the favourite accusation that the racists so frequently aimed at the black players – was about lack of commitment and not working hard enough. It was a charge that, in any given game, could be levelled at a lot of players, black and white.

The racists populated the terraces, too. Still do, I suppose, but hopefully in ever decreasing numbers. At West Ham and Villa Park we had to endure the usual banana-chucking episodes. Cyrille dealt with it in his own favourite way. He would grab the freely tossed fruit, ram it down his shorts and give further evidence that what they say about black men is quite possibly true. Brendan, on the other hand, simply peeled his banana and ate it, which brought a roar of applause from the Hammers fans and instantly defused a potentially nasty situation.

Racism does exist, it will always exist – you can't pretend it's not there, you have to face it as an issue for adult discussion – but it can be controlled properly in football by a mature, reasoned approach. I always said to my players: 'You are black, so what's the big deal? He's ginger, he's Welsh, he's a right t. . ., and you're black. Who cares?'

Obviously if individuals step beyond the reasonable bounds of banter to foul abuse, then you must come down hard on them. But it is a matter to be resolved on the shop-floor of this sporting industry of ours. If you allow the wackos, of both extremes, to become involved and label it heavyweight racial discrimination, you magnify the problem of what is mostly a minor disruption in football.

I have nothing less than admiration for many black players. Particularly the pioneers, like my own trio and, of course, Viv Anderson. I actually managed an all-black team, with the likes of George Berry, Bob Hazell, the Chamberlain brothers and Garth Crooks involved, in a testimonial for Len Cantello at the Hawthorns. But for all their popularity, there was never anybody to touch Regis. Just ask his own folk. With all due respect to Paul Ince, and he can bring in the lawyers if he wants, there was only ever one Guvnor – big Cyrille, naturally. To the black players, he was very definitely *the* man. They treated him almost like a godfather. When they were on the same pitch, as friend or foe, they made a point of walking across to Regis and shaking his hand. It was respect for him both as an outstanding footballer and also because of the way he has conducted himself and carried the flag for his race. Nobody has done it better.

I like, too, the manner in which John Fashanu has made his way in the world, accepting that in the twilight of his career he was burdened with a problem that took him to a courtroom to demonstrate his innocence. That apart, he made his mark and was a powerful leader among his fellow pros. Carlton Palmer is another. He, it's true, has made mistakes, but it was football dedication and real character that earned him his recognition with England. Paul Ince has made even more of an impact in the global game, dealing with the race issue in Italy in demanding respect by his demeanour and talent on the field. He was, remember, a bit of a tearaway as a youngster if the stories are to be believed. Since then he has been a single-minded, one-man show of a success story. Great. John Barnes is another who, in the way he played and also conducted himself in the public arena, has surely been an inspiration to so many wannabee black kids. Finally there is Paul McGrath, but I don't know what you would call him – English because he was born in London; Irish because he played for them; or black because that's what he is. See, there we go again in planting unncessary labels on people!

Seriously, no matter how much I genuinely admire that early, pioneering generation of black footballers, I have never been too happy with what came later. There was an alarming period, created by a more resentful, openly hostile element, when the race issue threatened to become very volatile. This second-wave of black players – not all but dangerously enough of them – seemed to be hellbent on stirring up the whole unsavoury atmosphere once more. I saw it as reverse racism and a worrying tendency that might destroy so much encouraging progress. This minority came into the game, brash and swaggering and full of arrogance, with an attitude that the world owed them a living, simply because they were born black. They certainly didn't do their race any particular favours and, absolutely no question, didn't behave anything like as well as the great black personalities who paved the way in earlier years. I accept that, during this time in the mid to late eighties, society in general was not as well disciplined or respectful either and the two syndromes might well be linked. But I still didn't like what I was witnessing and feared the mistrust and schisms might be an explosion waiting to happen. These latter-day stars weren't like the earlier generation, who were mostly happy guys, squaring up to the world's daily demands with a smile. Now all we had were growing men with a chip on their shoulder, so morose and sullen, and apparently reluctant to build relationships with their white team-mates. Maybe they had been brainwashed. Maybe they were innocents being exploited for racist purposes by more sinister forces who saw some mileage in their public fame. Ask me if there was a secret agenda, and I just don't know the answer.

What I can explain is the bizarre, perplexing events that surrounded the tragic death of Laurie Cunningham when he was still a young man with so much to achieve. I got the call from Spain when Laurie was killed in a horrendous car crash in the mountains above Madrid in the summer of 1989, hurled from his car as he returned from an all-night race meeting. He was only twenty-eight. It was my duty, not an easy one I might add, to break the desperate news to big Cyrille. I did that and then prepared for the funeral to be held in London. I had known Laurie a number of years, the manager-player bond had always been fairly strong, and I never had a doubt in my mind I should attend. But when I arrived at the funeral ceremony, the only other white man I could see was Liam Brady. It was eery. I couldn't figure it immediately, particularly as Laurie had so many friends among white footballers. But it soon became very evident that certain influences had been at work, involving what can only be described as a black brotherhood of people connected to the sporting world. They were apparently determined to turn Laurie's funeral into what I would call 'an event' for their own propaganda purposes. Brendan Batson, rightly in attendance, was absolutely furious about what happened. It was as if Laurie's funeral had been hijacked and completely stage-managed.

I should have been suspicious before I even left for London. At the time I was manager of Sheffield Wednesday. Two of my high-profile players were Carlton Palmer and Dalian Atkinson, both, of course, black. They requested a day off training to attend the funeral. I asked them if they had known Laurie personally. A shake of the head. Carlton said: 'I saw Laurie play. I respected him but I didn't know him.' When I questioned why they, then, should be there, they answered in unison: 'This guy in London says we have got to go.' I pointed out that a funeral was an occasion for family and close friends to pay their respects, not a vehicle for some kind of black power movement. They saw the sense of what I said, and didn't go. For me that kind of political manoeuvring was a highly undesirable and deeply worrying development. It was quite plainly a group of people, who could rightly claim to have been abused, but who now had their own agenda trying to manipulate the race issue for their own ends. It was racism in reverse and I am glad to say it now seems to have largely been diluted and dispersed.

There will possibly always be some element of conflict, cultural differences that won't easily go away, like the Rangers and Celtic hatred still festering in Glasgow. I hope that pessimistic view is one day proved to be wrong. But there is a racist factor – or rather a mockery of anyone who is different – in all walks of life. If you are fat you risk abuse, be an Italian in the wrong place and it happens, and look what befell a cult figure like Eric Cantona at Crystal Palace. He was targeted because he happens to be French. No, not for a single moment do I condone it, but I do believe so much of it is less sinister than we suspect. It is an unwanted aspect of our sporting existence, but in many cases it is merely employed as a language of retaliation or with the intention of antagonizing or belittling a rival. I know there is still a minority of clubs seen as anti-black, but it's hard to pick them out now in football's multi-cultural environment. They, too, are thankfully fading away. And, let's be realistic, any club in the world, no matter how racially sensitive, couldn't possibly turn their backs, surely, on a player like George Weah. It should always be the quality of the footballer, not the shade of his pigmentation, that determines whether he is good enough for any team. And, in my humble judgement, many of them are worth signing for the fundamental reason that they are, well, different.

Compared with white players, the black footballer is certainly blessed with a different muscle development that is of great benefit in most sporting activities. That's fact, not fiction, or even football fantasy. In most cases, it makes the individual more agile and flexible, athletic and very pacy. Sometimes they do struggle with stamina, but they have speed to burn. Also, and this might be something to do with their roots, there is an innate grace and flair about their game. Think of the Caribbean cricketers, for instance. That same easygoing, this-is-a-doddle-man approach is part of the make-up of the black footballer. In my opinion, and the record books are there to confirm the fact, they are a decidedly valuable asset in any side. There have been some magnificent black players as I have already pointed out. One that I missed is Ian Wright. You can loathe him, like him, or spit his name out like an insult, but he has been an exciting, productive, magical performer and comparable with any striker of the post-war era. Yes, even my favourite Three Degrees.

I've put one of them, Brendan Batson, under the microscope already. The other two, Cunningham and Regis, emerged at roughly the same time and were players of a classic kind, a very distinctive sporting breed. In terms of sublime soccer artistry, there was no one in the country quite like them for a period. I have already declared Bryan Robson as the best player I have consistently worked alongside. But, for a period of approximately six months, I wouldn't be able to split Laurie and Robbo in that judgement. During that spell, Cunningham was the greatest individual to be seen operating in our domestic game since the halcyon days of George Best. He was simply magnificent, capable of working and controlling a ball until it could be fairly defined only as a conjuring trick. At the time, I said that if Laurie ran in the snow, he wouldn't leave any footprints: his balance and grace were of such quality. He had phenomenal skill and yet, for such a creative player, he didn't leave you short on the sweat quotient either. He was a heartbreaker, a matchwinner, and a scorer of many superlative goals. I remember one in a floodlit game at Derby County. He shouldered himself inside, cut the ball in with the outside of his right foot and bent it in around the keeper's groping left arm. Drool, man, drool, it was of such perfection. Jack Charlton was watching. He gave me a tug later: 'Hey, Ron, you could travel the world for a year and not see a goal as good as that.' I grabbed his arm, escorted Jack downstairs to my office, and plugged in the video. 'Just watch this, big man.' The tape was of our game the previous Saturday and it showed Laurie notching up another goal that was a carbon copy. That was Cunningham. Just an incredible performer.

The culmination, or maybe it should be described as a crescendo, of his huge talent came on a spectacular night in November 1978, in Valencia. They boasted in their team the likes of Mario Kempes, who just happened to have won the World Cup with Argentina; Rainer Bonhof, celebrated star of the great German side of the time; and several Spanish internationals earning fortunes. That night Laurie swallowed them up and spit them out as if they didn't deserve to walk on the same planet. It was a performance on a par with that long-cherished exhibition of European brilliance by Besty against Benfica in the Stadium of Light in Lisbon. And, essentially, it was the game that signed and sealed Cunningham for Real Madrid. He was going nationwide at that moment and the bulging wallets of the Bernabeu weren't slow to write the next act. That winter, in the late seventies and very much a focal point in an exciting West Brom team, Laurie was moving towards a certain soccer destiny. He was to be a pioneer in the contract freedom being introduced to our game. And you couldn't blame him for being ambitious to take advantage. I was told, once our season finished and the summer sun beckoned, Laurie jumped on a plane for Spain and knocked on the famously impressive front door of the Madrid club. 'Will you sign me?' he's supposed to have asked. 'I would like to play for you more than anybody else.' True or false, I don't know, but my own hunch is that it was the special performance in Valencia that sold him, even if the financial details were nailed down in my kitchen in Sutton Coldfield.

When the delegation flew in from Spain it included Real Madrid's president, of course, and their general secretary. Bert Millichip, our chairman, was there with one of our directors, but mostly I was centrally involved in the initial negotiations. I had fixed the bartering figure at £1.5 million, more than twice the transfer record at that time. Chatter, chatter, chatter and then the Spanish secretary opens up: 'We can offer you £300,000 immediately for Cunningham.' My Yorkshire terrier Charlie growled menacingly at him. 'See, *señor*, even the dog knows that amount is a joke.' They laughed and then asked to use the phone to call Spain. I followed them to the kitchen. I grabbed a brown paper bag, ripped it in half, and scrawled £1.5 million on it. They penned £300,000. For the next couple of minutes we wrote down the bargaining figures, alongside each other in two columns, until we reached £900,000. There was a shake of the hand and we walked back into the lounge of my house. 'Mr Chairman, ' I said, 'if you ask these gentlemen for nine hundred grand, I think you'll find we have a deal.' And that's how the great Laurie went on his way, courtesy of a supermarket paper bag. Not long after that, he couldn't kick his way out of one after suffering a number of quite serious injuries, one involving his knee. It was a handicap, I suspect, that stopped him achieving what his talent deserved. The other inhibiting factor in Spain, I suppose, was his age. It was 1979 and he was still not twenty-three, but what can you expect any footballer to do when Real Madrid arrive on the doorstep, offering the status of overnight millionaire and also, just as significantly, the opportunity to play in that wonderful arena for a lad who knew he was blessed naturally. There was also the contemporary belief, rightly or wrongly, that Laurie didn't get the best treatment out there. But I've always known he should have been a world great, instead of a player of a few brief, splendid seasons.

I reclaimed him from the Spanish League while I was at United around five years further down the line. It was only a loan, just three months of Old Trafford employment, but within that time I recognized that the dazzling brilliance, that ability to drive defenders insane, was still very much part of Laurie's armoury. What was missing was the scorched-earth pace that planted him in a different dimension during the earlier years. But Laurie wasn't just a showman on the pitch; with his charismatic nature he could attract almost as much attention off it. I recall George Petchey, Laurie's coach during the maturing early part of his football life at Orient, reciting a story that captured his nature perfectly. Apparently, if he was ever fined by the then manager, Arthur Rowe, for bad time-keeping or some other relatively trivial breach of discipline, Laurie had an immediate money-raising solution. He would pop down to the local disco, give them a demo dance in some competition or other, collect the prize money and arrive at the club the next day to pay off his fine. As I said, he was a real mover and shaker, this boy.

But there was a fundamental professionalism about him, too. He could, for instance, have played for United in the 1983 FA Cup Final against Brighton, but didn't. Even now I still can't quite believe that he turned down the opportunity of playing at Wembley in a showpiece game being transmitted across the world. You would think it was a temptation too big for any player to resist. The day before, I saw Laurie testing a suspect thigh by running twenty flat-out sprints down one side of the Bank of England training centre at Roehampton. No problem there, then, I thought as I strolled across. 'You okay, Laurie?' The reply came in a second: 'No, I don't think I could last the distance.' Simple as that. Mostly, in that kind of situation, a manager has to pry deep into a player's mind to discover if he is really fit and, if he's not, prevent him from playing for the sake of the team. Seeing I was uncertain, Laurie repeated his opinion: 'I think I will let the lads down if I play.' There was so much at stake, remember, for an individual who was desperate to prove so much, but he took the hardest option of all. He didn't play. That was why, five years later, I was delighted to see him make the Cup Final after all. He was employed by Wimbledon as a sub in their historic victory over Liverpool. It was a reward he deserved.

The predictable spin-offs of an international career largely, and this was another mystery for me, passed him by. He only got a handful of chances, admittedly, but most experts would agree that Laurie failed the test. He was such an athletic figure, an unquestioned master of running at pace with the ball and beating opponents as if they were merely a mirage. I particularly remember one game for England against the Swiss. I just didn't recognize the man out on the Wembley pitch. He didn't express himself, almost changed personality as a player, when in the white shirt of his country. 'You have become a passing player,' I accused. 'That's not your game – you devastate defenders running with the ball.' It was as if he wanted only to be part of the team, instead of part of the action. The maestro wore a mask and it didn't suit him. But when he was challenged, Laurie always maintained that was what the England management of the time wanted from him. My swift retort was, surely, if that was the case, why the hell did they pick him. He could destroy anybody with his running and ball-skills, but there were plenty of others up and down our nation far superior at actually passing the ball. He lost the international battle in competition with Steve Coppell, who contributed highly for England, but hardly had Laurie's attacking instinct or inventiveness. Still, that's not an unusual result in our game, is it? He should have been a giant, one of the all-time world players, but he never quite reached for the stars. The last time I met him was in Madrid. He took me out to dinner with the president of his new club, Rayo Vallecano, and he was greatly looking forward to a new challenge. 'Wait until I get back to the Bernabeu,' he promised me. 'That's when I'll really show them.' Sadly, Laurie never made it that far.

Big C was the third component of the Three Degrees, of course. If Cyrille Regis had been granted the capacity to score scruffy, sloppy, dead-ordinary goals, then I assure you all he would have been the greatest goalscorer the world has ever seen. It's a statement that can never be proved, but I don't make it lightly, because this was one absolutely incredible footballer. Cyrille always had to notch with the exceptional, the full Oscar job, his weekly candidate for *Match of the Day*'s goal of the century. I won't ever forget his specialist finish against Manchester City at Maine Road. He started deep and rolled like thunder as he went past Mike Doyle, then Dave Watson, treated Paul Power like a roundabout, and chipped Joe Corrigan, one man-mountain of a goalkeeper. It was that good, the whole of Maine Road rose from their seats in collective admiration and saluted him with a standing ovation. City's own fans clapped and roared and couldn't believe it. The great Joe Mercer, then a

City director, turned to Bert Millichip and said: 'That's close to the best goal I have ever seen.' Bert, in all seriousness and straightforward as could be, replied: 'Mind you, Joe, he doesn't get one like that very often, you know.' Joe and me buckled up laughing at that gem.

I can also remember another jewel from Regis at Everton. He had just chested down a cross and volleyed a screamer into the net, when he collected the ball on the half-way line. Mick Lyons was built like something out of *Gladiators* but no matter. Regis just went round him. Big Mick, fast realizing he would never catch up with an escaping Cyrille, simply rugby-tackled him, wrapping his arms in a deadlock around the waist. It didn't make any difference. Cyrille merely dragged him forty yards or so, smashed the ball into the net from the edge of the box, and then calmly, almost disdainfully, unbuckled his assailant. Such power in a forward I had never witnessed before. He was built like a cruiserweight and had the pace, near enough anyway, of an Olympic sprinter.

That special goal against Everton came, funnily enough, on the night when Regis declared he intended staying at West Brom and, in the process, unravelled a week or two of football intrigue that stretched all the way to the high office of the President of France, Monsieur François Mitterrand. Or so I was reliably informed. Now, this is a story that needs a deal of explaining so it might be wise to give the background. I hadn't been at the Hawthorns very long and neither had Cyrille, who moved there as a nineteen-year-old – a late starter in the professional game. As a new arrival in the Midlands area I was booked into a local hotel where I found two French guys were staying as well. Initially, I was assured they were a couple of journalists doing a magazine shoot, specifically with Regis in mind. He hailed from Guyana, a French colony, and that – so I was told – was their angle. Soon, though, I sussed their ulterior motive after a member of the hotel staff confirmed their real identity: one was a soccer agent and the other was the general manager of St Etienne who had targeted Regis for very obvious reasons. Not only was he an exceptional player, he was also eligible to play for France in the 1978 World Cup being staged that summer in Argentina. At that time, Regis had not represented England so the route appeared uncluttered.

Enter Monsieur Mitterrand. In the background, so I was informed at the time, he was secretly tugging at the political strings to push the deal through. The French were prepared to pay something around £750,000, well above the record transfer valuation of Kevin Keegan, and a huge figure for a player who had appeared in no more than twenty-five senior games at West Brom. Fortunately, we managed to persuade Cyrille to stay with us. It must have been a huge temptation for him. And, in truth, he knew far more about the manoeuvres and possibilities than any of us. Even to this day, we have a laugh about how he knocked back two journalists who wanted to make him an instant millionaire. His final pay-off was a much better contract with West Brom, plus two signing-on fees. I gave him one as a little sweetener, an extra bonus, for staying loyal when he could have made a quick killing. What I didn't know was that an influential club director had already crossed his palm with club silver for the very same reason. But, as the years rolled by, nobody could ever deny that Regis was an investment without a flaw.

He would, in truth, have been an even more sensational operator in foreign football than he was in the British arena, although, understandably, I never mentioned that at the time. Cyrille, you see, was very much a burst player, athletic, explosive, dynamic. Yet, in our country and for a reason that has forever puzzled me, the tactical demands laid on the front players are the enemy of such natural qualities. We ask our forwards to work in defence, closing down on the clearance balls, charging around in what can often be a false purpose. My belief is that with a danger man like Regis, the important consideration is to conserve energy, not burn it recklessly, so that when the crucial opportunity arises he has all the power available to make it count. The strategists of the continental game understand that and allow their forwards to concentrate their efforts mostly around the box, and certainly in the attacking zones of the field. Abroad, he would have been a predator without peer. In saying that, I have got to concede he wasn't bad in England either; a committed professional with a great attitude and a person of tremendous stature, too. I can honestly say I have never in my life met a greater guy than Cyrille. Furthermore, he is probably the best centre-forward I have ever worked with in my teams. If he had possessed just an ounce of nastiness in his nature, Regis, no question, would have been the best of all time in his specialist position. On the subject of spectacularly exciting goals, this feller was surely the founding father of the species. With just a little of the competitive chemistry of, say, a Denis Law, he would have been terrifying, the complete master. In full flow, nothing could stop him.

As an international, Regis never quite made the impact you thought he would. I saw a couple of his games for England and particularly remember his last appearance against Germany. For me, he was our best performer. Others, with the actual power of hire and fire, thought differently and Cyrille disappeared from the global game almost before he had arrived. At the time the common theory among the football brotherhood was that Regis lacked anticipation inside the box. But I argued, then and now, that he had an asset not too many English forwards have ever had: the belief and bludgeoning physical power to pick up a ball and run at a defence from thirty, forty, even fifty yards. Ask any defender on the planet and he will tell you that is the striker from hell; the scariest of all opponents and the type that stops them sleeping at night. He used to frighten me and I was only sitting on the dugout bench. He should, I might add, have been in my line-up at United as well. I know that, Cyrille knows it too, and he would have been sensational. This was a footballer, like Eric Cantona in later years, simply born for the Old Trafford stage.

I wanted to take him from the Hawthorns when I left in 1981 but, politically, it was clearly a difficult transaction to even consider. After Robson and Moses followed me up the M6 to Manchester it became damned near impossible. West Brom were extremely sensitive about my departure and what they inter-preted as a defection by two of their top players. The subject of Regis was a no-go area. But, with the benefit of hindsight, I should have been bold, ignored the inevitable flak and gone in with a bid. Yes, very definitely it was a mistake of mine to stand back. Here was far more than merely a very good footballer. This was a championship winner, who had the capacity to change United's destiny. I'll always regret not making that decisive move but at the time certain factors made me hesitate and hold off. I had already signed Frank Stapleton and there was also the emergence of Norman Whiteside and Mark Hughes, two not insignificant figures, to consider.

Years later, I did belatedly try to take Regis from Coventry in exchange for Alan Brazil. Most of the details had been agreed with their manager, Don Mackay, but then we discovered Regis had a major problem with a thigh injury. Our medical advisers warned me the Regis injury might even be career threatening, and the transfer collapsed. We switched to little Terry Gibson instead. Enough said, I suppose. The Three Degrees became simply a part of my football history but they had already contributed immensely to my football future – their success at WBA helped build my management reputation.

CHAPTER FIVE

The Hell-For-Leather Glory Years

The Three Degrees were an integral part of what, on reflection now, I consider my most exciting times in management. It all started in January 1977. West Brom were a team full of colour, entertainment, enterprise and hell-for-leather glory. They were, for the most part, the type of players who stirred the soul, made the job enjoyable and worth doing. Off the field, too, we were a bit different. No, we weren't quite in the playboy category of 'win or lose, we'll have some booze', but we didn't live by the traditional standards either. It was down to the very nature of the men. They loved life, lived football, but knew how to sample the best of both. And they did. Often. Just as long as it was under control and not at the risk of damaging their football performance. Okay, they were free spirits but they also knew when to stand in line and obey the code of a professional player. It made it easy to be in charge. They were simply great to deal with. You could take them out for a night, even allow them a couple of real benders on the booze when the team was away for a week. But lay down the law about a ten o'clock training session and they were all there twenty minutes early, sharp, buzzing and ready for action.

You couldn't do any of that now. It's a different era. That level of personal responsibility, a pro's innate dedication, seems to be missing. Allow these modern-day players a drink or two and they end up like the wild bunch. But back in the seventies, setting off for a European tie, there was only one order for my players: champagne all the way. Once the plane left the tarmac at Birmingham, they were all given the chance to have two or three glasses of bubbly. No harm in that at all. It helped them relax. On one trip to Galatasaray in Turkey our 'happy hour' went even further. This particular European tie had been switched away from Istanbul to Izmir because of a disciplinary order from UEFA. The team hotel left, shall we say, a lot to be desired, like efficient plumbing and a place to have a meal. So, instead of hanging about in the doom and squalor of it all, I took the players out the night before the game. We found a pavement café, had a beer or two and a bite to eat, and relaxed. To make sure the mood stayed upbeat, only a few hours before kick-off I whipped them off to the local swimming baths and got them all involved in a swimming competition. By the way, we won the away leg 3–0. Moral there somewhere, don't you think?

The longest trip I ever embarked on with West Brom was, of course, the pioneering journey to China at the end of the 1978 season. It prompted the now immortal line, delivered deadpan by John Trewick when asked if he wanted to go on an excursion to the Great Wall: 'Why? Once you have seen one wall, you have seen them all.' As you can imagine, it was a three-week experience that took you back a hundred years in time and also thrust you, full-frontal, into the implications of the one-party state. There they all were, clad in those grey boiler suits, obeying orders, doing what the system demanded. All a bit chilling really. And I've never understood why the Chinese have a population explosion on their hands. Already in place is the finest contraception on the planet – ugly women!

We were the first Western football team to be allowed to enter China since the revolution and I have got to say, by the standards of the day, they treated us extremely well. The hospitality was generous, the hotels pretty good. But it was difficult adapting, even for a brief period, to such an alien way of living. Remember, Chairman Mao had been dead only a couple of years and the notorious Gang of Four had just been arrested, incidentally in a place called Hangchow where we based ourselves for a few days. Throughout our travels we were kept under the never-ending vigilance of the men in grey suits, all the same dyed-in-the-wool Communist Party officials, with one common task: to make certain we didn't see anything they didn't want us to see, or hear anything they didn't want us to hear. Eerie stuff and too paranoid for me. I laid a bet with the lads that I would have the top minder drinking champagne and smoking Havanas before the end of the trip. In truth, I never got even close to pulling it off.

The Big Brother mentality in China at that moment in their history was best captured in an episode involving Ian Woolridge, the noted journalist. For years he had been desperate to gain entry to the Red Empire and take a look for himself. I suspect his profession made certain that was nigh impossible, so he probably used our summer tour as the convenient vehicle for getting access. Whatever, it was soon clear to me that you would never describe Ian, for all his urbane charm, as the most appreciative fan of the Chinese way of life. In Hangchow, he was granted the opportunity to put his ideas into very forceful words and, in so doing, revealed a sinister insight into how the boiler-suit brigade occupied themselves in the twilight hours. One night, the players and staff headed for the top floor of the hotel for an evening of recreation, playing cards and having a natter. When we wanted to go back to our rooms, there was no way. All the lifts had been returned to the ground floor and very firmly anchored there. We ended up spending the night marooned away from our beds. Next day, old Woolers, itching for a story for the home market, cornered me for an interview. His theme was very evidently the dangers a group of expensive British footballers had been exposed to on what was supposed to be a friendship mission. What would have happened, he asked, if the hotel had caught fire? You could easily detect the drift of his piece and it wasn't going to be exactly complimentary to the Chinese. Anyway, Ian trots off, taps in his story and files it to London. Next morning, he was ambushed and challenged by delegation representatives – the spies, in truth – who complained about the hostility and criticism of the Woolridge article in the paper. They insisted he was wrong, unfair and had showed their country in a bad light to the Western world. They rattled on and on in their shrill way. And that's where their scheming came unstuck. Woolers had filed his story all right, but he had done that on Saturday night and it could not appear in the *Daily Mail* until Monday morning – twenty-four hours after the Chinese tried to reprimand him. We knew then that they had been listening in and his phone line back home had been tapped. We never had any obvious proof, but the suspicion was that the rest of us were under the same kind of high-tech surveillance.

Mainly thanks to Woolers, we had one very pleasant interlude in China when we visited Shanghai. Through his phenomenal contacts that spanned the world, we stayed in an old colonial hotel that, throughout all the revolutionary zeal, had managed to cling to some familiar British traditions. In keeping with such old-world charm we decided to add one further authentic touch – a game of cricket, between Gentlemen and Players, in the hotel grounds. The match was going very well until Ally Robertson, obviously representing the Players team, worried that his side were losing too many wickets, decided to intervene. With a certain amount of style and flourish, he grabbed a white towel and quickly ran it up a convenient flagpole. He was using it as a signal of surrender, something of a joke really, but for the Chinese it was a wounding insult. From behind trees and pillars, out of bushes, under stones, they came at us in very angry droves. Not one of us was aware that to the Chinese a white flag is a sign of disrespect and, worse still, an omen of death. We offered profuse apologies, and quickly abandoned the game of cricket, but our hosts were not easily appeased.

I had more hasty explaining to do when a couple of the other lads landed us in trouble later in the trip. As you can imagine, on such a wide-ranging journey and obviously recognized as a VIP party, we had no alternative but to attend banquets on a regular basis. We came to one huge dinner too many on the social diary and politely I gained permission for the players to miss it. It was a half-hearted excuse admittedly, something about the boys needing to concentrate on the next important game. But tolerance was shown and we were pardoned the formalities. Everything was fine until Bert Millichip, very much the leader of the China enterprise and a man who knew his destiny lay solidly within the football establishment, returned to the hotel foyer after the banquet. With him were other dignitaries, consular staff and their ladies, all ready for a nightcap before retiring. What greeted them were amazing scenes of a very well known West Brom star, Ally Robertson, chasing another naked team-mate, Derek Statham, around the foyer, primed to throw a bucket of cold water over him. For Bert it was understandably a huge embarrassment, almost a diplomatic incident. Some extremely hurried, placatory noises from me calmed the situation.

In footballing terms, we had few problems. Most of the games fell to us quite comfortably, including one in Canton when the crafty Chinese believed they had a secret weapon: long grass. They allowed the pitch to grow five or six inches more than it should, a ploy aimed at thwarting our swift and accurate passing game. The answer? Instead of playing it through, we knocked it long and found the head of Regis every time. They had no defence against his aerial expertise and within fifteen minutes we were six up, with Regis celebrating four of them. By this time, though, the attractions of the mysterious East were beginning to pale. I knew it was time to make the great escape and head for Hong Kong and the world-famous Happy Valley racetrack. You couldn't imagine two such vastly different cultures existing shoulder to shoulder but that, of course, was years before the 1997 handover to China. On reflection, it was a very enjoyable interlude in my life and some day I wouldn't mind wandering in China again, just as long as it was for a good deal less time than our three-week stay.

We had been invited on that trip because West Brom was then quite a high-profile football club and Mr Millichip an influential figure in the game. Bert was the supreme diplomat, an accomplished tightrope walker in any tricky boardroom situation. On one occasion, high on the agenda for discussion were new, improved contract offers for John Wile, Bryan Robson and Brendan Batson. The debate went on for an hour or two, with various people putting in their five pennyworth why they should get a deal, why they shouldn't, how it was costing the club a fortune, and so forth. There must have been six radically different opinions on the topic and, you know what, Bert agreed with every single one of them. Truly amazing. It was at that point, and I do genuinely love the feller, that I knew Millichip was destined to be a high-ranking name in the FA. His clever filibustering stopped me arranging the contracts for three crucially important players. As I left the meeting, Sid Lucas, a shrewd old

Brummie who really knew his football and the workings of West Brom, pulled me to one side. 'Now then young 'un,' he said, 'that's the first time I have seen you leave with your tail between your legs.' As it happened, it all backfired on the club sometime later because the relative financial security Millichip's plan gave West Brom made it easier for me to take Robson to Old Trafford.

If Bert was something of a diplomatic master inside the corridors of power, he stepped out of that mould when he was in the VIP box watching a game. Sitting next to him was an eye-bulging experience, believe me. Let me remind you, at that particular time in his administrative career, before his elevation to the FA's top job, Bert ran the disciplinary section. He was, in fact, the chairman of the committee dishing out punishments for all kinds of offences, among the more serious being dissent and bringing the game into disrepute. Honestly, if anybody should have been charged, it was Bert – for his abuse of referees! For as soon as a game started, he put his West Brom hat on and maligned the match officials as much as any West Brom fan would. It was embarrassing to hear him, match after match, berate officials with really savage criticism of their performances. He had a fixation about refs and many times his comments were completely out of order. He wasn't shy about outsiders hearing his opinions either. More than once, he said to me: 'Your centre-backs can't be doing their jobs, Ron, unless they have collected twenty penalty points by March.' And that, let us not forget, is a statement being delivered from the mouth of the disciplinary committee chairman.

In every other aspect, I always found Bert, a practising lawyer of course, completely fair. Possibly to the public he gave the impression of being pompous, even élitist, but he was not like that at all. He was a very friendly, helpful character and a resourceful and tough one when he had to be. He took on the mantle of FA supremo during a period of uncomfortable demands in English football. They were troubled times with our national game plagued by hooliganism, much of which we transported abroad, and with it the consequence of seriously damaged reputations. Bert, I must stress, dealt with it in as dignified a way as was possible for anyone in that onerous position.

Though everyone close to him at West Brom, even in his earliest years, accepted that Bert felt his ultimate destiny was at Lancaster Gate, the administrative heart of football, he held the position of chairman at the Hawthorns for many years. It was a far-seeing, influential football man called Tom Silk, however, who was a director and the real power behind the throne. He was, tragically, to lose his life while still relatively young in an air crash over France, along with his wife, while piloting his own light aircraft. If it hadn't been for football, I would have perished with him. A week earlier, in 1980, Tom flew me back from our game at Brighton. During the brief journey back to the Midlands, he asked: 'If you are doing nothing at the weekend, I am off to the south of France, would you like to join me?' It was obviously a temptation but I explained it was impossible because I had to plan for the League Cup tie fixed for Everton on the following Tuesday. So, reluctantly, I turned him down. Without that decision, you obviously wouldn't be reading this book. Come the evening of the big game at Goodison Park, as we were standing around in the hotel lobby waiting for the team bus, another director broke the sad news. Tommy Silk had been killed flying home. Tommy was an entrepreneur, a right laugh but a deadly serious businessman, and a visionary who knew what he wanted for West Brom. It's a fair bet that if he had still been alive, I would never have left for Manchester United. He would certainly have made it very difficult for me to leave. And, what's more, he would have made damn certain that West Bromwich

Albion maintained their status as a footballing power and did not suffer their later decline.

With a little touch of good fortune, during the headier achievements of the club, I might have taken them to the Division One championship in 1979. We were denied on the last kick of the season, finishing in third place, courtesy of a Trevor Francis goal which elevated his team, Nottingham Forest, into the runners-up position. But it was the big freeze of that winter that, quite literally, put all our ambitions on ice. Just after Christmas we topped the league, when the worst weather in decades cancelled West Brom's fixture list for a month. Finally, when we returned to competitive action at Anfield, we had clearly been unemployed too long. The team was match-rusty and we were beaten 2–1. Liverpool emerged with the title again, with a record number of points. West Brom finished on 59 points, a total good enough to win most championships of that era. We had also reached the quarter-finals of the FA Cup and UEFA Cup and played eleven games in twenty-five days at the climax of our interrupted campaign.

It was the following season, however, that I will for ever regard as the pinnacle of my time in management, the period when I fulfilled the demands and responsibilities of the task better than at any other time or anywhere else. The odds were heavily stacked against me in the summer, seeking new energy and purpose after the title disappointment the season before. Due to contract freedom, I lost Cunningham to Spain and Len Cantello, an impressive midfield anchor, to Bolton Wanderers. Tony Brown, a finisher who lurked in the shadows and pounced with better effect than any rival of that era, had packed his bags for America. Just as bad, Regis and England fullback Derek Statham were laid up with knee injuries that ruled them out for months. In other words, half the team that put us in with big-league potential had been wiped out. I needed to put the roof back on, even if the foundations remained sound. Allison's second-time regime at Manchester City was also under serious review and I took advantage of their clear-out. With the Cunningham finances, I took on board Peter Barnes and Gary Owen and also waiting in the wings was David Mills. He was my ultimate transfer disaster, the player who subsequently declined to such a degree I called him my albatross.

Millsy was supposed to be the midfield predator to replace Bomber Brown. It was, clearly, a challenge to daunt the very best and for David it sadly proved too much. For him, the move went belly-up from the start. He couldn't even find the right hotel, or even destination, for the signing on a Sunday morning. If that didn't tell us the deal was jinxed, and we should be praying already, nothing would. But to shorten the whole catalogue of disasters, anything that possibly could go wrong for David did exactly that. He suffered injuries, took a huge knock to his confidence, and from being an England squad player he slowly vanished from the scene. John Deehan was another signing from Villa who was intended as Regis's partner, but eventually repaid the investment as a centre-back. Barnes and Owen were also sound purchases, with Barnsey notching thirty goals as a winger in two seasons, and Gary playing at West Brom for seven years before his career was ruined by an accident at home.

With that team, for all its frailties and frustrations, much was achieved in a very short time. And that is what underpinned my professional satisfaction and left me with the inner certainty that I have never managed any team better than that. I overcame greater handicaps, leaped more formidable barriers than anywhere else. By Christmas, the high-flying dreams of the season before lay in ruins: we were plumb bottom of the division. Then I made a big decision. I introduced Remi Moses, who was nothing but a promising kid, into midfield to snap and snarl and keep everybody on their toes. He made his debut at Crystal Palace during the first week in February of the 79–80 season. We lost just one of the next nineteen games and finished a very respectable ninth. It was a testing examination of my management ability, but I had succeeded in keeping the whole outfit bubbly and bright when heads were threatening to go down. The following year, the resurrection of West Brom continued, and we reclaimed a position among the top three. I left with the club soundly based and endowed with quality players, only to return six and a half years later with a club close to my heart at the very edge of collapse.

I was out of work in September 1987, when the call came. Ron Saunders had just been sacked at West Brom. I was invited by one of the club's directors, Brian Boundy, an ally of the late Tom Silk and a good friend of mine, to take over the reins and return Albion to their glories of old. He assured me he was taking over as chairman and that's what persuaded me.

But when I arrived, the size of the crisis became apparent and I wondered what the hell I had taken on. The place was in disarray and close to being skint as well; there was a dangerous mood of depression, and not many players of real substance remained. The club was in a right old state. I was very much the crisis manager. On the day I moved in, West Brom were bolted to the bottom of the old Second Division. I set about the salvage operation. We survived the threat of relegation, basically because salvation was delivered by a lot of experienced, older, well-proven players bought in a decided hurry. I latched on to Andy Gray from Aston Villa for just £250,000. Kenny Swain joined us from Portsmouth, then Peter Hucker and Brian Talbot, all adding know-how, tough minds and a willingness to do the business. I took players that other clubs had discarded, performers who had enjoyed their most productive seasons perhaps five years earlier. The average age was thirty-four, but it didn't matter; this was a salvage operation, make do and mend. Next I integrated new-blood challengers such as Carlton Palmer and David Burrows, while adding the quality of Arthur Albiston from Manchester United. Then, let me be honest, a stroke of luck. It was the capture of Chris Whyte from America, where he had been playing indoors. Initially, we recruited him on a month's trial and he didn't let me down. His impressive performances guaranteed that when I moved to sign him permanently, other clubs were brandishing cheque books as well. Palace and Birmingham were just two and they were certainly able to put more cash on the bargaining table than me. Once again I was in the wars at West Brom with the debate focused on whether we could afford Whyte anyway. It was madness. They said he would bust the budget; I argued he would save the club. Now, just think about it. Over two years, Chris was going to cost the club exactly fifty-three grand and that wrapped up his wages, legal expenses and house removal fees. I slammed on the board-room table, hassled and raged, and seemed to have won the argument. Then I discovered a single director had refused to sanction the deal because there was an extra payment of just £1,400 in pay-as-you-earn contributions. I exploded. Our secre-tary informed me that the objection would stop Whyte playing in our next big league game at Ipswich. I reached for the phone, dialled the dissident director, and told him: 'If you don't back off and agree, I'll be round to your house and give you a whack you will remember for the rest of your days.' Very rapidly the Whyte package was smoothed on its way. Little more than eighteen months later, after I had left the club, they collected £650,000 for him from Leeds in a tribunal-fixed fee. I had to chuckle when I heard the same boardroom members who had squabbled over his original signing, now complaining they had been short-changed. Whyte, don't forget, was the footballer they had said wasn't worth even fifty grand. That's what you get with a certain breed of director. No logical or sensible direction – and a complete betrayal of their job description.

Second-time around for me at West Brom was mostly about that kind of pettiness and football frustration. I had to wheel and deal, call in a few favours, and almost sing for my supper to get the players an overnight hotel on away trips. The rate of exchange for the team to get their bedroom accommodation was easily agreed. I would do a freebie after-dinner speech at the hotel to cover the cost because the club, tight as the proverbial drum, refused to pay. The cause wasn't helped when my close associate Brian Boundy resigned over internal politics. Charming! I was shocked. I had returned only because I saw him as an important ally, the purposeful link between boardroom and manager's office. His departure left me feeling distinctly isolated. The timing couldn't have been worse, with a few bodies for shifting, though, on the whole, the team was showing signs of encouraging development. One transaction, in particular, comes to mind and that was the departure of Andy Gray. Good player, smashing bloke, but always the cock-eyed optimist was Andy. The enquiry came in for him from Graeme Souness, then with Glasgow Rangers. He offered £25,000, it seemed a good career move for Andy, so I agreed. I then called the great man, telling him: 'There's a club wanting to buy you and they are pretty big.' Typically, came the reply: 'Who is it? Milan, Barcelona, Juventus . . . er'. When I started humming 'Flower of Scotland', he twigged and soon disappeared to do a smashing short-term job at Ibrox. Not many weeks later, I was surprisingly calling the removal men in as well.

Out of the blue a message came that Atletico Madrid wanted

to speak to me. On the night of my Old Trafford sacking, remember, they had first been in touch, but the deal hadn't happened. Now they were back offering me another very exciting opportunity. It was only weeks into the new season in 1988 and, for me, a matter of a year served on a two-year contract with West Brom. I have never tried to hide my ambition to be in charge of a foreign club but there was also a personal commitment to a team in the making. The next step was predictably easy. I went to see the new chairman. His name was John Silk and he was the brother of Tom, but their surname was the only thing they had in common – they were complete opposites. However, John was the man calling the shots and needed to be informed. I explained the scenario and also that I would be perfectly happy to stay with West Brom on one important condition: they double my contract, not the finances but the time span. My reasoning, as I outlined to the chairman, was that if I had the guarantee of long-term job security I would take the club back to Division One in three years. I also spoke privately to a more sympathetic director, who promised to try to influence the board on the contract extension. The response from the chairman was, well, a little less than helpful. 'Once you get us into the top division come back, and we will then look at an extension of your arrangement with us.' Not much room for manoeuvre there, then. It rankled obviously. Just before that statement the boardroom praise of my achievement in reviving a sinking team, and a club falling apart, had been almost gushing. Now they no longer seemed so committed and, as the deal in Spain was worth a minimum of ten times my West Brom wages, there was little left to discuss. I saw myself being pushed towards one career conclusion.

I left, very much in the knowledge that I could never have had the same relationship with John Silk as I had shared with his brother. He struck me as a man not really prepared to invest the necessary sums in the transfer market. And with that regime disappeared any reasonable prospect of West Brom becoming a sizeably effective club again. Bobby Gould took over from me, managed to get them relegated, and was immediately rewarded with a two-year contract. So that was what the chairman wanted – somebody to take West Brom and guide them to the opposite end of the division. It's a real test to read the minds of these directors sometimes, isn't it? Seriously, though, I recommended they put Brian Talbot in as my successor, and certainly if I had stayed the trading of so much young talent would never have happened. Big money was too much of a temptation and they sold Palmer, Don Goodman and David Burrows. The cheque book was being waved, but it might as well have been the flag of surrender in signalling the end of West Brom as a significant force in our football.

CHAPTER SIX

The Menace Within

Hard men and even harder liquor were an integral part of football long before I entered the game. In my days as an apprentice at Villa, I can still remember incredible stories about grizzly old pros in the fifties and their off-field antics. So the prying eyes of the modern media focusing on the heavy boozing follies of certain of today's footballers is not exactly news to me. Or mind-blowing for that matter. I recall, as soccer kicked off in the postwar decade, tales to make any kid footballer's jaw drop. There were players then, legends of Villa Park, who broke from training at midday. Off they would saunter to the local pub and there they would down six or seven pints. Maybe they would enjoy a plateful of pie-and-chips into the bargain. And then they would return to run twelve laps before enjoying an afternoon practice match. What's more they could all play and, yes, what I am really trying to say is that there has always been drinking in football. I think what has moved menacingly into our particular sporting business in the last couple of generations is really wild drinking among the stars. The odd pint of beer, downed at the appropriate time, is not going to harm any well-prepared athlete, on a running track or a football field. For instance, the great Liverpool teams of the last thirty years, champions all of them, were famed boozers. Particularly, the side of the eighties that I considered the finest of the lot. It was part and parcel of their dressing-room culture that they obeyed one code in the leisure hours: sink it before it turns sour.

My own philosophy has never changed: as long as an individual didn't betray his club with bad social behaviour because of drink, and always performed to his potential on match day, then limited quantities of liquor at the appropriate time were acceptable. If a player irresponsibly went down the local most nights of the week for a drink, it's obvious he couldn't perform to a professional level anyway. That kind of maverick behaviour would soon be detected and dealt with. But I have never seen any harm in footballers, conducting themselves in a proper mature way, letting off steam with a few drinks after a match. Or even in a social atmosphere, say, one other night a week. Drinking among team-mates, and I stress it must be in moderation, creates dressing-room spirit or, as they say in the more modern idiom, helpful male bonding. I have no objection to that whatsoever.

Some managers are of a sterner mentality and have argued for a total ban on booze. How they would implement it I don't really know. Don't think they do either, if they are honest. They're what I call the pasta preachers. But it's never that easy imposing draconian discipline, without applying common sense understanding of the animal you are dealing with. Footballers are pretty basic human beings by and large. They all appear to have climbed out of the cot believing that once a rule is created, it is essentially there to be broken. Sure, the Italians have forged their international reputations on smart football, the good food guide and being booze-free apart from the odd whisper of wine. Well, fine. But we are not like that as a nation, by social instinct or upbringing. And neither are the Germans. They like a few beers, too, and it doesn't appear to have done them a great deal of harm, does it? I have to smile when I hear recently imported foreign coaches to the Premiership advocating a pasta-only diet and a teetotal regime. Let me explain that for every player who enjoys a drink in our country, there is another who abstains. It's the way it has always been. Always will be, too, because social drinking is a British way of life.

It could be argued that the fantastic financial rewards on offer in our game resulting in the advent of the overnight millionaire calls for greater individual responsibility. I understand that point, but the fact is that responsibility lies where it should do – with the individual. If you drink too much, your performances will suffer and your value as a footballer will diminish at a rate of knots, as will your high earnings. If you are smart, therefore, you take it easy and sensibly; it is in the interest of every footballer to look after himself correctly. Never kid yourselves that footballers have to make too many sacrifices. They have a better life away from the work place than most of you. They have the wealth, the personal prestige, the keys to open all the right doors and make life sweet. I have enjoyed that side of football as much as anybody. As for the Champagne Ron tag, forget it. I like the odd glass of wine and I love champagne, for sure, just as long as it is the best and it's been bought by somebody else!

When the England squad hit the bubbly bar in Hong Kong in the summer of '96 it provoked a bit of a stir. All of a sudden our heroes found themselves surrounded by blazing headlines and instant notoriety. It surprised me, it really did. The graphic pictures, admittedly, looked a bit loutish, but I could understand why Terry Venables allowed his players off the leash, if only very briefly, at the end of a tour. In his thinking Terry is a lot like me and clearly felt that granting the players some recreation time would help, rather than hinder, their preparations for the European championship finals. Take a look at the record book and it would be hard to argue that he was wrong. What did anger me, and was to be strongly condemned, were the incidents on the aeroplane flying them back. I don't want to know the names of the guilty, or even the innocent, because what happened was a collective responsibility. It was unacceptable, hooligan behaviour. And the whole party rightly had to carry the shame and condemnation for it. That was a one-off. More disturbing still, and appalling in my judgement, have been the incidents when younger players of the modern generation really have overstepped the line. I have seen them at certain football functions quite literally drinking themselves into oblivion. And they have done it just for the hell of it. We are not talking the odd pint or two here, but the really hard gear of vodka, tequila and the rocket-fuel concoctions that would put anybody in orbit. Now, *that* is plainly suicidal and has no place in any soccer environment.

But even worse, far worse in fact, than the wildest of drinking binges is the drug problem within football. It does exist and it is a truly alarming problem. It must be nipped in the bud without delay or it could escalate and swamp the whole game in a very short time. Yes, I see it as a greater threat to football than anything we have known in the history of the professional game. All of us are aware of Paul Merson's well reported drug addiction (which we are all delighted to see he has overcome) and the way it jeopardized his career. He is not, believe me, an isolated case. Nowhere near it. There are others in the Premiership, even now, battling the same kind of traumas. Merson might well have indulged in drugs of a serious variety, but through the nineties other players with top clubs have certainly had experience of using illegal substances. I know from my own time at Villa that drugs are used by footballers at the highest level of their trade. I found out through a test I arranged with the club physiotherapist. The test was supposedly random, but the motive was very definitely calculated. And the subsequent results proved my suspicions were clearly correct.

Physiotherapist Jim Walker and myself told all the first-team lads they had to subject themselves to blood tests. To this day, not one of them knows the secret purpose of it all. We explained the check-ups were necessary for routine medical records that the club needed to have. When the analysis was completed we discovered that at least two of Villa's stars of that era had taken an illegal substance. If the evidence had been laid in front of the FA, they would have faced the wrath of the football authorities and would almost certainly have been banned for a lengthy period. The drug that showed up in their bloodstream was cannabis, or pot, and it justified our private feelings about the individuals involved. Another of Villa's big names used to call me at home, so laid back I suspected he was horizontal, and I always figured he must be on something better than energy pills. There is also a well-known England international, with a long Premiership career behind him, reputed to be the biggest dealer in football. He cornered the drug market and, apparently, whatever substance you wanted, he would very quickly have it available. I have no substantive evidence for laying that accusation, but his reputation has long been well known in the game.

I don't know whether the use of heroin is all that widespread, but without question there is a fairly liberal supply of coke by all accounts. It seems to have become part of the younger generation's culture. Young people collect at discos, raves or other kinds of nightspots where drugs are in plentiful supply and very much part of the scene. Because of their status and wallets full of easy cash, footballers inevitably are seen as easy prey for the pushers. If the individual has no self-restraint then, bingo, the equation is complete and extremely dangerous. Addictions, by their very nature, are exactly that. But there is an easy way to stop it, slicing the problem to the core with immediate effect, and that is the random test. I know of one club, from London and with a reasonable Premiership record, that has carried out its own spot checks on players. They managed to get around the delay in having the results delivered, too. At Villa we used a blood sample and that process takes roughly a fortnight to complete. The London club I'm referring to employed a much simpler route via a hair sample. That way they knew the results from the lab almost instantly. The football authorities implemented their own drug testing regime during the last few years. With limited success, I might suggest. The reason? It allowed the chancers to gamble with the system in the reasonable knowledge they could escape.

I have always advocated a much more rigorous application of the tests. There is enough cash flowing through the game to finance even the most complex system. The players' union has millions stashed away and it must be in their interests to be concerned about the long-term welfare of their members. The other institutions, like the Premiership, FA and Football League, shouldn't be against dipping into their collective pocket to impose one necessary safeguard in the war against drugs in our sport. That is the fortnightly check of every member of staff, of every professional club in the land, to detect the drug cheats. The reason for the two-week rota is basic.

Within that period it is easy for the technicians to detect the use of an illegal substance. So it must rule out the random gamble. Instead there would be a compulsory test that would rumble the guilty few and protect the innocent majority. They are out there, too, playing their games and living on the edge. In my later management years I would bet that on any average Premiership weekend, there were probably a dozen players – and here I am being very deliberately cautious, even kind – playing with some sort of illegal substance in their bodies. And, what's more, knowing they were. They believed the odds were on their side in beating the random system. Mostly, they were right.

You would catch every single culprit if football would only introduce and finance its own drug surveillance squads. They would be expensive, but they are desperately needed if our threatened game is not to pay a far more costly price. Of course, the first step must be in detailing what is on the banned drugs list. This really does need examining. For years, players faced the risk of being accused of using an illegal substance after taking certain sleeping pills, a cough mixture or a cold cure. Now that was downright ridiculous. My plan of campaign must be focused on the footballers foolish enough to dabble in the *real* drugs, whether they enhanced a performace or more likely ruined your life. First offenders could be fined, counselled and warned. As the level of abuse increased, more draconian punishments would be necessary for second offenders until the stage was reached when the repeat offenders faced bans for life. After all, you see the impact of drugs daily on the American sporting scene. Their biggest stars have been shown to be involved heavily in drugs. And what happens in the States is very often rapidly transported across the Atlantic to Britain's shores. We can't afford the contamination. Drugs in football is a serious reality. It must be dealt with by proper controls and we can't afford to wait a second longer, no matter the financial cost.

CHAPTER SEVEN

Mad Max

I wasn't on drugs, and to the best of my knowledge neither was he, when I first met a wild and whacky football character called Mad Max. But he was very definitely like something from an hallucination. And maybe that's why I bestowed on him that particular nickname. His real name was Jesus Gil and he was for a long time the all-powerful president of Atletico Madrid. He was also the man who granted me my longest-held wish – to be a manager of a foreign football club. He was in the end, you might recall, the boss who sacked me and, as I have told many people since, I have had longer holidays in Spain than I lasted as his manager. It was a reign of exactly ninety-six days, a period in which I took Atletico from virtually the bottom of the League to third top, precisely three points behind Mad Max's most hated enemy, Real Madrid. But it wasn't enough and El Presidente, without a single word or even a two-second telephone call, put my head on the block in February 1989. The supreme irony, even worth a bit of a chuckle now, was that when Atletico dismissed me I was actually back home in England, loading my bags and furniture on to the van to move to a new home in Madrid. What you might call a case of pack 'em and sack 'em. But, hang on, we are rush-

102

ing ahead of the tale. Let's get back to where it all began with Mad Max.

Back, in fact, to the autumn of 1986, after my sudden exit at Manchester United. As I have mentioned earlier, on the night of my sacking party I received the first call from the Spanish club. It was merely a sounding-out exercise. They wanted to know if I was interested. My reply was predictable and, subsequently, the message came through that I would be put in charge of Atletico for the new season. As far as I was concerned, the picture was perfect. But, as they say, the best laid plans can often go wrong. Three months after the deal was set up, the president making the appointment suddenly died. At the time, it was explained, there would be a series of elections within the club to appoint his successor. Not to worry, they also insisted, because the late president's nominee would declare me as his choice anyway. First, though, we had to go through the formality of a London meeting at the Metropole Hotel. Somehow I survived that despite the barmy intervention of a close pal of mine called Phil Black. It was a very solemn event with a group of very refined and formal Spanish grandees. Discussions lasted some hours until a uniformed commissionaire moved in on the group and kept busily interrupting our dialogue. He became such a pest that, in the end, I told him rather brusquely to hop it. It was only then that I recognized it was Phil in disguise. Apparently, he had bribed one of the hotel staff to lend him the braided uniform and peaked cap. And while I was giving him the hard word, there he was, standing to attention behind my Spanish interviewers, and saluting me in the style of that famous Benny Hill character. I just about kept control, pulled off the interview and landed the job.

Then it was off to Madrid and the hustings. I can't possibly describe it any other way because the election of the Atletico president was run along the same lines as a political campaign back in England. There were parties, meetings, TV interviews, speeches in crowded halls, the lot. And it was during all the hollering and heckling that I first bumped into the man I was later to christen Mad Max. He was a front-running candidate in the race to become Atletico's next president, and you could see immediately he had a lot of clout and a mountainous pile of pesetas to back his bid. Señor Gil paraded Cesar Luis Menotti, the coach who led Argentina to their 1978 World Cup win, as his new manager. He also vowed to buy Paulo Futre, then European Footballer of the Year and recent winner of the European Cup with Porto. Something, you might agree, close to a dream ticket in any election. And Señor Gil wasn't finished. He also hired a whole train to take hundreds of Atletico's fans to their game in Zaragoza. So it came as no surprise to me when, at the end of a very hectic week in Madrid, he bagged most votes and immediately took office. That meant, of course, that from looking to have a place in the sun, I was, in the football sense, very much in no man's land. Back home the season was already underway in that winter of 1987 and, for the first time in many years, I wasn't involved. I was simply unemployed.

I was later appointed by West Bromwich Albion and persuaded to return for a second stint as manager there. I was setting about the task of saving my old club from the state of decay it had fallen into when, in October 1988, I got the call I never, ever expected. It was from an intermediary of Jesus Gil, the man who had stopped me landing the Atletico job in the first place, telling me I was his choice to be the next coach. By then Menotti had long gone. So had about four of his very short-term successors. Now it was my turn. And the start of an incredible reign in Spain and one of the most fantastic periods in the whole of my football life. Yes, it was exactly that even though it spanned no more than ninety-six days.

How can I describe Señor Gil? Well, if you remember the Phil Silvers TV show and a character in the series called Doberman, he was like him, only magnified by a factor of at least two. Jesus was a big man, around 6'5" built like a fighting bull and with a larger-than-life personality – at times almost beyond the normal rules of sanity. He never kept his mouth shut for more than an hour. Controversy was his favourite, almost obsessive, game and did he love hogging those headlines. He strutted around all the time and left me with an impression of what the Italian dictator Benito Mussolini must have been like in his days of power. Whenever, for instance, Mad Max arrived for a match, he made such a grand entrance to the directors' box it was almost farcical. Quite literally, he was a VIP figure who commanded instant attention, as supposedly adoring Atletico fans swarmed beneath his balcony singing songs and football anthems in praise of the great man. Impressive it was, too. Only later did I discover that every single cheerleader was actually on the president's payroll. Without the wage packets stuffed with pesetas they wouldn't have been anywhere near the place.

One morning the local edition of *Marca*, a famous sports newspaper in Spain, dropped on my desk. There, plastered right across the front page, was a picture of my boss. He was dressed in, of all things, a convict's uniform and his huge, jowly face peered through the bars of a prison cell. Now, you can imagine Peter Hill-Wood or Martin Edwards doing something similar to make a public point, can't you? Exactly. The whole stunt was apparently connected with some particularly disparaging remarks he had levelled at the Spanish footballing authorities. As a result, the FA bigwigs slapped a ban on Gil and shunned him as an undesirable in the game. This was his public reprisal.

Shortly afterwards, just days before one of world soccer's greatest, most spectacular derbies – the collision between Madrid's great rivals Real and Atletico – he created more havoc. I had been in management a long time, admittedly, but this fixture filled me with excitement, apprehension, a touch of fear maybe, and wonderful expectation. I couldn't wait for it to happen. Suddenly, on the Wednesday morning building up to a great weekend in my life, with the whole of Spain transfixed by the derby preparations, I was confronted by another of Mad Max's wilder outbursts. A local journalist told me that the president, in his latest blockbuster for the papers, had warned that Atletico would be sending only their most junior team to play Real. I thought for a second or two it was a joke. By the look on the reporter's face I quickly realized it wasn't.

The explanation was that old Jesus, at his rampant best, had insulted his contemporary at the Bernabeu, Mendoza, and couldn't easily be forgiven. Apparently he had accused the eminent Mendoza, of being the sort of man who would break into your ranch and steal your chickens. Now, to the English mentality, that kind of jibe might appear mildly amusing. To the Spaniards, you couldn't possibly say anything more derogatory. It was like an act of war. The upshot was that, inevitably, the Real hierarchy were enraged and Gil was summarily banned from attending the big game. Just as inevitable was the retaliation. He vowed that his first-team stars wouldn't be allowed to show up if he couldn't be in attendance. Only the kids could play, that was his final word. It wasn't mine, very definitely not. 'The Atletico team that will be in the Bernabeu on Saturday will be our very best – and you can bet money on that,' I told the local pressmen.

When the day dawned, the president didn't show. He had landed himself a new role and was acting as co-commentator on the game from the nearby TV studios. You couldn't turn the spotlight off him too easily. Even so, come half-time, he was on the mobile phone to me. It was 1–1 and he was delighted, lauding us all and praising one of the great performances in history. They were his words, not mine. But, yes, we were handling the biggest of occasions very well. In the end, though, we lost 2–1 to a goal in the ninety-seventh minute. You had the impression it might have been played into the next decade to secure Real their win. And victory came courtesy of a scandalous free-kick decision.

What's more their famous goalkeeper, Francisco Boyo, took out four of my players in one-on-one situations in much the same way that the notorious German goalkeeper Schumacher brutally buried the Frenchman Batiston in the World Cup of 1982. Amazingly no action was taken against Boyo although, curiously enough, two of the Atletico players were sent off. Later, neither one was given a suspension when a disciplinary commission watched video evidence of their supposed crimes. Yet Boyo, viewed as the innocent by the referee, was banned for a then record nine matches for his on-field activities. Read between the lines and you might get some notion of the, what shall we say, idiosyncrasies of the Spanish League in that little affair. When I was later cornered by the press boys, all hungry for a blazing-mad headline, I remained deliberately calm. '*Nunca criticamos el árbitro en Inglaterra,*' I told them in my limited Spanish, which translates as, 'In England we never criticize the referee.'

The morning after, all the papers applauded me as the 'polite English gentleman'. Little did they know my real feelings on the subject. There were suggestions, naturally, that just as happens back home with the likes of Liverpool and Manchester United, in Spain also officials tend to favour the big clubs. Certainly that particular *árbitro* did not do me, or my unjustly treated players, any favours. That Sunday afternoon, mind you, when I walked into the Vicente Calderón stadium to watch our second eleven, Atletico Madrileño, I could hardly believe what happened. As I entered the official box, the 13,000 crowd rose to their feet as one and gave me a very emotional standing ovation. It was, apparently, in recognition of the team's gallant performance against Real and also my own diplomatic reaction to the result.

I certainly needed some comforting after what had gone on the night before. Not just the result either. A few of my closest friends from England had popped over especially for the game. Afterwards, I invited them all to a wonderful fish restaurant, despite the players pleading for me to return with them. What I learned later persuaded me they might well have been right. Because when the team bus arrived back at our ground, the delighted, beaming president was waiting for them. 'I'm so proud of you all, you are my heroes,' he told them. And with that he handed each player £5,000 as a personal bonus out of his own pocket. Needless to say, I missed out, so that proved to be the most expensive fish and chip dinner I have had in my entire life! Another glimpse, you might say, into the wonderful world of dear old Mad Max.

Strangely enough, for all the uncertainty, I always felt I got on well with the president during my brief stay. You just had to accept the bottom-line: you were living on top of a time bomb and one day the explosion would surely claim you. It seemed that if a coach wore a suit Gil didn't quite fancy, that was reason enough to hand him his cards. Once one of his managers was fired for nothing more sinister than losing two friendlies – and they were in pre-season. Colin Addison, my immediate replacement, was sacked at half-time during a Cup semi-final. I once saw a whole broadsheet page of Gil's appointments and dismissals. From memory, I was the third longest-lasting manager. I was almost tempted to ask him for a testimonial.

You were left with the distinct feeling that much of the aggro might have arisen not simply because of the immense power he wielded, but from the fact that he was something of a media junkie. He loved publicity of any kind. When I first met Gil in Marbella, he wanted the TV cameras in the room while I actually negotiated my contract. I stood firm, cleared them out until the nitty-gritty had been agreed and I had sealed the exact terms of employment. But for all his flaws, he was very generous. I ended up with a three-year contract, worth £250,000 a year, increased by exceptionally good bonuses for taking Atletico to success. I did, as well, find him a very magnetic character, always with a smile filling his face, and positively beaming as we climbed the league table. When I joined, Atletico were third bottom and in a certain amount of turmoil. Within weeks, I lifted them to within two points of leaders Real Madrid. We also reached the quarter-final of the Copa del Rey, the Spanish equivalent of the FA Cup. At the time, we felt confident we were developing a side to win trophies. Very rapidly, the dressing room had been transformed from a morgue into a place of celebration and achievement. That was important, I felt. After the Madrid derby, when some of the players poured out tears of frustration, I arranged to take them all out to dinner on the Monday night. It was something of a tradition in Spain. If a player notched a hat-trick, or was celebrating a birthday, he would invite the whole team to his favourite restaurant. A good atmosphere was created this way and the danger of footballing cliques developing was avoided.

So, I invited all the lads to this smashing old restaurant in the heart of historic Madrid. The invitation didn't extend to the president. It didn't matter – he still turned up. Midway through the feast, he rose to his feet to deliver, with all the considerable panache and charm he could muster, the address of El Supremo. He congratulated all of us, told us Atletico's team spirit and commitment was greater then than at any other time in the club's history. In other words we were on a roll and he was with us all the way. From memory, I think that speech poured from Gil's lips exactly three weeks before I got the chop. And so, understandably, I had not the slightest hint that the P45, or whatever it is called in Spain, was almost in the post.

Sure the situation was always going to be volatile. That was accepted as a natural law of life at Atletico. I just made up my mind, virtually from signing the contract, to enjoy every single second it lasted. The dismissal, though, when it came, was still weird. In an exceptional week we had just played three games, winning two of them and drawing the other. First, we made the trip to Murcia and beat them. Next, we headed for Valladolid and inflicted on them their first home defeat of that season. Finally, we tackled a tough fixture with Celta Vigo and drew when we had chances for another victory. We were only three points behind Real Madrid and very much in championship contention. Amid a very hectic first-team programme, I was summoned to an important policy meeting with the president. It was a Friday night, with those two recent victories under the belt, and everyone seemed at peace with the world. Including Señor Gil, I might add.

I headed for his offices in town. There we discussed a sudden transfer development over the Portuguese forward Futre, Atletico's most important player. The president explained that Silvio Berlusconi, the Italian TV tycoon and owner of AC Milan, had offered £6 million for Futre, a figure that was far in excess of anything offered at that time for any player in the world. Gil looked at me and demanded: 'What would you do, if we accepted this money for Paulo?' Very quickly I got my mind into gear. I laid down the plan of action to replace a great performer. First, I told the president, I would move to sign Jürgen Klinsmann, then an impressive young forward at Stuttgart. Secondly, my target would be Thomas Hässler, another great German I had just watched playing in a European game for Cologne. Thirdly, I would return to United with a £1 million offer for Bryan Robson which, at that time, I suspect they would have accepted. In Spain, playing just one game a week, Robbo would have been a sensation. Around this time I had also investigated a return to the pro game for Mark Lawrenson. He had retired with a long-term achilles tendon problem. But, again, one match a week in Spain would surely represent a stroll for Lawro. He, too, was keen on the idea, but because of financial complications over an existing insurance pay-out to Mark when he packed it in, and Liverpool's resistance to surrendering his registration, the ambitious proposal never got off the ground. With that initiative dead, and as the final and boldest move of all in my strategy, I promised Gill that I intended prising the great Butrugueño and Sanchis from Real Madrid. Their existing contracts were about to run out and we could secure them for nothing. It was a very convivial meeting, the president liked my transfer options, and also fully approved my idea to set up a reserve-team league. He knew we had a squad of twenty-three players and a lot of very good footballers who didn't get much more than a game a month, if they were lucky, because of the underdeveloped structure of Spanish football.

I was just ready to leave and link up with the players for the Vigo match, when I was asked to remain in my seat. The intervention came from Manolo Raborra, initially appointed as my interpreter, but over those few months of my management clearly revealed as the president's spy in the camp. You couldn't swop socks without it being passed on, if you know what I mean. Anyway, Manolo the message-carrier rose from the table, looked across at me and said that the president had a favour to ask of me. 'He is too shy, Ron, to ask you himself,' he said. I almost fell off my chair. Now anybody who knew Jesus Gil for merely a minute of his life might have said many things about him – but shy and retiring, do me a favour. The special request involved a complicated matter concerning a defender called Andoni Goicoechea. Remember him? You must do surely. He was the Spaniard who became infamous overnight as the Beast of Bilbao when he made a tackle, if it can be described as such, and left Maradona's leg in two pieces, almost in different parishes to be exact. When I arrived at Atletico he had been signed up by Gil but, subsequently, had suffered a very serious injury. He had been laid up for months on end. Now, apparently, the president wanted me to play him at Vigo. Strange, I thought. No, madness really. The lad could hardly run at that stage. In fact he was still a virtual cripple at that time. I burst out laughing: 'You must be joking, I can't do that.' Now this is where the complications started to develop. It transpired that little more than twelve hours after our Sunday game with Vigo, the president was due in yet another courtroom.

Just before my appointment, the sacking *señor* had fired four of his top players, including the Atletico captain, because they dared to speak out against him. They were due in court, too. But first it was the case of the club's recently dismissed doctor. He had been with Atletico for something like twenty-five years but was then seeking alternative employment. One of the statements he had made was that in his opinion the injured Goicoechea would never play again. It appeared the president's favour was for me to play the still-injured Spaniard that weekend to strengthen his legal argument in fighting the wrongful dismissal claim by the departed doc. Now Goico was a smashing big feller, a footballer who had operated at the highest level, but there was no way he could be risked in any competitive game. It was ridiculous and the president's request was denied. I never thought any more of the matter as I left the meeting. Whether that refusal played a significant part in my dismissal I won't ever know for certain. I'll just allow you to draw your own conclusions. The plain fact is we drew with Vigo and, as had been planned for a while, I flew home during a two-week lull in the Atletico programme to pack my bags for a permanent return to Madrid.

At midday on that crucial Monday, I was packing all the gear away when I received the call that shook me to the core. It was my assistant, Colin Addison. 'Ron, I don't know what to say,' he almost stammered. 'They have just offered me your job.' Then a slight pause. 'The only thing,' he added, 'is they haven't improved my contract.' I just couldn't believe what he was saying. I challenged him: 'So you have actually accepted it, then?' He mumbled something and, hurriedly, was gone. Naturally, I have to admit what I saw as his disloyal behaviour did seriously strain relations between myself and Addo for a long time. I thought he should have displayed far more loyalty and waited for me to return quickly to Spain to resolve a very strange affair. Since then, as they say, a lot of water has disappeared under the bridge and we have settled matters. But ask me why Colin accepted my job and, even now, I can't provide any reasonable, logical answer. At the time, there was absolutely no call from the club to say I had been sacked. It was only when I put a call into Raborra that I received any kind of confirmation. 'Has something material happened?' I asked him. He was evasive. 'Just tell me, do you want me to come back?' He replied: 'I don't think so.' I attempted to fly to Spain three days later but was fog-bound at Heathrow. My legal adviser, already over in

Madrid, suggested it was wiser for me to stay put. 'It's just mad out here. Don't bother coming back. We will have to sort it out in court.' *Adiós España*, like it or lump it.

Within a fortnight, Sheffield Wednesday revealed an interest and I took that job as Peter Eustace's replacement, initially on a short-term arrangement until the end of the season.

Back in Spain, meanwhile, the litigation rumbled on over my compensation. There is a legal obligation there to pay in full whatever is due from a contract if the employer terminates the agreement. There were a few squabbles, naturally. They accused me of running back to England to line up a new club at home. It was a preposterous allegation. Nothing could have been further from the truth. I loved it in Madrid, it was truly football happiness for me, and the record in just over three months wasn't too bad either. It read: played 15, won 11, drawn 2, lost 2, and I don't think anyone reaching that level of success in this country would be at the slightest risk of losing their job. All the same, even with the benefit of years to reflect on my experience, I still think of Jesus Gil as an impressive character. Not by a million miles does he rank as the worst chairman-figure in my career. He was very powerful, maybe too powerful for the stability of the club, and he also surrounded himself with a right load of minions, for want of a better description. And that's being extremely polite about them. But if you laid down the law to Gil, as I did in banishing him from our dressing room forty-five minutes before the kick-off, he respected the decision. Even if I did need to put a right gorilla of a guy on the door to make sure the keep-out order was never breached.

I never exchanged a single word with Jesus Gil for roughly three years after the sacking. The next time I bumped into him was while I was doing a TV commentary when his team faced Manchester United in a European tie. He came bounding across to me at Old Trafford. His opening line was: 'Olá, it's my favourite enemy,' then he burst into gales of laughter and grabbed me in a typical bear-hug. As I have emphasized, I always got on fine with him and I believed, still do in fact, that he respected the fact that I would never kow-tow or buckle to his bullying. To this day, though, I have never been given a sensible explanation why they sacked me at Atletico. Various stories have been bandied around, most of them ludicrous, and the daftest of all claimed that I spent too much time out of Madrid, that I took the team to the holiday beaches of Spain instead of the training ground. Hand on heart, I never did that even once. It was also maliciously suggested I used a racist remark to the Brazilian star Donato. That, too, was a blatant lie.

As official confirmation that I was nothing less than the innocent party, Atletico eventually paid up my contract in full. What's more, I have returned to the club several times since and been made extremely welcome by everyone there. Miguel Gil, the son of Jesus, took over executive control and, I have got to concede, the whole place seemed immediately to reflect far more stability. Raddy Antic, who used to play in England with Luton, remained as coach for a considerable period and Atletico had great success under him. But, without boasting too much, I am convinced if I had been left in charge for longer, Atletico would have been celebrating real achievements on the field even earlier.

Honestly and truthfully, I haven't the faintest idea why the end came so suddenly with the team very much on a roll. All I know is it was a huge disappointment for me, possibly even greater than leaving United. Spanish football, you see, was very much my kind of game. It was the sport of the people, involving the blazing passion of both star players and the humblest of punters, and that is what guaranteed its great appeal to me. I have never forgotten what happened once in Madrid when my wife Maggie and I were out strolling along the famous shopping streets of that wonderful city. 'Look who's over there,' pointed Maggie. It was Sevey Ballesteros. He had just won the British Open and was arguably the best golfer on the planet. Yet not a single Spaniard gave him a second glance. He was my hero and he was ignored by his own people. Next day, I remember telling the players who I had seen. 'Who?' they yawned. 'Oh, yeah, you mean that golfer.' They couldn't have cared less, or been more dismissive. Now if it had been Butrugueño or Futre, they would have been mobbed and buried beneath a mass of humanity. Because of this fierce commitment to the game, even the most high-profile players never gave me any problems.

I can only ever remember one footballer betraying his profession, even in a minor way, while I was at Atletico. One of the reserve team defenders had a night out on the town during which he paid too much attention to a whisky bottle. By the time I arrived for training the morning after, it seemed the whole of Madrid was mortified by the shame of it. Everybody from the dressing-room cleaner to the president's staff were muttering about the disgrace and shame of it all. The player was duly punished and that was the end of the episode for me. But it demonstrated the Spaniards' acknowledgement that it is a great privilege to play football and earn good money for it – something that seems to have disappeared from our own ranks. Spanish players know what a great blessing has been bestowed upon them and, no matter how prestigious their position or reputation, appreciate that fact. I never had another problem, other than with Señor Raborra. I suspect he stands somewhere at the centre of the mystery of why my reign in Spain was suddenly swept aside.

The first foreign offer of my career was laid at my door in my spell with West Brom towards the end of the seventies.

Philadelphia Fury put on the table a hefty financial package amounting to $50,000 a season which, three decades ago, was a lot of lolly to turn down. But I did, reluctantly, because I felt scuttling off to America then wasn't exactly the wisest career move. After I finished with Coventry in June 1997, the cash temptations proved even tougher to resist. Besiktas, the well-known Turkish club, offered me a tax-paid inducement of £600,000 a year to manage them. Again it was a no, and by now you must consider me a candidate for the white coats. Down the years, I was also approached to move to Istanbul to manage the Turkish national team, while Nantes, during the 87–88 season when Mo Johnson played for them, wanted me to go to France. Little did I know then that my ambitions abroad would be realized in Spain. All too sadly, though, the dream survived for less than a hundred days.

I could, in fact, have returned very swiftly when both Seville and Valencia tried to tempt me back with lucrative coaching offers. Las Palmas, also part of the Spanish League, wanted me as well around the same time. But the trouble was I had committed myself to trying to bail Sheffield Wednesday out of relegation danger.

CHAPTER EIGHT

Wheeling And Dealing

Even though my experience abroad was brief, it was still rewarding and it also swept aside one of football's most-quoted clichés. You know the one I mean: that once anybody leaves Manchester United, whether he be player or manager, they are well on the way to an unfavoured destination, namely the scrapheap. Or, at the very least, that departure must inevitably mean dropping a few rungs down the ladder of achievement. My career record, I hope you'll accept, disproves that particular argument. Atletico, with a crowd following much greater than anything witnessed even at Old Trafford, can hardly be described as a backward step. Supporters of Sheffield Wednesday and Aston Villa, my next two clubs, would rightly maintain that there is life after United, too. And after beating Alex Ferguson's favourites at Wembley with both those teams in two packed-out Cup Finals, do I need to say more? What I will add is that, ironically enough, after working in Spain I felt even better equipped to manage a club of United's stature. I suggest that Fergie might agree, after those early years of torture in a very tough job. He survived an extremely hazardous ride between 1986 and 1990 when, people better informed than me have since suggested, he might have been sacrificed if United

Left: John Nash, the man who won me over in one conversation and got me on the management ladder. NORTHAMPTONSHIRE EVENING POST

Above: As manager of West Brom – a team full of colour, entertainment, enterprise and hell-for-leather glory. SPORTING PICTURES (UK) LTD

Below: Training during my second stint at West Brom. David Burrows, now at Coventry, is on the extreme left. ACTION IMAGES

The Three Degrees – Laurie Cunningham, Brendan Batson and Cyrille Regis – were an integral part of what I consider as my most exciting times in management.

WOLVERHAMPTON EXPRESS AND STAR

Returning from West Brom's pioneering trip to China in 1978. We were the first Western football team to enter China since the revolution.

THE MAIL ON SUNDAY

Joining Manchester United in the summer of 1981 and winning a manager of the month award.

MANCHESTER EVENING NEWS

Signing Bryan Robson for Manchester United was something I thought would never happen. Robbo, it goes without saying, is the finest, the greatest, the most rounded and accomplished footballer I have ever been blessed to work with.

MANCHESTER EVENING NEWS, MARK LEECH

After a couple of false starts I finally got the chance to manage in Europe. At Atletico Madrid I met the one and only Mad Max, Jesus Gil.

Bert McGee, the old Sheffield Wednesday chairman, promised Maggie and I that we would love Sheffield because it reminded him of Rome! STEVE ELLIS

With Trevor Francis, who would become my successor when I left Sheffield Wednesday. STEVE ELLIS

Above: Welcoming Carlton Palmer to Hillsborough. Below: Roland Nilssen who signed from Gothenberg, lived his football life according to a strict professional code. Here we are celebrating Wednesday's League Cup victory. STEVE ELLIS, COLORSPORT

Above: Following my heart rather than my head and joining Aston Villa, the club I supported as a boy. This is my first press conference with old Deadly.

WOLVERHAMPTON EXPRESS AND STAR

Left: Steve Staunton. I will concede that there was a touch of good fortune when I prised him out of Liverpool.

WOLVERHAMPTON EXPRESS AND STAR

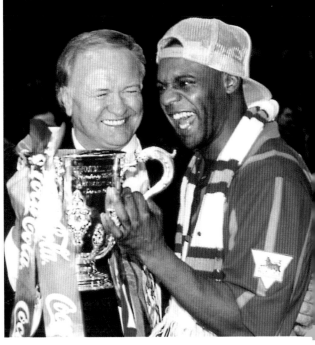

Above: Mark Bosnich. One of the finest and most athletic keepers in the land. ACTION PLUS

Above: Celebrating winning the League Cup with Dalian Atkinson. He was, without doubt, the fastest footballer I have ever seen in my life. SPORTING PICTURES UK LTD

Below: Before I ended up as one more Ellis statistic, Villa managed to beat Inter Milan in the UEFA Cup. Here is our winning penalty. COLORSPORT

Above: Avoiding relegation with Coventry. EMPICS

Left: At Coventry I played Dion Dublin at centre back for the first time, maybe laying the route for his England future. COLORSPORT

Right: When I left Sheffield Wednesday, there were cries of Judas. It was the magnetic, mesmeric attraction of turning a football possibility into reality that brought me back to football and a return to the club. ACTION IMAGES

Left: Brian Clough – my all time No. 1 manager, with his assistant Peter Taylor. EMPICS

Below left: With Gordon Strachan at Coventry. EMPICS

Below: With Andy Gray, my assistant at Aston Villa. I had always admired his enthusiasm and knowledge, and felt he had the background to become a first class manager. ALLSPORT

Still the only manager to win three major trophies with three separate clubs. With Manchester United we won the FA Cup in 1983 (above left) and again in 1985 (below left), with Sheffield Wednesday we won the League Cup in 1991 (above) and with Aston Villa the League Cup in 1994 (below).

Right: With my
wife Maggie.

Below: With
Norma Lane,
secretary at
Sheffield
Wednesday and
my dad Fred.
His telling
words, 'You will
never know
unless you have
a go,' got me out
of the building
game, and into a
different ball
game. STEVE ELLIS

had found a suitable alternative. Since then he has enjoyed more than a decade in charge, has merited his success, and demonstrated that if patience is preached in the boardroom, the right man will deliver the proper rewards.

More and more though, in the closing seasons of the nineties, you feel that the game has become more pressured, an atmosphere mainly created by a new wave of directors. The ego polishers, I call them. The loadsamoney generation, mostly from a background in the City or the commercial world, who arrived with a wad and believed overnight they had the qualifications to be a football boss. It was not a trend, I hasten to add, that overwhelmed United but, yes, it was a club changed dramatically from the one I managed. It developed into the home of a sporting industry, more of a financial institution than the headquarters of a team famous for playing in red. I accept that the whole structure of football in general has altered significantly since the time I was there in the eighties, but no club clung more tenuously to the commercial bandwagon and progressed further on it than United.

They have benefited hugely from the financial revolution. United arguably slapped more in the bank from television revenue in a single season than we had as our total turnover between '81 and '86. Then, of course, there was the twenty-odd million, and climbing, from the replica shirts, the souvenir trade and the truly incredible Megastore. No question, it became a very different ball game for Fergie than it was for me. He stood as manager of a club able to compete in any arena with the likes of Barcelona, Real Madrid, AC Milan and Juventus, all the giants of the global game. In my time that just wasn't possible. I spent a little over £7 million, and recouped £6 million of the investment. It was called balancing the books and I was made very aware of the hard financial rules from the first day I arrived.

I don't intend to give an impression of jealousy. Far from it. I enjoyed my time with United. It was a great adventure and I am certainly not envious of what happened later. I loved to see them sitting on top of the football pile so often, at least when they weren't challenging me at another club. I left to create a little record of my own, anyway, as the first manager to lift three major trophies with three separate teams.

My United experience wasn't exactly without its rewards either. Two FA Cup Final victories, another Wembley appearance in the League Cup, never out of the top four and a few semis, too – not bad. Then there was the youth development, a facet of United's place in the national game rightly emphasized during the Fergie era. I was quite proud of what happened in my time. You don't get much better than Norman Whiteside and Mark Hughes as home-produced talent. Well, do you? The only difference, as I see it now, is that after my departure United have made a great play with the general public and in nationwide headlines about their production of superkids. It was not such a high-profile topic when I was in charge and I never meant it to be. But nobody will ever convince me that the massive change from my decade to Fergie's domination wasn't all about finances. Not counting out the pennies any longer, but having bank vaults full of the stuff. And being prepared to invest it in the finest players around. That was the significant mind shift that transformed everything.

Take my experience with Mark Lawrenson in 1981. I wanted him, made our play before Liverpool, but lost out because the money wasn't immediately available. In Fergie's time it just wouldn't have been allowed to happen. No way. Then, of course, the classic case of missing out on Gary Lineker before he joined Everton as Andy Gray's replacement in the mid-eighties. The old enemy, balancing the books, was to blame for that, too. Long before Howard Kendall made his successful bid and lured Links to Goodison Park, I had been busy sounding out the possibilities. I spoke to Gary's adviser, Jonathan Holmes, fully aware that Lineker was out of contract at Leicester in the summer of '85. I also knew he quietly fancied joining United. The snag was finding the funding. My most likely option was to trade-off Frank Stapleton, which I tried to do. Two foreign clubs, Bordeaux and Mechelem in Belgium, were interested. Frank wasn't. He refused to leave Old Trafford at that time, and so it was a matter of reverting to plan B. I got back on to Holmes in the hope that he was prepared to accept a delay until I could raise the transfer cash from other sources. I asked him to shelve our deal for a few months. Tentatively, he agreed. From the feedback, I understood at the time that Gary didn't have much objection either. The proposal was for the player to agree another twelve-month contract at Filbert Street and stay there until I could conjure up the necessary big ones. Fine. At least it was until Gary was no more than thirty minutes from putting his name to that new contract. In stepped Everton, whisked him away for talks and that was the end of another transfer plan. Cash flow, you might say, effectively made sure United would never benefit from a torrent of Lineker goals.

The repercussions have never been lost on me. It would be reasonable to assume that if Lineker had joined United then, and delivered the goals you would expect from a performer of his calibre, my job would surely have been saved. Because the one asset we always lacked in that period at Old Trafford was a high-powered, prolific finisher. Most of our other units functioned just fine. We were blessed with good team balance, had abrasive and creative factors in midfield, and were sound enough at the back. The only thing missing was a truly instinctive predator. Stapleton, unquestionably, was an impressive line-leader, arguably the best centre-forward in the land for a time. Young Hughes was very similar, a link-man and a linchpin of the attack, who created the spaces for other people. Neither was, though, the out-and-out poacher I felt we needed. So, in those days, the goals had to come from various sources: Robbo piled in with a few, the wide men contributed too, and Frank and Sparky offered their ten or fifteen apiece. Oh for a Lineker, a footballer able to turn candidates into champions, as he demonstrated very swiftly at Goodison Park.

I remember a conversation I had with Jimmy Greaves around that time. He was heavily involved in television, had trailed Lineker around the Midlands, and felt he was the best young finisher he had watched in more than twenty years. You might say it took one to spot one, but I don't think too many people imagined Gary would become as great a striker as he eventually did. Certainly I didn't. But he could, and definitely should, have played for United.

Lineker was the one we missed and another international, in the shape of David Platt, is the one who supposedly got away. Or, more precisely, the one I let go. I've never considered that to be the case and quite a few people in the game would readily support my view. Platty, in truth, is an example of the young lad, who never looks as if he's going to make it, and then turns himself into a superstar. Brilliant, first-class, and I applaud him for it. At the end of every season, managers agonize over the future of the latest batch of promising kids, and need to select one or two for the heartbreaking cull. For the unfortunate discards, Platt is the name to remember. He is the footballer, maybe above any other, who proves there can always be a come-back around the corner.

Even now, years later and with the benefit of hindsight, I see Platt's departure from United as the right decision at the time.

Consider the facts as they were then. He was a young centre-forward in those days, not a midfield runner capable of nicking important, match-changing goals. And he was stranded in a queue behind a whole bunch of more promising youngsters banging the door down and begging for their opportunities. Hughes and Whiteside, of course, were the big two. Then there was a lad called Scott McGarvey and another, Nicky Woods, regarded by many envious clubs as a major star in the making. Sadly that potential was to be wrecked by a serious injury. But what it meant was that in a pecking order of five or six front players, including the men established in our first team, David barely got a sniff in the reserve side. What he was then was a sound lad, an admirable worker and a very conscientious player. He deserved a break, another club where the ladder might be easier to scale.

He could have stayed at United another year, but I figured it wiser to do a ring-round for Platt's benefit. I offered him to his home-town club, Oldham, but they declined. Like everybody else their preference was for young Woods, but he wasn't going anywhere. Eventually, I gave Dario Gradi a buzz at Crewe in 1984. David was nudging nineteen at the time and, to be strictly fair, they took him after some persuading; basically on my recommendation as much as anything. For a while, Dario, well respected for developing youthful talent, remained unconvinced. He viewed Platt as a very average performer. Then, apparently right out of the blue one summer, the lad arrived for pre-season training and simply blossomed beyond belief – the classic late starter. Subsequently, he got the opportunity to clamber back up again with a move to Aston Villa. Even at that stage, Dario concedes, he never realized how far Platt's development could progress. So much so that Crewe didn't even insist on including incentive clauses in his contract, traditionally seen as extra transfer cash based on future success and international appearances. They just asked for a flat fee and sent him on his way. At Villa, David did reasonably well, helped by their status and the fact that they were on an upward charge from the old Second Division. From there, you might say dear old Platty enjoyed a gradual rise to overnight fame. He was smuggled into the England set-up, very much as a fringe player, and then Bryan Robson got hurt. Bang! The dice rolled the right way, David slammed in the winning goal against Belgium in the 1990 World Cup Finals, and the story of his career became something akin to fantasy football. The rewards of Italy's Serie A, the glories of Juventus, next Arsenal, and an unstoppable ride to the kind of personal achievement nobody would ever have foreseen or predicted. I've always suspected that if David had stayed another couple of years at United, heading nowhere fast and floundering in the reserves, his destiny would have been to remain a very ordinary player in a mediocre team. He would never have been an item in the English game. But he grabbed his chance, and the blessing of a very strong, single-minded streak in his character carried him where he wanted to go in his profession.

Much the same might be said of Peter Beardsley, another class act allowed little chance to give the grand performance at United. Another regret? Well, in a way, yes – but once again special circumstances prevailed against it happening. I first saw Peter playing for Vancouver Whitecaps when we took them on in a summer friendly in 1982. It was immediately plainly obvious to me that he was something of a player. I took him on a three-month loan. Unfortunately, most of the time he figured in the reserves and only managed one senior game in a League Cup tie down at Bournemouth. Once again a key factor in reaching a decision was the log-jam of forwards ahead of Beardsley. So, too, was the £500,000 fee demanded by Vancouver, a quite significant pile of dosh in those far-distant days. Brian Whitehouse, the reserve-team manager, counselled me with the sound advice: 'Pete's a very handy player, but it's still half a million. I have got a lad already here, who is as good if not better, and he's cost us nowt. Sparky will do that job, just give him the chance.' That's exactly what I did, although when Peter packed his bags I urged him, on his return to Canada, to get busy in an attempt to get the fee cut. Then we would definitely be interested. Not long afterwards Newcastle's manager Arthur Cox made the investment and little Peter ended up in the Second Division with Keegan, Terry McDermott, Chris Waddle and company. They sheltered him from the public glare and immediate expectations in a way that would never have been possible in Manchester at that time. In retrospect, I wish I had landed Beardsley, but if I had taken him it would have halted the development of Hughes. Swings and roundabouts, as they say, and certainly it worked for the benefit of Beardsley. Like Platt, he found a far less difficult route to the top.

They are the decisions, any manager realistically appreciates, that can come back and kick you right where it hurts. Mostly, I hasten to add, when the full facts are not, or cannot be, placed in the public arena for reasonable debate. The issue of Mark Hughes, even more than Platt or Beardsley, and his departure to Barcelona is just such a case. Before I set out the background let me establish one undeniable truth: not for a moment did I want Sparky to leave and I did everything in my power to persuade him to stay. But money talks. I emphasize the point because of a statement Fergie, my successor at United within months of the deal that took Hughes to Spain, was responsible for virtually as he turned the key in the door. He was astonished, he said, about the transfer and insisted he could barely believe the club had allowed such a talent to move abroad. Fine words, false premiss.

It was a deal taken out of my hands in an equation of contract complications and personal ambition. But more of that later. Of initial importance is the remarkable development of Sparky from unknown to high-priced foreign export in little more than eighteen months.

When I first saw Mark Hughes he was coming up sixteen and whacking a ball around in United's indoor gym. I was less than knocked out, I can promise you. He looked morose and unenthusiastic and his football was worse. To put it simply, he was downright slipshod and lazy, just the opposite of the bright and lively kids I love to banter with in training. I muttered something to the other coaches along the lines of, 'Well, he's not up to much, is he?' Next, I clocked him in our youth team at Leeds when they had a very powerful outfit. Once again, he looked sluggish and less than impressive. Then, in an instant, Sparky left me gobsmacked. I had almost given up on him at the moment he collected the ball, beat four defenders as if they didn't exist, and smuggled the pass through for a Whiteside goal. 'Hang on, lads,' I said, 'maybe I've been a little premature about this geezer. He's a player all right.' In a matter of a few seconds, Hughes had shown me the kind of quality that was later to become his trademark at the very highest level. It was just that he was slower than the rest in establishing himself and making an impact. When he did, it was like a warhead exploding.

He made his United first-team début as a left-winger in a League Cup game at Oxford in late '83. He scored, too. But it wasn't until the following season, 84–85, that, almost meteorically, a major hero of the postwar game suddenly took over. He was a warrior who played his heart out – a performer to stir the soul of any red-blooded supporter. He was also homegrown. He couldn't fail, could he? And he didn't. Boil it all down, add the factor of Terry Venables and a kid from nowhere on peanuts money. It was a headache waiting to happen. As Sparky had emerged so suddenly, he was only then picking up around £200-a-week on a reserve-team contract, a deal due to expire within eighteen months. If that was allowed to happen, United, at the very best, would collect just £200,000 for Hughes if he decided to leave. We needed to act fast and we did. A new pay deal was urgently put in place and Hughes signed on at United for another five years. There was just one snag, a real crippler at that. His agent insisted on a buy-out clause being inserted, which compelled United to allow Hughes to consider his options should a foreign club pursue him with an offer of at least £2 million. What could the club do? We were over a barrel. If we backed off, Hughes could quit for buttons. Sign him up and at the very least it was £2 million, then a British transfer record by a considerable distance. And that is exactly what happened. Okay, it was very much the second-best option, but it was some kind of protection. And it was only unbuckled by a bit of bad luck and the intervention of one man. That man was, of course, El Tel himself.

Barcelona appointed Venables as their new coach just as Sparky was being hailed as a sensation in England after less than two seasons at the top with United. If the Spaniards had recruited a foreign coach, nothing would have happened, but Venners knew all about Sparky and he pictured him as the perfect foil in a dream partnership with Lineker. Circumstances simply conspired against us. I know everybody raised their eyebrows when the sale went ahead, but they didn't know I had spent some weeks behind the scenes bending Sparky's ear about it all. I desperately wanted him to stay. I tried to convince him that it was too early for him to move abroad. He had less than two years' experience of top football, he wasn't married, he would be just a well-paid recluse in Spain. Most of my warnings, unfortunately for him, would prove uncomfortably true. But there were massive temptations for Sparky, not least being the financial rewards. At United his wage had been considerably improved to around £1,000-a-week basic. That was a bit of a wad in England; but in Spain it was a round of drinks. Barcelona lured him with ten times as much. Really, it was no contest, I'm sorry to say.

So off Sparky trotted, still wet behind the ears, very immature in the football sense, and understandably so with such limited experience, and maybe not yet properly equipped mentally to survive in Spain. Over there, the foreign import is always the first target for any hostility when things go wrong. It can leave deep scars in even the most committed and confident footballer. Sparky understands this now. The tragedy is that, if he had delayed his departure from United for just three or four years longer, he would have been an absolute sensation abroad.

His contemporary at United, of course, was Norman Whiteside. And what a player he was! Tell you what, with another yard of pace, he would have been the greatest player in many generations. Norman, ironically enough, joined the club on the same day that I did in the summer of 1981. More correctly, he actually signed apprentice forms after being attached to United as a schoolboy, even though at that early stage he looked about thirty and played with equal maturity. The sad thing was that no sooner had he arrived in the camp than he was gone, packed off to hospital for a cartilage operation on the knee that ten years later was to bring a premature end to his career. He was missing for a while and the first real glimpse I had of his ability was when he scored that Hughes-created masterpiece at Leeds in a youth team fixture in 1981. Some goal, some footballer. His only handicap was a lack of sprinting speed. With that extra gift, he would have been the most complete player to come out of these islands since John Charles; in other words the best in Britain. Even so, he was still one of the outstanding contributors of his generation. His game was all about intelligence, awareness and the perceptive pass. At times, his skill was astonishing like the Wembley goal where he employed an Everton defender as a screen to fool Neville Southall and bend that FA Cup Final winner past him in '85. In the modern jargon, big Norm always had the advantage of seeing the big picture. He knew exactly the position and availability of every player on the pitch at any given moment. Therefore he could pick team-mates out with uncanny accuracy to punish the opposition. Yet, wrongly, that was not always the image of Whiteside presented to the general public.

Too often, and in a serious distortion of his talent and contribution to United, he was cast as no more than a thug. Norman was tough, a strong and very powerful opponent, but he was never cut out to be a hatchet-man. Not on your life because, to put it simply, you could always see him coming a mile off and move out of the way. It was the only part of his game that was predictable. He would come roaring in like a runaway locomotive, the crowd would be up on their feet, and ninety times in a hundred the intended target would be gone and waving farewell. Honestly, I would always prefer a tango with Whiteside than a tussle with Sparky. In the physical sense, he was far more dangerous. Norman was a wholehearted heavyweight, while Sparky had some cunning about him. Craftily, he would bide his time and wait his opportunity. Between the two of them, it was no contest really. Not for a moment am I trying to suggest the Irishman couldn't look after himself. He certainly could, but there is a significant difference between doing that and being spiteful or malicious which is how Norman was sometimes depicted. In one game at Anfield, I remember a certain Liverpool player calling Whiteside a coward. Frank Stapleton questioned his sanity and urged him not to suggest it again – in case Norman got to hear him next time. Frank was an international team-mate of the player in question and I think it was very sound advice. In telling him to button the lip, he was doing his fellow countryman a distinct favour.

Not so lucky was another even more famous footballer in Spain. Norman was barely seventeen when he played for Northern Ireland in that wonderful World Cup tie when Gerry Armstrong's super goal beat the host nation in Valencia in 1982 to make the quarter-finals. I was there doing television. At one point Norman tackled Juanito, the absolute darling of the Catalan crowd, and for a moment I thought the Spaniard's orbit might deliver him into the commentary box beside me. The home fans predictably went ape, screaming for Whiteside's summary execution or worse. He didn't bat an eyelid and just stared down at his fallen foe as if to say: 'Hey, *señor*, do you want some more of where that came from?' Mostly, though, Whiteside was a juggernaut out of control with the horn blaring, enabling the majority of opponents to escape without too much damage. It was his guile, artistry and footballing sixth-sense that I appreciated far more. Often I would tell him: 'Norman, don't worry about that other silly macho stuff – just kill them with your ability.' In my opinion, most of the time he accepted the advice and did exactly that. In Bryan Robson's absence through injury, I even made Whiteside United's captain when he had only just turned twenty. That footballing honour is the true measure of the real Norman Whiteside. He had the perfect temperament and remained unfazed by the most demanding occasion.

Like Hughes, Norman was, unwittingly, fundamental in Alan Brazil's short career with United. And maybe a factor in what I consider the unfair accusations of panic-buying in my final year at the club. Certainly, Brazil should never come remotely close to being placed in that category. He scored thirteen goals in twenty-nine first-team appearances at United and I would never condemn that record as a poor return. My reasoning for wanting Brazil had been straightforward. I figured he would be a useful foil for Stapleton; I knew he had been the beneficiary of Arnold Muhren's midfield supply at Ipswich and I believed the partnership could surely blossom again; and, finally, he had a proven record for scoring goals. In the end, he lost out for two reasons. Number one was that he was rendered redundant as a serious candidate for the front line by the emergence of Whiteside and Hughes. Basically, the pair of them made it impossible for me to pick him. The other reason, as time went by, was that Brazil just couldn't cope when the United crowd turned nasty and started hounding him. Possibly I didn't help, either, when I presented him with his début at the expense of Norman, already something of a cult-figure with the terraces as a product of the United youth system. That was Whiteside's special identity; poor old Brazil was a come-lately outsider. He seemed to allow the crowd reaction to upset him so deeply that, eventually, as a sub it looked like he preferred to warm-up in the tunnel. There was no rhino hide to protect him from the barbs. Sad, really, and also a disappointment for the whole club.

On reflection, I would consider it was a transfer deal without any great margin between profit and loss. Seemingly unable to cope with the crowd's venom, though, unfortunately Brazil clearly had to go. We arranged a swop with Coventry, the first intention being to recruit Cyrille Regis in the exchange. That was duly sabotaged by an injury scare, with our medical experts insistent that it was too risky to take Regis on board. Pity that, he would almost certainly have strutted the Old Trafford stage better than most. So, in the end, the transaction revolved around the arrival of Terry Gibson. I considered his extra pace might provide attacking variation for us. It was a theory that never had a chance to prove itself. In truth, the whole scene was just too big for Terry. He couldn't handle it and, if I had to hold my hands up to one transfer gamble that failed, it would have to be the signing of Gibson. Not Peter Davenport, though, whom I also recruited around the same period. Dav, let nobody fool you, was a good player and capable of operating in a number of positions. At United, he boasted a goals record of one in three which is always respectable. And whatever else the cynics might suggest, Davenport spent three years with United and then they sold him at a profit. How can that be considered an expensive mistake?

Another reasonably cheap purchase who, at £500,000, cost marginally less than Davenport, was Jesper Olsen from Ajax. Yet he still represented my most extravagant foreign investment for quite a long while. Jesper rapidly got to grips with the English mentality and our different tactical ways, and looked, initially, as though he would deliver huge dividends for the side. He had plenty of quality in the locker and his first season, when we won the FA Cup in 1985, was certainly encouraging. Next time out, I figured, he might even develop into a contender for Footballer of the Year. Olsen's early promise was largely undermined by a serious injury, though, and I have to concede that eventually his fame came via the front pages rather than the back. That was unfortunate because Jesper was an extremely gifted winger and, off the park, a nice enough bloke. What might surprise the English football public is that people in his native Denmark, and also in Holland, remember him as a very different character. They saw him as a fiery, explosive little so-and-so on the pitch. I didn't have to wait long to have first-hand experience of what they meant. In fact, you might even say I had a ringside seat. In all honesty, Arthur Albiston delivered an early warning about

Olsen's suspect methods on the training field within days of the Dane's arrival. 'It's going to go off out there, gaffer, unless you watch it carefully. Jesper is definitely a bit naughty,' he told me.

Those self-same words ran through my mind at the very next session. It was a little razz, a five-a-side between the first team's players and I was in the sweeper role in Remi Moses's side. Suddenly, Jesper burst through with the ball but overran it. In stepped Remi, tidied it up as neatly and efficiently as he always did, and started up a counter attack. Next, almost a full second later, Jesper carried on through with the challenge and almost cleaned out Moses. I couldn't believe it, neither could Remi, but his survival instinct clicked into gear faster than you could blink. Instantly, he adopted a crouched and well-primed stance, almost a cloned image of the boxer Marvin Hagler. Then bang, bang, bang, blood was spurting all over the place and Jesper was in a sorry heap on the deck. I moved swiftly to intervene. It wasn't necessary. That particular one-sided contest was well and truly over.

The only outside witnesses were two Danish reporters. I attempted to smother any leaking of the incident by quickly talking to both of them. My tack was that it had been a simple collision of heads, but they weren't fooled and, I suspect with the cooperation of Jesper, the whole story hit the headlines. Inevitably, it triggered a few problems within the camp and taught Jesper the painful lesson that it wasn't a wise move to go around kicking people, particularly one Remi Moses. I have already discussed the physical threat of Whiteside, Hughes, Robson, and also the likes of old bruiser Kevin Moran, but of all of them the one I would not have liked to tangle with was Remi. He was the original silent assassin. Jesper, in a second or two, discovered that he had a team-mate as useful with his fists as his feet.

I dealt with the issue without delay by calling the two players together in my office. Apologies were offered all round and I took immediate disciplinary action against Remi with a fine of two weeks' wages. Certain outsiders demanded even more draconian action, like moving Moses on to another club, but I never considered that as an option. Remi, for a start, had not provoked the incident, he had been more sinned against than sinner, and while not condoning his retribution, I fully understood his reaction. Let's be honest, too, and concede that scraps between team-mates will always happen inside a training camp. Football has its physical side and tempers are bound to snap at times. It was just that this particular incident received more publicity than I would have wanted and more than any other I have witnessed. That, I must say, could hardly be avoided with sorry-sight Jesper's eyebrow full of stitches for a while. He learned from the experience though. From that moment on he always made sure he was in Remi's five-a-side team, never the opposition. Wise man, wouldn't you say?

Well, at least that was within the confines of the Cliff training headquarters. Outside their protective boundaries, Jesper landed himself in another serious scrape that involved a Dutch taxi-driver and, eventually, yours truly. It happened in 1986 when we played in a four-team summer tournament in Amsterdam with Ajax, Dinamo Kiev and a South American side. We had already qualified for the final and were due to face Jesper's old club, Ajax, on the Sunday afternoon. When the preparation work had been satisfactorily completed on the Saturday morning, I freed the players for a walkabout and shopping trip in the city. But the curfew was applied – 7.30 for dinner back at the hotel, or else. Suddenly, with that deadline only seconds past, our physio, Jim McGregor, not the best man for hiding a problem, grabbed me. 'Seven are still missing, boss.' I was annoyed. Immediately I thought of Robbo and the other big hitters such as Whiteside, Moran and Albiston. I couldn't have been more wrong. This time, would you believe, it was John Boy and the rest of the Waltons. In other words, Jesper, Chris Turner, Gary Walsh, who was on his first big trip, Peter Barnes, Mike Duxbury, Terry Gibson and Clayton Blackmore. Hardly the crew from hell, and that's what seriously concerned me. It was so unexpected for that lot to break the curfew that I even feared they might have been involved in an accident. Then, around ten-thirty, Duxbury and Gibson were spotted sneaking back through the hotel lobby. They were given the third degree and it transpired that Jesper had decided to show them all a few of his favourite old haunts in Amsterdam. He had a bee in his bonnet at the time because he knew I had left him out of the team for the showdown with Ajax the following day. He had been wounded and this was retaliation time. And the rebel leader decided to take his baby-face pals with him on the town. At some stage, he finished up with more facial damage, not quite in the Remi category but serious all the same, after a minor fracas with a taxi-driver.

I left Mick Brown, my assistant manager, on dog-watch patrol around the hotel corridors to wait for the others to arrive back. Still fixed in my mind is a mental picture of a growling, grumbling Mick, certainly very unhappy at being kept out of his bed, so you can imagine the reception for the stragglers when they returned. Particularly as it was nearly dawn, roughly 3.30 in the morning. They had enjoyed their night of freedom and enjoyed a few drinks. What they didn't relish was the first punishment. I ordered an eight o'clock wake-up call for every one of them, plus a fresh training kit at the bottom of their beds, followed by the order: 'Right, you lot, it's a six-mile run around the park with McGregor and then I want to see you all when you get back.' My original plan of action was to send Jesper and his six renegades back to Manchester on the next plane. But that proved impossible because both Turner and Walsh were involved and I would not have had a goalkeeper for the Ajax game. It would have been unfair to spare them and banish the rest so they stayed. I couldn't understand how the whole group could be so brazen and stupid. It wasn't just irresponsible, it was dumb. They must have known they would be found out. They were and it proved very expensive. Back at Old Trafford I immediately docked two weeks' money from their wages and warned them that any future breaches in discipline might well see them paying an even heavier price. In effect, they would be putting their United careers at extremely serious risk. Episodes of player misbehaviour such as this, I have to admit, were rare during my six-year administration at United. Mostly, I recall them as wonderful seasons of football adventure and personal pleasure. No small measure of success either. For a while, it was a dream job but never, as Fergie appears to have considered it since, a club where I felt I could fulfil my football destiny. There was too much else to be attended to on the Atkinson agenda.

CHAPTER NINE

The Dream Turns Deadly

It was in the summer of 1991, June to be exact, that I faced a management decision with far more emotional impact on my life than anything that happened at Old Trafford. To be truthful, I doubt that I have ever dealt with a greater, or more demanding, dilemma in all my years in the game. Just weeks earlier, I had celebrated the most successful season in Sheffield Wednesday's modern history: promotion back to the First Division combined with winning the League Cup, the club's first major trophy in fifty-six years. Maybe as the manager I could be accused of a shade of bias, but I genuinely felt we had the foundations to build one of the country's best teams. And that, pure and simple, was my big dilemma. Because, amid all the euphoria at Hillsborough, I had suddenly received a phone call that was to alter the whole focus of my career once more. It came, via an intermediary, from the chairman of Aston Villa, the aptly named 'Deadly' Doug Ellis. He stands, probably in a minority of one, as the only club chairman in the English game I always knew I could never comfortably work alongside. But here he was, offering me what I had always wanted: Villa, you see, were *my* club; I had followed them since boyhood. Now, on my seven o'clock morning drive to Sheffield every day, I suffered the agony of zooming past their training ground. That, I accept, was my fault. I could have solved it with a move to Yorkshire, but it still amounted to my daily dig in the ribs, the reminder of what I had always really wanted. For years and years, I had privately considered Villa to be my ultimate destiny as a manager.

So, when the bait was dangled, I was hooked. The small problem of a productive relationship with my employer, Mr Ellis, was conveniently buried at the back of my mind. Much the same way went the knowledge that I would be surrendering arguably the most satisfying job I have ever had, at Wednesday. It was a case of heart ruling head in many ways. Personal desire, rather than other professional considerations, pushed me remorselessly in one direction. Until, that is, an eavesdropper literally dropped me right in it and caused much unnecessary aggravation for all parties involved. Somebody apparently overheard a so-called secret telephone conversation between my accountant and Villa's legal representatives. The local radio station in Birmingham got the tip-off and, suddenly, it was broadcast nationwide that I was heading out of Wednesday, bound for Villa Park. But there was an extra complication to this already tangled plot. The story broke on a Friday morning, just hours before I was due in Sheffield for the open-top bus parade of the steel city. It was Wednesday's long-planned homage to their fans in recognition of a wonderfully successful campaign. Originally, I had planned to go ahead with the official tour and then break the news of Villa's approach to the board later. With the secret in the public domain, blasted across every newspaper you could lay a hand on, that was impossible. The unfortunate leak meant that when I arrived at the ground, I was met by hundreds of Wednesday fans pleading with me to stay.

I hurriedly held a private meeting with Dave Richards, the club chairman, and another influential director, Cliff Woodward.

They counselled me against leaving a good job half-finished and then, 'What about those great supporters who want you to remain here?' So many doubts, so much searching of conscience. You will understand the scenario. The pressure was on and, in an emotional state rather than a rational moment, the decision was reached: I would stay at Sheffield. I knew in my heart it was wrong and the Wednesday players round me at that time have subsequently told me that my body-language said it all: they knew I was being torn apart.

Still, once the civic reception was over, I made my escape and drove back to my Worcestershire home. Quite unexpectedly, on the following Tuesday afternoon, I was lounging around in the back garden, soaking up the sun and very much at peace with myself, when the door chimes went. It was, lo and behold, the Villa chairman and his secretary, Steve Stride, the friendly persuaders so to speak. I had no prior knowledge of their arrival; they just turned up to add weight to the negotiations begun seven days earlier. I think they had quickly got the vibes from what had happened in a hurry at Sheffield and rightly antici-pated there had been no real conviction about my decision. In an hour or two of arm-twisting talks, Mr Ellis considerably increased the financial package which, in all honesty, wasn't the decisive factor. Still, I had again been convinced I should manage his football club. By that stage, I was committed. I had no alternative but to meet the Sheffield board to attempt to secure my release amicably; if that wasn't possible, I would have no choice but to resign. I knew it could only lead to grief and hostility, but it was the lifetime 'I-wish' job for me and I couldn't resist.

Next day it was the road back to south Yorkshire and another brief discussion with Dave Richards. He, I appreciated, was in as much of a predicament as I was. Preferably, I wanted the comfortable exit; for him that was potentially too hazardous a route. He explained that if he allowed me to go by mutual agreement, he would have to answer to the directors and the supporters. The only option was resignation and, no bull, it was the hardest decision I have ever taken. I knew I would take flak; I understood that. The Wednesday fans had their own reasons for feeling betrayed. Their agenda was different from mine and they didn't know everything that I knew.

Exactly a year before, for instance, I had been discreetly sounded out about a move to Villa before they appointed Joe Venglos. But at that time I had just taken Wednesday into the Second Division. I felt an honour-bound obligation to stay, shape a team for the promotion campaign, and help them back to the major league. A year on, without being aware of that approach, Dave Richards suggested: 'Give us one more year and then move to Villa next summer.' It was, of course, an impossible request to fulfil. Everybody in football knows it's a game in which everything is down to timing and, if I ignored Villa's overtures, more than likely the opportunity would never come my way again.

Proof, though, that my relations with Wednesday's inner sanctum were still professional, is that they asked for my recommendations on a replacement. I immediately put forward the name of Trevor Francis. At that time he had been with the club for two years, knew all the first-team players, appreciated that the playing staff was sound and was familiar with the whole workings of the place. He understood, like me, that the team only needed tickling along to be a success. So it proved. In 1993 they finished third in the championship race, reached Wembley twice in the FA and League Cups only to lose on both occasions to Arsenal, and relished a few more well-earned moments of high achievement. I believe the majority of Wednesday supporters, although initially niggled at the way I left, very rapidly came to appreciate the longer-term benefits of my time at Hillsborough. Certainly, in the weeks and months following my departure, I was grateful to receive many generous and appreciative letters from them. So much for the Judas role, then? Well, not quite.

In the quirkish, often bizarre and fatalistic manner that football deals with its principals, there could be only one opening fixture the 92–93 season. You've got it in one. My new club Villa, thanks to a very mischievous computer at the FA, had to travel to play Sheffield Wednesday. They were waiting for it, of course they were, and that was only the media. They stoked up the tension to such a fever pitch, you would have thought I was set to be strung up by my ankles from the nearest lamppost. Even my newly appointed assistants, Andy Gray and Jim Barron, had almost swallowed the propaganda. Jokingly, they refused to sit alongside me as the team bus arrived at Hillsborough – just in case the sniper missed and got them instead. In reality, there was a bit of jostling, a few jeers and, naturally, the cries of Judas. But, honestly, I've endured worse ear bashings from Maggie, my wife. Even when I appeared on the touchline, the reaction of the Wednesday public was decidedly mixed. It was as if they felt they had to protest, subject me to a bit of verbal stick, but there didn't seem much conviction or genuine venom about their reaction. I swear there was even a small ovation from a certain section in the main stand. There was little to applaud, at least in the opening minutes, from my Villa team. David Hirst and Danny Wilson banged in a couple of goals to expose our first-day uncertainty and fulfil the wishes of the more vengeful elements. But Cyrille Regis, thanks to some advice from old warrior Gray to rattle Wednesday's goalkeeper Chris Woods with the physical stuff, delivered some relief and a good goal just before half-time. Dalian Atkinson, a former Wednesday forward, added to their pain with an equalizer, and another of my new signings, Steve Staunton, claimed the winner. After a victory like that, and particularly at the start of a new season, there was only one place to go. The health farm, of course. And that's where I ordered the Wednesday bus to take us. It's got to be the best place to recover from a hangover, hasn't it? Oh, and yeah, Judas picked up his share of the bar bill.

Ironically, if Joe Venglos had taken my advice a few months earlier I wouldn't have been in the job anyway. As the previous season was drawing to a close, I supervised Wednesday's reserve team at Villa. Joe, such a nice bloke and a coach of proven credentials, was coming under fire as Villa flirted with relegation. I remember the *Birmingham Mail*, after one crushing, five-goal defeat by Manchester City, coming out with a screaming headline that demanded: 'Go, Joe, for Christ sake go.' It was vicious, vindictive and unnecessarily nasty. And also totally unjust treatment of a football man who arrived in this country with a deservedly well respected reputation. Joe had demonstrated his knowledge in charge of the Czech national side; his problem was understanding the mentality of the British players. He was used to a more spartan regime and could never come to terms with, for instance, footballers wanting a drink after matches. Long before the recent invasion of foreign coaches, he fell victim to a clash between different sporting cultures more than anything else. I discussed all the ramifications of that at our reserve game and also told Joe that if he genuinely wanted to stay at Villa, he must never quit. He knew certain individuals were undermining his authority and attempting to squeeze him out. I told him to stick to his guns. I meant it, too. In a matter of weeks, though, he clearly decided it was time to cut his losses and he left Villa Park by mutual consent. Once I stepped into his job, I soon realized that restructuring needed to be quick and positive. Without any delay, I recruited Andy Gray as my assistant. I had always admired his enthusiasm and knowledge and felt he had the background to become a first-class manager. Instead, Andy would later decide to take a different route within football's broader reaches and become a match analyst with Sky.

Others, at least as famous, had also opted to fulfil long-standing ambitions elsewhere before I even arrived at the club. David Platt was a case in point. Towards the climax of the previous season, Bari had tried to tempt David to join them in Italy. His immediate reaction, at least in public, was to confirm his commitment to stay at Villa for a further season until his contract expired. Within two or three days of the start of the pre-season build-up, though, I assessed his attitude in training and reached my own conclusion. David's heart just didn't seem to be in it any more. It was pretty obvious to me his football focus had drifted elsewhere and, rather than mess around, prompt action was needed. That was to take the Italian lire, help David on his way, and rebuild the team with his transfer fee. So I stayed behind to meet the Bari delegation while the rest headed for pre-season preparations in Germany. Chairman Ellis was also away, talking another good game I suppose, on holiday in Majorca, but I dutifully kept in touch with him by phone. Within a couple of days I nailed down the deal for Platt's move: a cash fee of £5.5 million, plus two friendly matches that Bari guaranteed would give us a further £500,000. Everybody seemed satisfied, even the Italians, who packed their bags and went home.

I shot off to Hanover to join the first team and, within a matter of days, Ellis returned to England to complete the transfer formalities. Nothing could have been simpler or so I thought. But then he was on the line saying he was under siege from the whole media circus and that the Italians were trying to browbeat him into accepting less money for Platt. My reaction: 'Tell them to clear off then, Mr Chairman. Believe me, they won't dare return without the player.' The Latin mentality would not allow the Bari directors to lose face with their fans after promising them the famous England international. Not long after he was back on the blower, boasting with the news that that he had finally struck a deal. You can imagine my surprise when I was told it was now £5 million, plus the guarantees. It seemed to me that we had lost out on five hundred grand. I think that if we had held out, they would have paid the higher amount. Still, the cash was in the bank and Platty was off to Serie A.

It left me with more negotiations that I most definitely kept under very close personal control. We needed new players, and fast. In a matter of weeks I had wrapped up virtually a new Villa team. Steve Staunton, a blinder of a deal at £1.1 million from Liverpool. Over to Spain next and just over £2 million the pair for Dalian Atkinson and Kevin Richardson after their brief experience at Real Sociedad. Paul Mortimer, a £350,000 turn-around signing, who lasted three weeks before returning to Charlton. Darius Kubyski, £200,000 agreed with Legia Warsaw. Shaun Teale, a snip at £375,000 from Bournemouth and, of course, a longer-term investment in Ugo Ehiogu. He cost me just forty grand and must now be worth in excess of one hundred times that figure. While at Sheffield, I had seen Ugo playing for West Brom in a youth team. He looked some prospect and I pressed their then manager, Brian Talbot, to sell him. He wouldn't budge. But Ugo was only on an apprentice's contract and when that expired he had no desire to stay at the Hawthorns. Clubs were notified and we moved quicker than the rest to snap him up. I also took my old pal Cyrille Regis from Coventry on a free transfer and, suddenly, the team was doing okay. It was not, though, the finished article. Within three months I knew what we needed above all else. We were short of a young goalkeeper. Nigel Spink was on the staff and Les Sealey, a forceful dressing-room character, had also joined us. But I needed a younger version, an ambitious kid to develop and bring through. Initially, I focused on David James at Watford, a quite impressive prospect when I checked him out, but we couldn't get down to the nitty-gritty of doing a deal. Then the name dropped like a newly minted penny: Mark Bosnich. It had to be him.

If you need any reminding of his early background, Mark spent his teenage years at Manchester United but was turfed out of the country under rather stringent work-permit regulations. Nobody doubted his high-level calibre; it was his ancestry that was the problem. But, on the grapevine I heard he wanted to return to England and have another crack at the pro game. Brian Whitehouse couldn't have been better placed to give me the briefing. He had been Bossy's reserve-team coach at United – now he was my chief scout at Villa. Perfect. His verdict: 'If you have the chance of signing him, don't hesitate. Go get him because he could be the very best.' Andy Gray put in a call to Jim Leighton, formerly Mark's senior team-mate at Old Trafford, and Jim was positive and applauded Mark as the best young keeper he had ever seen. Enough said. So next all I needed was a chainsaw to tackle a massive tangle of red tape. At United, Mark's problem was a lack of international caps, a regulation enforced by our own players' union to guard against the English game being flooded by cheap foreign imports. When his student's permit expired in 1991, at seventeen, he had no option but to get the plane back to Oz. I think the idea was for Mark to stay out of the country a year or so, grab a few more caps, and return to United. But I never had the vibes that that was the proposition Mark really fancied. Still, his personal ambitions couldn't resolve the bureaucratic stand-off we faced. In short,

Mark didn't fulfil the international appearance criteria so the door remained firmly shut. Then, suddenly, I had the key thrust in my hand. 'Has he got a girlfriend in England?' I asked. 'Yeah, he's courting a young lass in Manchester.' Quick as a flash, I suggested: 'Why don't they just get married? Then he won't have a problem.' Just call me heart-of-gold Ron! And so it was that, in no time, they walked up the aisle and straight into the arrivals hall at Heathrow.

When Mark first arrived, though, I had little doubt about one fact. I feared I had dropped a right clanger. He had, apparently, been enjoying the life of a beach bum back in Aussie while playing a bit of spare-time football in Sydney. He was very rusty. Worse, he was very overweight, about two stone to be exact. While humping that sort of luggage around, he didn't appear exactly agile either. The whispers, meanwhile, were coming in that United were not all that pleased about our signing manoeuvre. Something about being gazumped, I think was the complaint suggested, and at that stage I was tempted to let them have him even though we had done absolutely nothing wrong. Anyway, we ended up in front of the beak, summoned by the FA on some kind of charge I still don't understand. The fine was a nominal £35,000 and, to this day, I am convinced that if our chairman hadn't been part of the FA hierarchy nothing would have happened. It was politics, a bit of diplomatic strategy, a nonsense just to show the establishment aren't men behaving badly. To complete the story, Mark shaped up very well eventually. He can be headstrong at times, a little impulsive in his decision-making, but there can't be any questioning of his development into one of the finest and most athletic keepers in the land. At the price – only thirty-five grand remember – an absolute steal, too. So was Shaun Teale, who might even have made an England squad or two without the handicap of his missus. If they had a team for mischief-making, she would have more caps than Bobby Moore, believe me.

We took Shaun from Bournemouth on the say-so of Harry Redknapp, a good pal of mine, and because they were close to being skint. It was a gamble, but I had few worries after Harry's generous recommendation. 'I'm telling you, Ron, that this lad will be a hell of a player.' But, at that stage, he never mentioned Teale's wife. Carol was her name and that old pop song comes to mind, 'Oh, Carol, you are but a fool . . .' Shaun was never much of a bother. He got on with the job, forged a tremendous central defensive partnership with Paul McGrath, and I know Terry Venables seriously considered him for the international squad. But he was his own worst enemy or, put more accurately, maybe that title was a toss up between Shaun and Mrs Teale. She was an absolute terror and the flashpoint for so many problems at the football club. She was forever moaning and complaining, ringing up people with bits of mischief, and jabbering on to the press about matters which should have been of no concern to her. After a while I chatted to Harry Redknapp about her, seeking helpful advice on how I might control a tricky situation. 'Shaun's quite a good guy, but she's a living nightmare,' he told me.

Carol could never stop poking her nose into club affairs and, inevitably, it had to have long-term repercussions for her husband. She once, quite arbitrarily, packed him off to hospital for a nose operation that our medical people had advised could well wait until the end of the season. Later, just before we beat Manchester United in the 1994 League Cup Final, a petty, mischievous little story appeared in one of the Sunday papers, claiming that United would be clad in Armani suits for Wembley and would be collecting huge bonuses as well. By comparison, Villa would be on peanuts and be dressed like paupers. Coincidentally, some of the boys told me that these were the same things that Mrs Teale had been saying in the players' lounge beforehand. When we got to the game, the suits were identical and our bonuses were greater than those of the United players. Shaun was a sound pro, and a powerful stopper, but he allowed his wife to rule so much of his football life that in the end it just became impossible for him to survive at Villa.

He might even have been our most influential player in that Cup Final, but in the summer that followed the Teale family made another tactical error. They decided to go on a month's holiday to Florida. Fine, except that he should have had a hernia operation before leaving for the States. When he returned, roughly two days before we reported back for pre-season training, Teale booked himself into hospital for the surgery. I, unfairly, took my anger out on Jim Walker, our physiotherapist and one of the most conscientious and dedicated men in the game. His answer: 'I know he should have had the op a month ago, but he refused. His wife said he must have the holiday first.' The consequences were severe for Teale. It meant he was absent for our start to the season and, more crucially, it guaranteed his defensive shirt went to Ugo Ehiogu. Very rarely to be worn by Shaun again, I might add. The new formation, with McGrath in the other defence slot, didn't please Teale, obviously, but there was only one reply: 'It's your own fault, son.' Even after I left the club, he didn't figure in the first team too often and very rapidly took the long slide down several rungs of the ladder. First it was Tranmere, then Preston, and now . . . well, maybe Carol will give us a call. In something like four years, Shaun moved from part-time soccer to being a Wembley hero, and to this day it's my view that if he had stood up to his missus the way he faced big, hulking strikers, he would have enjoyed plenty more seasons at the top. I can honestly say that Mrs Carol Teale supplied me with more unnecessary aggro, hassle and problems than all the other football wives I have come across put together.

Most of the others were sweeties, though, and that very much applied to the Mrs Staunton. I was lucky with Steve too. I signed him for a little over a million and, with the cheap-day arrivals of Bosnich and Ehiogu, I had recruited three of Villa's stalwarts of the nineties. They cost me, in total, no more than £1.25 million and very quickly their collective valued soared to something in excess of £12 million. Now, Doug, that's what I call sensible big business. With Staunton, as I'll always concede, there was a touch of good fortune when I prised him out of Liverpool. Graeme Souness suffered a huge amount of criticism over the sale and has confided in me it was his worst decision at Anfield. He has always regretted it, but the circumstances were stacked against him at the time. It was the period of the three-foreigner restriction in European competition, with the Scots, Irish and Welsh included in the prohibitive equation. Souey had three left-sided defenders and, in David Burrows and Gary Ablett, he had two who were English. The odd man out was Irishman Staunton, so he was the obvious one to be sacrificed. But after Souness's sacking, Liverpool attempted to take Staunton back. I played the only bargaining card I had at the time: 'What would happen, Stan, if we gave you more money than we have ever paid any footballer?' Stan stayed.

With Dalian Atkinson scoring goals, a transitional season climaxed with a run to the FA Cup's sixth round and a respectable seventh place in the League. But to make a reasonable charge at the title, I felt we were short of a top class right-sided midfield player and a high-calibre striker. In the closed season the first of those problems was solved when another of Staunton's former Liverpool colleagues, Ray Houghton, joined us. He was an infectious, inspirational footballer much in the way Gordon Strachan had developed at Leeds United.

To solve the striker problem focus once more switched to Merseyside – and Dean Saunders. He was known to be unsettled and I discussed a deal with Souey. At £2.3 million, I was assured, we could sign him. Back to the chairman and it was Deadly in deadlock. While he had agreed with me about the priority of another goalscorer, at the very mention of an immediate hard cash investment he dithered and dallied. And then he dithered some more. For two or three weeks the signing saga dragged on until it reached the proportions of farce. One afternoon I smuggled Saunders into my house. He was unhappy at Anfield but to make the move to Villa he needed to take a drop in wages. I felt some friendly persuasion was necessary to demonstrate our faith in him. The chairman, meanwhile, tried to meddle and cut and fiddle a deal, as sometimes was his way. Meanwhile Deano, predictably I suppose, started to lose his belief in the move. I did, too. It was early in the 92–93 season and we lost 3–1 in a midweek fixture with Chelsea. I snapped at Ellis: 'Why are we messing about? When is this deal going to get done?' He replied: 'I can come up with a better package if I do the business with Liverpool myself.'

Two weeks had already elapsed and, significantly, a local Birmingham radio station opened their sports programme with a fans' phone in. The calls centred on the issue of the chairman and his reluctance to dip his hand in his wallet. I read the script. Next morning, six hours before we played Crystal Palace at home, the phone call came. It was Doug. 'What is the present situation with Saunders? Can we still buy him?' Deliberately niggled, I answered: 'The situation's the same as it's been for a fortnight, chairman – course we can buy him.' To encourage matters along, before the match I went out on the pitch to announce we had secured Saunders. What I do know as an absolute fact is that we could have had Deano two home games earlier, one of which we lost in front of the lowest attendances of that season.

With one of those fixture ironies that fate so often throws up to add a little spice to football, Saunders completed the formalities just in time for our next home game – against Liverpool, naturally. He underlined an emphatic début performance with two goals and we despatched Liverpool back up the M6 in miserable mood, forced to accept a 4–2 defeat. Immediately, Saunders' linking play and understanding with Atkinson was smooth and powerfully effective. It certainly suited big Dalian, an immensely talented footballer but somebody for whom the words 'work' and 'rate' didn't link and had long been eliminated from his dictionary anyway. With his ability he should have been an England player. Correction, he should have been a world player; a fifth of the price but certainly three times the performer Stan Collymore could ever be. But that is another story. What is beyond dispute is that Dalian believed that alongside Deano he had a partnership created in the sporting heavens. They got on so well they roomed together. Deano, a sparky little wind-up merchant, told me of an early bedroom chat between the two of them. 'Hey, gaffer, I've just told Dalian that the deal is I'll do all the graft, all the running, getting into the corners, dragging away the defenders. All he has to do is drop short and do the damage. I tell you, gaffer, he just shot bolt upright in bed and said: "Deano, I've been looking for a partner like you all my life – this is magic." His big brown eyes, gaffer, were the size of dinner plates.' The scene was set for the sting. At the team meeting I plonked Dalian on the front row, making him the centre of attention. I then briefed him on his role, using Deano's scenario except deliberately reversing their roles, and waited for his reaction. A look of horror filled his face, and he broke out in a sweat, the first one of his life probably. And the whole place erupted in a belly roar of laughter from the other players as long practised mickey-taker Deano neatly wrapped up another victim.

For several months many in the game accepted this pairing was as dangerous a combination as you could face in England. Until, cruelly as far as Villa were concerned, Atkinson suffered a serious, long-term hamstring complaint that kept him out of competitive action for much of that season. I will for ever be convinced that if the Saunders–Atkinson partnership hadn't been split we, and not Manchester United, would have been the first Premiership champions, in 1993. Villa completed the campaign as runners-up, admittedly some distance behind United, but I still reflect on a strange Saturday during the climactic run-in when we dropped points in a goal-less draw with Coventry. More significantly, it was the same fateful day that Alex Ferguson's team, losing 1–0 at home to Sheffield Wednesday, were, by some freakish time-keeping, allowed to score twice themselves in seven minutes of extra play. At the end Fergie and Brian Kidd, captured for all time on that video clip they still show on television, danced around like demented souls waiting for the straitjackets to arrive. Carlton Palmer, then play-ing for Wednesday, confided in me later that, with his team controlling the match and winning it easily, he asked the lines-man about the time left on the clock. He was told two minutes. It was five minutes later before Steve Bruce scored the first goal of his highly influential double. And that moment, I readily concede, was the first time I felt the fates would conspire against us and deny Villa the title, despite an impressive run of three victories in the next four games.

I strongly maintain, though, that if Atkinson had only been fit to lead the closing charge, nothing, not even United, would have stopped us finishing at the head of that particular pack. At times, Dalian could drive you nuts, and often did, as our countless bust-ups during that important period would surely testify. For all the barneys, I couldn't help admiring and liking the guy. I can remember standing there rollocking him more than once only for the pair of us to finish up in a heap of laughter. He had such an endearing charm about him that the fans, and the folk even closer to him, all fell at Dalian's feet. In raw potential, not to say football talent, he was blessed. Such power and pace to burn, he was without doubt the fastest footballer I have ever seen in my life. If he made up his mind, or was motivated enough, he could be outstanding in the air as well. But he was also infuriating because of his often lazy, almost disinterested approach to his game. That, believe me, was always the cause of my lost temper.

Nowhere did it rage more violently than after a goal-less draw at Chelsea in February 1994, when, within the privacy of the dressing room and with an admittedly calculated motive, I deliberately provoked an incident with Dalian. Initially, the loaded silence was broken, typically, by Deano as the inquest started. 'Well,' he said, 'you have got to blame us, me and Dalian. It's our fault because we never took our chances; never scored, never did this, never did that.' I stood there, simply testing reactions. Then, suddenly, I jumped in and snapped: 'Deano, you are out of order. No way can you blame Dalian. You can't fault him for missing chances. How can you do that? He's not even been over the half-way line all game. It's near impossible to miss chances when you don't even run up the field.' I was determined to goad the big feller and force a response. Dalian started rattling back, an angry babble of self-justification, so I went further, and further, pushing him to the very limit. As he headed for the shower room, I followed and chided him some more. He turned with a scowl and threatened me. 'Tell you what,' I said. 'You will have to put a lot more energy into doing anything like that than you ever did on the park. And listen again, pal, you might have to take a lot more punishment into the bargain.' That was breaking point. He lunged for me, there was a scuffle, players and the staff dived in to break it up, and it was all over inside a minute or two. I think I hit Jimmy Barron, and Andy Townsend also took a whack from someone but it was all unintentional of course. As for the two of us, I don't think we landed a blow on each other. We didn't even suffer a graze. Usual footballers' scrap, in fact. I straightened my tie, tugged the jacket into place, and left. Slap, bang into John Motson, in fact, who asked for the usual TV interview. 'Why not, Motty, let's go and talk now.' If he had only known what had happened just a few seconds earlier and barely ten yards from the site of the interview, he would have had quite a story to tell *Match of the Day* viewers. That, though, was the matter closed; no carpeting, no disciplinary punishment and no fine. After all, it was my premeditated act of provocation that caused the ruck.

Usually, Dalian wasn't the aggressive type. Just the opposite, in fact, and arguably that was the root of his under-achievement. His most fundamental weakness, mind you, was always with money. Hand Dalian a pound and he would go out and spend a fiver. He was always extremely generous with an ever-increasing circle of, shall we say, friends, which I always worried could eventually cause his downfall. Lovely feller, complex character, and I did try various tacks to get through to him and motivate him to deliver his true potential. I'm not sure I ever succeeded. I used to tell him that he had more ability than Alan Shearer, that he should be in the England squad, and, as he was always screaming for more money, that there could be only one route towards the major profit margins. 'Why don't you play like you really can all the time? Because if you do, Dalian, all the rewards in the world will be yours. You can be one of the top players, earning the sort of money Shearer picks up.' Then, and I still can barely believe his words, came the reply: 'You pay me what they pay Shearer, and I'll play like him.' So I intervened again: 'What if I pay you Romario's wages, can you play like him, too?' It was a quite remarkable, even astounding, philosophy, I think you must agree. But Dalian didn't see anything strange about his logic. For instance, in the season when Shearer walloped in forty-odd goals, Dalian had bagged just fifteen, yet he ambushed me with the opinion: 'I have still had a much better season than Shearer.' Quizzical look. 'Oh, really, how do you make that one out?' There was no hesitation: 'Because I have a Cup medal in my pocket and he has not.' It is damn nigh impossible to get through to a player with that kind of mindset. For him the law of least effort always applied.

After I left Villa, Dalian joined Fenerbahce in Turkey. Within a very short time they played Galatasaray, their arch-rivals, who had Graeme Souness as coach, and Dalian had a special incentive to win. The club president's son, apparently, promised him a Mercedes sports car if he scored two goals. Inside the first fifteen minutes Dalian was celebrating a hat-trick. He got his car and then didn't bang in another goal for Fenerbahce for ages. That's my boy!

His place as the terrace favourite was rapidly taken by Dwight Yorke, his much younger successor of immense natural ability. He was always a lovely kid, who, and this might sound corny, always carried a Caribbean smile that was like a daily dose of sunshine at the Villa training complex. In my first season with the club, he smacked in an impressive ration of goals into the very high teens. Then a serious injury interrupted his progress and by the time he was fit to return, the Deano–Dalian bandwagon had started to roll. Only once did he cause me a moment's trouble and that was when he teamed up with Bozzy the Aussie.

Goalkeeper Bosnich could be a little headstrong at times and he certainly stepped the wrong side of the disciplinary line with Dwight. It was during the period of the three-foreigner restriction in Europe and, having to juggle my team for a tie with Inter Milan in September 1994, I decided to play back-up keeper Nigel Spink because not only was he useful but, more importantly, he was English. That left Bozzy out in the cold, along with Trinidadian Dwight. They decided to break the curfew and go for a night out together before the European match. Unluckily for them, Portsmouth and my old mate Jim Smith, were in town to play Birmingham. He was subsequently told by his players, allowed out after they had played their game, that they had seen both Bosnich and Yorke in a nightclub about midnight. Jim was soon on the blower: 'What about your boys last night? Not very professional, that kind of behaviour, is it?' I erupted. When I hauled the two lads in, they very sheepishly admitted their late-night escapade, born out of sheer frustration and a bit of bravado, and got heavily hit in the pocket to such an extent their bar bill looked like buttons.

The summer after our disappointment in the title race marked the arrival of Andy Townsend. He cost £2 million and, because he was thirty, I was always told the economics didn't really add up. Well, with the benefit of history and hindsight, it is very easy to underline that with Andy as skipper, Villa always qualified for Europe and also collected two major trophies. When he left they also banked a hefty portion of the original investment, so once more, dear Deadly, it wasn't too bad a piece of business, was it? One of the trophies, of course, was the League Cup, when we triumphed over Manchester United at Wembley, with the epic semi-final against Tranmere and Dalian's special contributions along the way. That, let me just add, was the finest United side in many a generation and included the likes of Eric

Cantona, Paul Ince, Mark Hughes, Andrei Kanchelskis and Steve Bruce, yet we still defeated them 3–1. Two weeks before the final, Peter Schmeichel was ruled out after a red card dismissal and Les Sealey, a goalkeeper who had yo-yoed between Villa and Old Trafford, was given the Dane's job.

At the time, Les, in all candour, was not really the focus of my thoughts or tactics. I watched United very closely the week before Wembley when they played Arsenal. Cantona, already proven as the catalyst of their team, was in threatening form, but I rapidly decided to abandon any notion of man-marking him. Instead, I figured we must compete, in both muscular aggression and mental strength, with Ince and Roy Keane in the United midfield. It meant, naturally, scrapping Villa's usual system of play and also led to an unavoidable dose of serious disappointment for the likes of Garry Parker and Ray Houghton. I employed Saunders as a lone striker, with Atkinson and another speed merchant, Tony Daley, as flank attackers. They were there to keep United's fullbacks heavily occupied while also having the capacity to break out very quickly. Then there was the big selection surprise: the summons for a young unknown called Graham Fenton. Until well into the afternoon build-up, he didn't have a clue he was playing, but he had long been a fixture in my mind. I wanted, no, correction, I needed his physical presence and energy to buttress the Villa midfield. It was a strategy that I also felt would force Cantona to do most of his best work away from our box. It worked like a dream, too. Atkinson grabbed the lead, Saunders built on it, and then Sparky Hughes nicked one for United with six minutes to spare. But disaster for both them and the unfortunate Kanchelskis was waiting to happen. The Russian handled to stop another goal, the penalty was smashed in by Saunders, and poor Andrei was sent off. We had the Cup and, still, chairman Ellis looked decidedly grumpy.

During the London celebration banquet, I wondered if he had other much graver priorities filling his mind. Like my future, for instance. It never occurred to me – why should it? – that after finishing tenth in the League with a largely experimental team towards the end, and with a major Cup in the boardroom display, I would be on my way out in no more than a dozen games with Villa. That's the boot business, as they say.

Before I ended up as yet one more Ellis sacking statistic, Villa managed to beat Inter Milan, one of the outstanding teams of European football, and a useful gentleman by the name of Dennis Bergkamp, in the UEFA Cup. The Italians did us in Milan through a penalty from the Dutchman. Back home, our perfor-mance was of a calibre not witnessed at Villa Park in years, and we finally emerged the winners in a penalty shoot-out. Up on the gantry that night was Kevin Keegan in his role as television pundit. At eleven o'clock on that famous Thursday, Kevin was still commentating on Villa's heroic deeds in the knowledge that by three o'clock on Saturday his Newcastle team would be play-ing us. He must have loved every minute of our attempt at all-night football.

Just for the record, we played very well against the Geordies but eventually lost 2–0 when there was just nothing left in the energy tank for the Villa players. Next it was Manchester United and then the Turks of Trabzonspor in Europe. In the final minute of the home tie we lost on the away-goals rule. By Saturday, Ellis was on the box, broadcasting to the nation his considered thoughts on yours truly. His delivery was something along the lines: 'Ron Atkinson is one of the three best managers in the country.' Five days later he radically changed his mind, decided I wasn't anything of the kind, and sacked me.

It followed the midweek game at Wimbledon when, coasting at 3–1 up, we had Townsend sent off. The Dons dragged us back to 3–3 and with the last kick of the match Oyvind Leonhardsen smacked in the winner. That Thursday morning, Deadly's secretary, Marion, called me and asked me to show at the ground thirty minutes earlier than planned. Honestly, even at that late stage, I didn't see what was coming. I was ushered in to see the chairman, whereupon Ellis, in very formal language, informed me that the club had decided to part company with me and end my services. Everything was left to the legal people while he, apparently, exited by the back-door route, the first time Villa's esteemed and most public official had ever done so. At the front door, I might add, were the waiting media, reinforced by a growing band of puzzled and not very pleased Villa supporters.

The overwhelming reaction from the club's terrace support was an immediate demand for my reinstatement. The local radio stations, along with most newspapers, ran polls that revealed the universal opinion that it was Ellis who should go, not me. On that very day, and on every day since, I have never been persuaded that my departure was a purely football decision. Other contemporaries, closely aware of the various machinations at Villa, have since led me to believe that view is the right one. My sacking was more to do with personal relationships or, more correctly, the lack of them. It's never been a secret that from day one of my management of the club, Ellis and myself were destined not to get on with each other. Deep down I knew that all along, and it was only my long-held desire to be in charge of Villa that wrongly compelled me to breach a golden rule. Through my football life I always maintained I worked for the people who employed me and not the club where I happened to be. At Villa I worked for the club in spite of the chairman and backed by the conviction I could handle it. Possibly I could, and probably he couldn't. Close friends have since suggested I would have survived if I had been prepared to be a little more humble with Ellis. When I accepted the job, he had turned to me and asked: 'Do me a favour – don't ever take the mickey out of me in public.' If the request hadn't been so pitiful, it might have been funny. I wouldn't have believed a sixteen-year-old office temp coming up with that, never mind Lord High and Mighty Ellis. The problem, a rather sad one too, with old Douglas is that he has a great deal of difficulty in laughing at himself. It seems to me that he is a man with barely a whiff of humility in his bones; unless his authority is respected and reinforced at every turn, he finds it a struggle to even communicate.

For instance, we used to have daily dealings by fax. There was I, just up by the Belfry golf course at Villa's countryside training ground, and a few miles down the road was Ellis. There was a phone by his elbow and at least two in my office, yet he clearly didn't think it was, with apologies to BT, good to talk. Advice, instruction, discussion, everything, all happened by fax. It was as though we were on a war footing. Maybe we were. At the height of the Saunders transfer stand-off, when Ellis was having his customary hard time with restless fans impatient for the deal, one of his famous faxes dropped on my desk. It was funnier than a Freddie Starr script. His secretary sent it to me with a command – yes, it was a command and not a request – to insert a special paragraph or two into my programme notes. The insert had to read something along the lines of: 'During my time in football, I have found Doug Ellis to be as good and helpful a chairman as I have ever had in the game. Blah, blah, blah. Not only does he support me financially, in making every effort to bring in high-class strikers, he also gives me the benefit of his huge experience in the game. So much so that I often use Mr Ellis as a sounding-board for both my tactics and team selections etc, etc.' That, and I know it might be terribly hard to believe, was what he expected me to put into my programme notes and feed to loyal Villa fans. When I called back the chairman's secretary, half-thinking it might all be a joke, she informed me that much more of similarly worded diatribe had already been, shall we say, pencilled out of the fax. But that didn't stop the programme editor bombing me with phone calls to see if my notes had been done and were ready for print. He, I gathered, was being badgered almost by the hour with inquiries about it from the chairman, although Ellis, I must stress, never actually spoke to me about his weird demands. He was never a great one for individual confrontations. No, the direct approach, face to face wasn't Douglas's strongest point, I have got to say.

If he had broken the habit of a lifetime and picked up the phone, mind you, he would have been given very short shrift by me. It caused a bit of a stir when I showed the infamous fax to the press boys. From that day, because of the sounding-board reference, they referred to Ellis as the Ironing Board. He, of course, revels in being known by his nickname of Deadly, perhaps in the misguided belief that it conjures up the image of a powerful football figure able to deal ruthlessly with whoever crosses his path. Excuse me, I'm sorry I even got round to mentioning that. This, after all, is a book about fact, not fiction.

Whatever the truth of Ellis's character, it was frequently suggested to me that I should soft-pedal and be a little more manager friendly to the great man. I had to be cuter, they told me or, in my language, a bit more snivellingly subservient. Fine chance of that. Examine Villa's history and you will see why. Nobody could have been more respectful, er, subservient, than Jo Venglos and it didn't save him. You couldn't unearth a more pleasant, polite and approachable guy than Graham Turner and Ellis still chopped him. So I worked on the premiss that I had to get results to keep the job; that was my only protection. Let's, therefore, reflect on the record. In three seasons with the club, I finished second, seventh and tenth in the League and also won the League Cup. Not world class, but not bad either, and yet I still disappeared when it suited Ellis. I had a great rapport with the Villa fans, a mutual affection even, and he didn't like that. It was a point of envy. Ellis, within his ivory tower, envisaged himself as the sole focal point of the club. Adulation, though, was never going to be Ellis's closest football companion. Whatever he might think, he is not a very popular chap in the Midlands area or, as a matter of plain fact, inside the game in general.

So what was Ellis really like? Like the chairman from hell? Hey, hang on, there are such inhibiting factors within this country of ours as the laws of libel. I must proceed with caution, therefore, and just reveal some of the less damning episodes of our relationship. Like the trip to Florence to play Fiorentina in a friendly. Some of the backroom boys, not exactly flush on Villa's wages, went out for a drink in one of the local bars. Everything was swinging until desperately seeking Douglas walked in. Very quickly, it was champagne on the table from Ellis and very much yachty talk, most likely to impress a gathering of girl singers in the place. Ellis, of course, had a lovely boat anchored up in the Med. The champers flowed, and in an upmarket place like Florence it didn't come cheap. Anyway, just to shorten the story, come last orders, old Douglas was nowhere to be seen. He had sidled out without a word of farewell, or a flash of bank notes, and the Villa physio and another member of the staff were left to pick up the bill. They had enjoyed a couple of lagers apiece, that's all, and the damage amounted to nearly a thousand pounds. They told me the story later and I was blazing about it.

Next night, the scenario was repeated only this time I made sure I was also sitting in the bar when Ellis strolled in. When it came to pay time, I deliberately allowed him to be on the very doorstep of the exit, before I bellowed: 'Hey, isn't it about time you weighed in for this one?' It has always been maintained that Ellis has the hide of a rhino, but that night he looked distinctly uncomfortable. He mumbled some words I couldn't make out and tossed his lire on the table, but no way did it take care of the bill. At the club, he would also invade my after-match gathering in the manager's office, even though he had a room of his own the size of a banqueting-hall. As soon as he arrived, the party ended and everybody made their excuses and left. I wonder to this day if Ellis ever understood why. If he hasn't, I'll let him in on the secret. They were all bored rigid by Deadly's tedious, never-ending fishing stories and couldn't stand his company anyway.

It was by the riverbank that the Deadly nickname was bestowed on him – by Jimmy Greaves of all people. And, yes, it was supposed to be another joke at Ellis's expense, but that was another thing he never twigged. Greavsy was taking part in a TV programme in which Ellis was screened doing something of which he had some knowledge. Makes a change, I suppose. As Doug hauled out the fish he quickly dispatched them with a bang on the head and up came the quip from Greasy: 'It's Deadly Doug.' Ever since the legend has grown that the nickname came about as a result of the Villa chairman's penchant for dismissing his managers. Another untruth exploded.

He might, I suspect, have been called many other names in his time, some of them a deal more crude and to the point, if only the general public had known what really went on at a particular Villa AGM. During the meeting, a proposal was made that the new stand should be named in honour of the chairman, the Doug Ellis Stand. He appeared to be quite overwhelmed with the formal suggestion and that's when I was left cringing with embarrassment. Why? Well, because I was already well aware that this particular proposal had previously been discussed by the full board and very much with Ellis's approval. It was merely another insight into the peculiar mindset of a man whom I had never liked.

How would I sum him up or describe him to a complete stranger to our football shores? First, let me say it wouldn't take long and, secondly, I would pray that they understood Anglo-Saxon in its crudest form. It might be a more succinct way of getting the message across. For a start, he is a classic case of a man full of his own self-importance to a degree you could barely believe. I doubt if he has ever had too many genuine friends, if he has had any at all. The people he claimed as friends always looked like toadies to me, flavour-of-the-month characters who then rapidly vanished into oblivion. To be blunt, and that's his well-favoured approach anyway, without Aston Villa, Ellis would occupy a very empty world. He was, I suppose, for want of a better description, best categorized as a career football chairman. He networked his way into the FA establishment through Villa's status in the game. I know he would have loved nothing more than to be the top man at Lancaster Gate; fat chance of that, Douglas old boy. I believe the other factor in his football life that probably still rankles with Ellis is that he wasn't connected with Villa when the European Cup was won in the eighties. He had lost his boardroom position during an internal squabble, even though his links with the club span many years. He started out, though, as a Birmingham City supporter and had a directorship with Villa's fiercest rivals for a while. He very briefly held a similar position at Wolves and, it's long been understood that, when Ellis was an outcast at Villa Park, he made an approach to Manchester United and offered them his services. They declined. He would be less than amused to discover what people in the game really think about him. Just give us a call, Doug, and I might be able to help in that direction.

He loved to tell a tale or two himself. Like the one that Andy Gray who, incidentally, would probably have stayed at Villa if Ellis hadn't forced the issue with Sky TV, loved to relay to the rest of us. It concerned Ellis's claim that he had invented the revolutionary bicycle kick while playing for a British XI that included the likes of Tom Finney, Frank Swift and Stan Mathews. But I was always puzzled by that story because at other times Ellis let it be known he played as a goalkeeper with Southport. Or was it Portsmouth? Unfortunately, Deadly sometimes seemed to get his wires crossed. When we recruited Earl Barrett, for instance, it was very embarrassing to be at the signing ceremony when Ellis mistook him for Paul Warhurst. Hey, don't laugh, it's an easy mistake to make. They were, remember, once both playing for Oldham Athletic at the same time, even if one is black and the other white.

In reality, apart from the odd inevitable collision, I didn't have too much conflict with Ellis – for the simple reason that I didn't seek it. Mutual acquaintances have long suggested that if I had been less forceful, I would have been Villa's manager for life. What they meant was I had to be subservient, to bow and scrape to placate his huge ego, to be a yes-man, and, in truth, that was never a possibility. It was a point of principle that I could never even be tempted to play such a role merely to save my position. I knew my survival depended on results, naturally. When the sacking decision was delivered, it was arguably the first time in my three-year reign when Ellis must have sensed he had the upper hand. At the time, Villa were languishing third bottom; it wasn't a situation that was irredeemable and I felt confident of lifting the club very quickly up the League. Even then he got it wrong and completely misread the mood of the Villa public.

Almost universally they wanted me to stay and Ellis to go. He replaced me with Brian Little, who only managed to scramble out of the relegation trap in the final game of the 94–95 season. The word from the street was that if Villa had not escaped, Little would have suffered the chop as well. Ellis was always prepared to sacrifice people if he was in any way at risk himself; there's never been any doubt about that. To his credit, and this I readily concede, Ellis must be congratulated on Villa's emergence in the Premiership. He has exploited the huge finances involved in modern-era football and now he has a very well-appointed club under his control. Nothing wrong with the castle, it's the Englishman inside that bothers me.

CHAPTER TEN

The Money Men

Very often, because of where I live, I am asked the question: How do you get to Coventry? If I can hide the smirk for a second, there is a rapid and smart reply: 'Easy. Lose six on the bounce at Villa.' It's a joke, of course. And roughly, perhaps, about as funny as my exit from that forever famously struggling club in the very heart of the Midlands. My time at Highfield Road was brief, full of intrigue, relegation campaigning, and backroom manoeuvrings until, in the end, it was almost a case of management by committee. But, then, what would you expect with a Member of Parliament suddenly introduced, complete with a sizeably impressive wallet, as a new occupant of the boardroom?

Geoffrey Robinson, businessman, player investor, offshore expert and eventually a New Labour minister of some headline celebrity, was always referred to by the whole backroom staff, not by his name, but simply as the Money Man. In view of later more public events it couldn't, I suggest, have been more appropriate. The fact is, though, he didn't barge his way into my football life until well into my sixteen-month period of management at Coventry. For that I offer my belated but no less grateful thanks here and now. But, hang on, I'm being just a little hasty, leaping too many awkward hurdles too soon.

167

It was another director, in the shape of Mike McGinnity, whom I had known for some time, who was far more significant, initially at least, in what happened to me at Coventry. It was February 1995 when Mike made contact, little more than three months after my enforced departure from Villa Park. Briefly he explained he was acting on behalf of Brian Richardson, the Coventry chairman. The question was fairly blunt: did I have an interest in taking over Coventry, inevitably clamped yet again at the wrong end of the table? 'Now, that's got to be a difficult proposition to consider,' I told him. 'For the basic reason that you already have a manager in place in Phil Neal, and he's a close friend of mine.' A little more urgently he suggested that, although Phil didn't know it at that stage, he was already history as far as Coventry were concerned. So, once again, he repeated the question. I flat-batted him, naturally, and told Mike that if and when they implemented their decision to sack Neal, then that would be the correct time to make their approach. It was an awkward issue for me to deal with because, during my brief unemployment, I had trained with Phil and his players and they had made me very welcome. His No. 2, Mick Brown, was also a long-time friend and my former assistant manager at Manchester United. In fact, not many weeks before Coventry's job offer, I had been in their directors' box when a fan leaned across and demanded of the chairman: 'Why don't you give Ron the job and get rid of that Neal?' It was extremely embarrassing and particularly uncomfortable because a certain Mrs Neal was sitting alongside me at the time. From that moment, I vowed never to attend another match there and I didn't during Phil's time.

That deliberate, self-determined position, though, didn't halt the moves to dispose of him. Coventry were eliminated from the FA Cup at Norwich and, inevitably, with the pressure mounting on him, he needed a result – desperately so. It happened that weekend with a League success at Crystal Palace, but on Sunday morning the call came. Hand on heart, I advised them to allow Phil a little more time. There was, sadly, to be no reprieve. Mike McGinnity told me: 'It's not a matter of that any more; the board took the decision about changing the manager on Thursday night following the Norwich result.' It didn't alter my position, not immediately anyway. I explained that I had always rigidly obeyed a policy of never accepting a job until the current occupant had been told, treated properly and had all his financial dues counted and fulfilled. That stance wasn't going to change just for Coventry's benefit.

Phil, clearly sensing something was amiss, attempted to contact me on the mobile. I got the message late, too late in fact. In truth, that day my thoughts weren't exactly focused on football matters. Des Anderson, once part of the management set-up at Derby County with Dave Mackay and a very close personal friend, had been rushed into hospital with a serious illness. I was preoccupied with that trauma and never got back to Phil to discuss anything. The following day, the Coventry board revealed they had parted company with him. Within forty-eight hours, they were knocking on my door and setting up a deal. A week later I was in charge. That's football and there is no time for crocodile tears. We all understand the rules.

The brief was pretty basic. Coventry, then familiarly placed in the bottom two, needed saving and I had a few hectic weeks left to do it in. Longer term, the arrangement was for a two-year commitment as manager while, in the meantime, grooming some young blood to take over. In the initial discussions, the name of Gordon Strachan was mentioned. So, too, were Ray Wilkins and Chris Waddle. Of greater immediacy was the prime task of notching up a few results, and very rapidly the crisis situation eased. We enjoyed a run of seven or eight games without defeat, which even included a memorable success at Anfield when Peter Ndlovu smashed in a hat-trick, something that Liverpool had not surrendered at home since the Shankly era. For our next match, Villa away, I invited a Sky camera crew along and they were able to record a standing ovation that will live in my memory for all time. It was from the Villa fans and, in a highly emotional manner, proved that there are other fine rewards in this business than merely the amassing of a hefty bank balance. I don't suppose the reception was lost on old Deadly, either.

Still, it was not the time to dwell on the immediate past. The focus now had to be a more productive future at Coventry and so I looked once more in the direction of Gordon Strachan. By that stage, Howard Wilkinson, his manager at Leeds United, had made it clear to Gordon his first-team playing days were over. For him, it was a different destiny and a new responsibility with the reserve ranks at Elland Road. I persuaded him to move on, although he needed little ear-bending to take advantage of the opportunity offered by Coventry.

He arrived with a clear and fundamental desire to learn the managerial ropes from me, but it was pretty obvious, just seeing him play on the practice pitch and in a solitary reserve match, that he was still far better than any other player we had on the Coventry books. This L-plate novice in the management game was the expert we needed on the pitch. For instance, we made a trip to Tottenham with relegation worries gripping the mind and Gordon delivered one of the finest performances of wing play I have ever witnessed. In all honesty, I don't think Justin Edinburgh has ever recovered from being mullared, to use an insiders' football term, that night. The little feller ran him daft and we won 3–1. From being among the dead men, suddenly it was salvation. The last game of that '95 season was a party hats affair with my old comrade Joe Royle, whose Everton had also been rescued from relegation.

That summer I was back on to Joe and agreed a very swiftly completed deal for David Burrows, a specialist left-back whose qualities I appreciated from his youthful days at West Brom. Next, it was Kevin Richardson, my skipper at Villa and a midfield expert with long-proven assets of leadership and invaluable experience. At Villa, strangely, they dismissed him as a spent force, but a good three years later Southampton still considered Kevin a player of consequence in signing him from Coventry. John Filan, a useful goalkeeper, arrived from Cambridge and, in a smoothly arranged swop, Paul Williams moved in as Sean Flynn went in the opposite direction to Derby. These were all vital pieces but John Salako and Paul Telfer were even more important to the overall plan. When Salako's proposed transfer to Keegan's Newcastle collapsed on medical grounds, it meant a huge economic bonus for us and we secured him on a significantly reduced fee. The cost of Telfer from Luton was a million, and that left me with a budget-priced supply line through the middle for Dion Dublin and Peter Ndlovu. Isaias Marcus, such a talent from Benfica, was to be the midfield hub. Unfortunately, he didn't survive long due to an almighty bust-up with Gordon. Great pity that. Even without our special foreigner, we did okay, despite a punitive scale of injuries and an even more worrying catalogue of red-card dismissals. It all made for a highly unpredictable existence.

My whole strategy was centred on what might well be described as mid-market buys and that, as you might have guessed, guarantees little more than mid-table ambitions. I attempted to sign Andy Linighan from Arsenal for a cheap-skate £300,000. It was that kind of loose-change exercise until, suddenly, although I wasn't aware of it at the time, the Money Man made his first appearance. The chairman broached the subject with the invite: 'If you could sign any available centre-back in the country, who would it be?' I immediately responded, it had to be Chris Coleman of Crystal Palace, with a ball-park figure of up to £3 million. Generous to a fault, at least with other people's cash, the chairman continued: 'Would you like him and one other, maybe a front player?' Now this was getting silly, particularly as Coventry were hardly known as the listening bank back then, but in for a penny, in for a pound. The name of Noel Whelan had long been in my mind. He was a player who Carlton Palmer, his Leeds United team-mate of the time, always praised as a footballer of immense promise. At that stage, identities of possible targets were kept strictly secret, but the club decided to put out the powerful message that Coventry were on the move. They had, promised the chairman very publicly, something in excess of £5 million to spend on new players. He didn't reveal the details, not even to me, but I suspected he had unearthed a football-minded benefactor from somewhere. We were in the money; great – and I wasn't going to ask too many prying or inconvenient questions. Something along the lines of beggars can't be choosers summed up my position perfectly.

Most of my efforts were directed towards prising Whelan from Elland Road, where he was a product of their youth development programme. With the aid of a usefully influential Mr Palmer that was eventually achieved. But, even now, I have to concede surprise that his Leeds valuation was an extremely modest £2 million. It was a price fixed, I suspected, because Howard Wilkinson needed to recoup his transfer investment in Thomas Brolin and Tony Yeboah. Ideally, he would have opted for a trade-off with either Rod Wallace or Brian Deane but, unfortunately, those players didn't have the same market value.

It was a transaction I deliberately kept very quiet. I appreciated that Whelan was certainly a highly coveted talent and the understandable fear at Coventry was that any leak would leave us vulnerable to counter-bidding from any one of the major clubs, including Liverpool and Manchester United. With nothing less than devious intention, I laid a false trail by telling the world I was really in pursuit of a midfield player. In due course, Whelan arrived safe and sound on our doorstep and he settled in very quickly, demonstrating his undoubted ability and proving an extremely lively asset to the squad. As a front player, in fact, he was nothing less than brilliant, even though he has now been converted to a useful midfield player.

In the meantime, I had set up negotiations for Coleman, another young player with an impressive pedigree. But, as so often happens in football, a strange twist of fate undermined, and eventually destroyed, my plan for a new defence. We played Blackburn Rovers, the Premiership's reigning champions, at our place one glorious Saturday afternoon and walloped them. Their manager, Ray Harford, somewhat disenchanted with his defence, didn't delay his initiative to put matters right. Annoyingly, he bid for Coleman and wrapped up the transfer, courtesy of Jack Walker's well-endowed wallet, very quickly. There was an easily available option in Liam Daish, a different kind of defender admittedly, but a strong man who performed a very useful job for us. Eoin Jess, a player Gordon had always fancied joined us from Aberdeen, even if he found the transition from Scottish football something of a rocky experience.

But, even with the reinforcements, it was the familiar rolled-up sleeves and relegation routine for Coventry. With six games left, not to put too fine a point on it, we had a dagger at the throat and were locked, grimly as always, in the scramble for survival.

Worse, next on the agenda were Liverpool and Manchester United – such a comforting thought in a time of crisis. Liverpool was the home game and, for all my natural instincts to go for most things with adventure and enterprise, I knew this was very definitely not a fixture to try and football our way through. It was a case of being physical desperadoes for a change, with aggression, determination and application the essential demands. We had to play it the ugly way, and we did, and we scraped in with a one-goal win. Next, up to Man U. That, tragically, was the occasion when our centre-half David Busst suffered the horrendous leg injury that finished his career and almost caused the great Peter Schmeichel to faint at the scene of the accident. The only consolation, and I use the word advisedly, for David was that, coincidentally, the opposition was United. Within two days of the injury, we all knew his career was over and immediately I called Alex Ferguson. After only a minute or two of that conversation, Alex had promised to bring United to Highfield Road for a testimonial, so at least David received, deservedly so too, a generous financial pay-off to help him plan his future outside the game. It was almost twelve months later, while idly flicking through a football magazine and seeing a vivid photograph of the incident, that I fully appreciated the real horror of Bussty's broken leg. Bravely, the lad tried to go through rehabilitation, clinging to an always forlorn hope of a miracle, but his leg was such a total mess there was never the remotest chance of a comeback.

While old Bussty was being nursed back to health, Coventry displayed their survival instincts. In the last six games of the campaign we collected eleven points. In one of them, for the first time and maybe also laying the route for his England future, I played Dion Dublin as a centre-back. The fixture was at up-and-under Wimbledon and, with Daish suspended, I flanked big Dion with Richard Shaw and David Burrows. 'Every time they bomb it in,' I told him, 'just head it away. Don't get fancy dan on us back there. It's a very simple job.' And, no question at all, Dublin obeyed the instructions to the very letter. He had a blinder and I have been led to believe it was that dual-purpose ability that persuaded Glenn Hoddle to call him up for our international squad. We won 2–0 and the victory brought Coventry's eventual salvation ever closer. On the final day of the season, we stayed up, and that close call brought to an end the toughest, most emotionally testing, and professionally trying few months of my whole career in management.

In February 1996, we discovered that my dad, Fred, was seriously ill and that news really shook me rigid. People in the game always referred to him as Duracell for reasons that didn't need any explanation. If there was a football match being played, you couldn't keep him away. When he saw the specialists and the life-threatening problem was uncovered, the advice to the family was to forget about surgery and leave my dad to enjoy the last few months of his life. Fred would have none of it. He demanded the operation because he had vowed to himself he would see in the millennium and that ambition wasn't going to remain unfulfilled if he could help it. While he waited to go into hospital, he kept watching Coventry's games as always, and turned up for the lousiest, most miserably dull match I think I have ever seen. It was against Bryan Robson's Middlesbrough and it finished 0–0. Both sides were lucky to get that and the pair of us should have had points deducted for a truly terrible performance. With typical humour, and bearing in mind he had only weeks to live, Fred leaned across in my office and whispered: 'I've got to tell you, before watching that I thought it was me who had problems!' Fortunately, the next fixture was West Ham and, you've guessed it, it was a carnival of a contest, full of incident and flair, finishing up two apiece. Fred was happy again: 'Now that's how I expect your teams to play.' Not long afterwards, my dad had his voice box removed and, poignantly, when we saved ourselves from relegation all he could do was raise his head off the pillow in hospital and give me the thumbs-up. With so much uncertainty, both personally and profession-ally, surrounding me at the time, they were the most pressured few months of my football life.

It was in the summer of '96 that the managerial ground began shifting rather strangely beneath my feet. Matters that should have been within my control started to slip away, or were, more to the point, loosened from my grasp for no very good reason. The initial unease was planted in my mind when I entered into negotiations to sign Carlton Palmer. He was always a player subjected to a fair amount of ill-advised criticism, too many people focusing on his weaknesses rather than his strengths, but I believe he has proved those cynical observers conclusively wrong. Anyway, I was never anything less than a committed admirer of Carlton and I decided he, along with his Leeds team-mate and South African striker Phil Masinga, would be valuable assets for Coventry. I spoke to Bill Fotherby, then the Leeds executive in charge of transfer affairs, and we agreed an overall package of £2 million. Not a bad investment, I thought, and unquestionably one that represented value for money. But my own chairman, Brian Richardson, clearly felt differently. He was reluctant to talk business on Palmer and that was strange because usually he revelled in all the wheeler-dealer activity, so much so that we used to joke he was really a frustrated manager. He was worried about his off-field behaviour, and the player's reputed drinking habits. I just reminded him: 'If you worked on that premiss, about a player having a social drink in his off-duty time, you would never have taken Bryan Robson to any club in the land.' The discussion, at one time, also involved Gordon Strachan. 'Hey, Gordon,' I said. 'You know the bloke, you have played with him, what do you think?' He answered: 'Yes, I genuinely think Carlton is a good player, a really good player.' And then, after a short pause, he added significantly: 'Having said that, I don't think I could handle him.' I found that admission simply staggering. He was a player made to measure for Gordon. Palmer was always committed to the work ethic on the training ground and gave nothing less than 100 per cent on the field. Yet Gordon, with the chairman as an ally, clearly didn't fancy this bit of football business. I walked out of the meeting, thinking their collective attitude was very definitely a little weird. It was the first inkling I had that things might not be too clever for me. Because Gordon, let me explain, had also dropped another hint: 'You must remember, Ron, you are finishing at the end of the season and I'll be left with the task of handling Palmer.'

I remained philosophical about my position even though I knew the vibes weren't that good. Roughly a week later, my suspicions were strengthened. The pair of them walked in one morning and suggested they could sign Gary McAllister, Gordon's long-time pal, for £3 million. My reaction: 'Well, if you think you can get McAllister, you had better go and get him. It's all down to you now.' Certainly, I felt that other people were muscling in on my territory and attempting to call the shots. I even made the deliberately biting comment: 'It looks as though we are now managing by committee. We should leave it to the appointed decision-maker, don't you think?' The fundamental message was clear enough, even if they didn't want to listen. I was opposed to the McAllister signing because, at whatever price they agreed, he was never going to be of value to Coventry. My opinion should not be misinterpreted. Look, I always regarded Gary as a smashing player and an outstanding pro. If he had moved to Liverpool that summer, instead of Coventry, I'm tempted to believe he would have helped them beat Manchester United to the championship. Furthermore, I don't think he ever had a chance to justify his fee at Highfield Road. At that time Coventry needed a grafting powerhouse of a player to build their midfield around, not a linkman like McAllister, who sees the responsibility of playmaker as far more important than shedding buckets of sweat and blazing it box to box.

It was always going to be hard for Gary on the field of play and even tougher off it. He had problems in the dressing room that, in fairness, were not entirely of his own making. The other players knew of his association with Gordon, seeing him as a buddy of the junior boss, and in a football environment that is always ammunition for cynicism, even unstoppable hostility under the surface. Wrongly, the majority felt certain information was being fed upstairs from the squad. That never happened in my time, I promise you, but it still provoked serious resentment. Reports that he was picking up £20,000 a week caused more envy of McAllister. I could appreciate that some elevated quarters of the club believed his signing would make an important statement about Coventry – that they were a club of some status and could attract the most gifted players in the game. Fine, but could Macca play, and apply his particular skills to an optimum level, in a team near the bottom of the League? That's not a churlish question, but a realistic assessment of what the team needed during that period. And it needed Palmer and Masinga far more than it cried out for McAllister, talented lad that he was. His signing, surely, was the first signal to the football public that the money men were moving in on the club and expected their wishes to be carried through.

Meanwhile, back at the training ground, and attempting to

reflect this new era of transition, I decided I had to make radical changes, too. I'm being sarky, as you will probably have gathered, but I did do a bit of tinkering myself that summer. I decided to grant Gordon a little bit of a freer hand and put him in control of all the pre-season planning and preparation. He took on more of the first-team responsibility. Soon we should see if he had learned the basic lessons of the management game.

For whatever reasons, we got off to a terrible start. After the first five games we had a grand total of one sodding point. It was time for immediate action, bruised egos and all, and the arrival of a physical trainer called Roger Spry, a fitness expert who has applied his trade all over the world and has worked alongside me at several clubs. Sharpened up, and with the players' physical conditioning much improved, we started clocking up the right results. We lost, I think, just one of the next eleven games. One man, clearly, remained unimpressed and he was, of course, the aforementioned Geoffrey Robinson, MP and new boardroom presence, otherwise known as the Money Man. His influence started to tell. Even to this day, I can recall an episode with dear Geoffrey at Arsenal in October 1996, and I still don't really know whether it had any bearing on my Coventry future or, more correctly, lack of it. Immediately after the game I met a journalist friend of mine, Ken Jones, and invited him to the boardroom for a brief chat. As I strolled into the lounge, our favourite Member, surrounded by his own friends, beckoned me across. Apologetically, I said: 'Geoffrey, very sorry, I'm struggling at the moment. I'm under pressure and have to see someone.' Whether he interpreted that as a snub, and was embarrassed or offended by my manner, I don't have a clue. I certainly had no intention to be rude. But within a matter of weeks I was effectively history at Coventry.

Mr Robinson's personal connection and input at the club were somewhat strange. He didn't involve himself in the daily running of Coventry's affairs, despite being a bona fide member of the board; what he did was finance all the deals for the chairman. He was very willing to invest his personal wealth in new players, by and large young players, which was never too bad an idea. Certainly, with the heavy finance freely available, I had no complaints whatsoever. It appeared, though, that others had their grievances. Just a couple of weeks after the Arsenal episode when, incidentally, we ruined Arsène Wenger's first game with a goal-less draw during a our run of one defeat in eleven, I got an inkling that all was not well. The chairman half indicated, nod and a wink style, he was receiving bad vibes from certain quarters. 'It's nothing I can't deal with,' he reassured me. Much later in the chain of events, when my fate had been well and truly sealed, Gordon confided that immediately following our home game with Sheffield Wednesday, Robinson gave him the tug and said: 'I want you to run the show from this point on.' Ironically, it was at the stage when I believed the team was starting to perform. Few goals were being conceded, and after the nightmare start to the campaign there was a solidity and control about us. In truth, I felt more confident about our potential and prospects than at any other period of my management. Which, put another way, meant I just didn't have the remotest idea that someone was waiting around the corner to sort me out with a fairly blunt instrument. The following fixture was a Monday night Sky match at Everton and that was the weekend when the chairman started getting twitchy.

His behaviour was explained as I motored down to the training ground on that Sunday morning in November for the final preparations. The summons for a meeting with the chairman was passed down the line. Quite bluntly, he told me the decision had been reached three days earlier, among the ivory tower people, that I should stand down from the manager's post. 'If that's what you want, that's what will happen,' I replied. Crucially, I would be in charge at Goodison Park and then relinquish my responsibilities. I didn't think it was necessary, I didn't like the proposition either, and I certainly didn't believe it served the best interests of Coventry at that time, but they called the shots. Of course, I was angry and upset at the timing, but it was something else that really stuck in my craw and left me boiling with rage. In advance of any confirmation following the chairman's informal discussion with me and *before* the match, the whole damn affair was leaked. There it was, chapter and verse, plastered across the pages of a newspaper. In actual fact, a reporter had called at my home after I had left for training on that Sunday morning. He, apparently, wanted to question me about the changes at Coventry before the chairman had even spoken to me. There was never any proof of a direct feed of the story, but the chairman did some surreptitious checking on my behalf. He confirmed there had been a deliberate leak and, of course, the original decision remained unaltered. I will for ever remain convinced that the purpose was to put the issue in the public domain so the chairman could not withdraw his support and backtrack on my removal. I had no opportunity to influence events. It was a *fait accompli* and by the time anything was officially disclosed I had been declared a fringe item. The message-carrier, sorry, I mean the chairman, told me that, as planned, I would stay at the club with the title of Director of Football, whatever that was meant to describe. It was window-dressing for a role that, in this country at least, has never been properly defined and carried through. It still stands as a title without a task.

Long before my removal from effective power at Coventry, during the previous summer to be exact, I had challenged the chairman on how he envisaged my future. It was a simple request: 'At the end of this season, what's going to happen to me?' Obviously there was a measure of concern on my part. I told him guidelines had to be firmly laid down, the areas of demarcation between Gordon and myself needed to be established. Brian Richardson, I have got to say, was pretty hazy in drawing the parameters of responsibility. In fact, there never were any. The topic, inevitably, was back on the agenda during that November weekend and I have got to say Gordon was less than enthusiastic. He wasn't anywhere nearly as surprised as I that he was, prematurely, about to take my job, either. Everybody else in the club could barely believe, or accept, what was happening. Not Gordon, though. When the three of us huddled around a table to discuss the imminent change, I asked the chairman: 'Okay, if that's what you want, who does what from now on?' Pause. Then, 'I'll leave it to the pair of you to sort out,' he suggested. Which, frankly, was impossible and he must have known that. So, from that day to the final severing of my links with Coventry, the matters were allowed to drift along. From my point of view, the whole affair was a farce, a joke that increasingly became less than amusing. The formal announcement was delivered after the Everton game when we managed to emerge with another draw. Because I knew the scenario, the scheming behind my back, I found the experience very uncomfortable. Gordon arranged a party when we got back from Goodison at a pub near the training ground, and even that went badly wrong. Two of the players had a punch-up and Noel Whelan left only to get breathalyzed just up the road. Not exactly the most encouraging omens for the immediate future, you might agree.

Still, big Noel kept his place in the Coventry set-up and eventually settled down as an exceptional asset. I felt like a spare part. Unless I was specifically asked to do something, I deliberately stayed out of the club's working environment. Certainly when it came to anything concerning the players, I just didn't get involved. I went along to scout the opposition, check on possible player targets, and if my advice was ever sought I gave it generously. I wanted to earn my corn, obviously, but what I wanted even more was to make sure nobody could point the finger and accuse me of interference. In the immediate aftermath of my losing the job to Gordon, Coventry lost three of the next four games, including a humiliating home defeat to Gillingham in the Coca-Cola Cup. It was disastrous, particularly when the impressive, always improving results of the weeks just before were considered. Some of the senior players badgered me on the phone. They begged me to return to the training pitch where they felt I might be able to steady the ship. Adamantly, I stayed away. Why? Well, in truth, because I had been ordered to. What they didn't know was that I had approached Gordon earlier, once more attempting to resolve the conflict of responsibilities, and said to him: 'I will ask you a question: for the next home game where would you expect me to be?' Almost coldly, he answered: 'I would expect you to be away from here, scouting probably.' That reply told me a million things, but only one mattered. Loud and clear, it was the message that Gordon wanted to do his own thing with me as far away as possible. That was his prerogative. Nobody, let me stress, ever told me I wasn't welcome at the training ground, but I felt like an outsider and so I went my own way.

All through the second half of that season, all I could do was stand apart and see a club in a dreadfully alarming tailspin with results getting worse by the week. With five or six weeks to go, we lost 3–1 to West Ham. I was raging, and not just at another terrible result. I could see from the comments filtering out of Highfield Road that I was being set up as the fallguy for the failure to escape relegation. Ron the Patsy, that was me. It was black propaganda stuff. The damage, they were suggesting, had really been done while I was manager. Not, for pity's sake, while Gordon had been in charge all the way back to November, some two-thirds of the season. Funny old game, as Greavsy always says.

It was time for the Atkinson is Innocent campaign and a phone call from John Motson inspired it. He had been commentating at the Hammers game and was on to me within hours. 'Ron, I don't know if you can do anything about it, but I'm telling you that this Coventry side is going down.' I said: 'Snap, I could have told you that.' Motty rattled on: 'Somehow or other, you have got to get back in there and help.' My parting words to him were: 'I know, John, because if I don't I'll end up carrying the can. They are focusing on me and looking for the best alibi already.' The week after that secret little conversation, Coventry were staring down the barrel with a nice sociable, friendly excursion to Anfield and Liverpool. What was that I was saying about when one door closes another is there to slap you in the face? I decided there was only one thing to do. I had to break my self-imposed exile and head for training on the Monday morning. I did. Gordon was waiting as I walked in and asked: 'Look, what do you think is going to happen next? Because, I'm telling you, from a distance it appears that you are going down unless something dramatic takes place.' He pondered and didn't really reply. He was very much in a corner with nowhere to go. Not long before he had brought in Alex Miller, an old-time buddy from Scotland, as his assistant manager. Now, he's a fine bloke, but I wouldn't have thought he possessed the right depth of experience of the English Premiership to be of too much help to little Gordy right then. And, what's more, he's never exactly been the colourful, bouncy, expansive sort of bloke to rouse a dressing room full of suicidal footballers.

To be fair to Gordon, for all his natural fighting instincts, I had the very definite impression that he secretly thought Coventry were on the way down, too. I was there to offer him an option. He knew, I reminded him, that my record down the years against Liverpool was second to none. 'It's your choice, wee man, but why don't you let me get among the lads for a few days for a jolly-up? Let me get their chins off the floor and I'll go up to the game with you at the weekend. If you want, we'll do that. If you don't, just forget I mentioned it.' It took him seconds to agree it seemed a sound idea. Atky is back, Atky is back, hello . . . well, not quite. I got the boots on, got mixed in with the boys again, had the crack and a little razz or two, and everything seemed to be buoyant. Then Gordon pulled me towards the end of the week: 'You know, if you are coming up to Anfield with us, I would prefer you to sit in the directors' box. Okay?' Obviously, that wasn't part of the original script so I asked him why he wanted me out of the way again. He told me: 'I don't want people to get the idea that I can't do the job.' Startling stuff, really. So I travelled with the team, had a bit of a laugh, livened up Saturday night with a few quizzes for them, and then, if you like, got back into my 'civvies'. We won the game 2–1. Sure, we had the luck and Liverpool didn't, but we worked very hard for the reward and David James did us a favour. He dropped a couple. If we had lost that match, Coventry would have been bottom of the League and, it's a fair bet, would have been relegated. But, suddenly, the mood had changed. I worked with the players another couple of days and we beat Chelsea 3–1. It appeared the arrangement was working smoothly and serving a purpose. Others, clearly, were not so convinced and, on pure instinct, I felt something was wrong. I had fixed to watch a game at Southampton and then, following the Liverpool pattern, I would join the team. No, said Gordon, adding: 'Alex Miller's going to that match and then he will join up with us.' Okay, Gordy, I thought, I have got the message, and from that point on I stayed away completely. The main satisfaction for me was that Coventry secured their place in the Premiership and I wasn't going to be a scapegoat for the follies of someone else.

In those final, unhappy, cold-shouldered months I had the feeling I was an embarrassment to some people at Coventry. My intention had always been not to rock the boat but, with the benefit of hindsight, I should have taken a different course after the fiasco of the Everton weekend. I should have turned round and simply demanded: 'Pay me up now. Just settle my contract and I'll be gone.' Plainly, there were certain factions within the club that wanted rid of me; I shouldn't have hung around. In all honesty, though, I do believe I played a critical role in Coventry's survival that season. My gut feeling is that if I hadn't got involved in the Liverpool preparations, the team would have lost at Anfield and relegation would have followed. There were other consolations. Two of my final tasks at Highfield Road were fixing up the return of Roland Nilsson to English football and bartering the arrival of Darren Huckerby. Two pretty useful farewell presents, I think you might agree. Gary Pendrey, my first-team coach, had wanted us to buy Huckerby some months earlier when he was still with Lincoln. Newcastle nipped in ahead of us, and we had to be patient. But when Kevin Keegan purchased Alan Shearer for £15 million, and with no reserve team on Tyneside, bodies had to be moved. We were happy to accommodate. We got Huckerby for £750,000, a budget price really with the transfer market in such an inflationary spiral. Funnily, the day he arrived, I greeted him with the less than chirpy welcome: 'Great, you have only been here ten minutes and I have got the sack.' In truth, there was no slamming of doors, clearing desks or packing bags for me at Coventry. I didn't storm off. Everything just seemed to fizzle out and my short reign with them was over.

So what role did Gordon Strachan play in what so many considered my premature demise? It was the big question that wouldn't go away during that turbulent period in my life. I have never been critical of Gordon at any stage and, in all honesty, I still genuinely don't know what part he played. Some people, very knowledgeable about the situation, have raised the question repeatedly: 'Do you think Gordon turned you over?' My reply has never wavered. NO. Both my wife, Maggie, and myself have always maintained that we never thought it was a case of a man we had known for years being underhand and mischievously looking after himself at my expense. There was only one area that troubled me during the whole sad business, and that was Gordon's serious lack of support at the crunch meeting with the chairman. As I stated earlier, he didn't seem in the least surprised, or uncomfortable, with the scenario. Yet many other football people I know in the same situation would have loyally said: 'Hang on, chairman, this is not a done deal. Before we do anything, I want to have a chat with the big feller. Things need to be discussed. If he's not happy, I'm not happy.' If the roles had been reversed, that is exactly what I would have done. And if that had happened, I might well have walked away and relinquished everything at that particular moment. Bearing in mind that our relationship stretched over something like fifteen years, I think the little feller should have spoken to me in some depth and detail about the management switch before the final decision was made. I would certainly not have done anything to endanger Gordon's long-term position at Coventry and, if that had been an issue, I would have walked away. But I was left with no room for manoeuvre. As a consequence, many of our mutual acquaintances are far more suspicious and antagonistic towards Gordon than I have ever been. I've never spent my career looking over my shoulder. I don't regret bringing Gordon into the club at all. I just feel that he should have stood by me with more conviction when it came to crunch time. And that, as far as I am concerned, is the end of the matter.

There was very little evidence that my new role, with the grand title of Director of Football, was ever going to work – either for the benefit of the club or myself. As I stated earlier, the people able to make the important decisions refused to draw the guidelines or give me any encouragement. So it was a dead-end job or, maybe more correctly, a job going nowhere. I roamed around Europe a time or two, tipped off the club about possible targets without anything much happening, and scouted for Coventry within our own shores. Very pleasant, very cushy, but very unrewarding too. Yet I still argue that, if properly defined and with the right football-based person in the job, it can be of great value to the game in this country. On this one we must copy the Continentals because they have got it cracked. Only one man, and on a lesser scale than is practised abroad, has succeeded in filling the role, and that was Lawrie McMenemy in his latter years at Southampton. Mostly, in this country, we just play around the edges and that was very definitely the case at Coventry. My vision of the Football Director's job is to operate more in the province of the chief executive. The responsibilities should encompass being the direct link between the playing aspects of the club and the financial apparatus of chairman and boardroom. The duties, in my opinion, should involve taking care of all footballing matters, excluding the coaching, selection and preparation of the teams. That means long-term policy, dealing with player contracts, negotiating transfers once the coach has pinpointed targets, and generally creating a better under-standing and an easier working relationship between board-room and dressing room. Uli Höness, the famous German inter-national, for example, has carried out these tasks with typical efficiency and success at Bayern Munich. Abroad, it is the Football Director who is the man of power and influence while coaches come and go. It will happen in this country, too, and sooner than many people suspect.

CHAPTER ELEVEN

People I Wouldn't Go On
Holiday With

This, let me warn you, is destined to be the shortest chapter in the book. For one very good reason. It is a focus on some fairly high-profile characters I have long since swept with a fair amount of contempt out of my life, and for that reason alone I don't want to dwell too long on this particular subject. In polite terms, let's just say that all of them have been crossed off my holiday-invite list. They are people who have left me with an intense dislike of how they behave and treat their contemporaries. Fortunately for me, encountering this sort of character has been a mercifully rare experience, so it means this part of my roam down memory lane can be remarkably brief, if a little more brutal than usual. Tommy Docherty and Malcolm Allison, to name but two, have tended to have that raging-bull effect on me in the latter years.

By and large, I'm not the type of person to have regrets or misgivings. I know I have been a lucky bloke to have worked for more than a quarter of a century, collecting some very healthy rewards, in a job that is rightly the envy of most. Along the way, the vast majority of people I have mixed with and worked alongside have been perfect company and professional in their behaviour. However, in a business that is so volatile and success-demanding, you are bound to get a fair share of the mavericks. You are going to have the occasional falling out with them. In a game of passion and conflicting interests it's inevitable. I have had blazing exchanges of opinion with people I still regard as bosom buddies. But then again there's a minority who fill an entirely different category. They are the household names trapped for ever in the Atkinson no-go zone; the untouchables, as far I am concerned.

Top of the list is the aforesaid Tommy Docherty. It may, or may not, be a well-known fact that Docherty and I are just not compatible. In truth, it's perfectly reasonable to suggest I hate and despise the little so-and-so. These are carefully considered words that I don't use lightly and wouldn't direct at too many other people in my long career. I see Docherty as an opportunist who has leached off the game; a man who is nothing but a liberty-taker. I didn't have a cross word with him when I managed in the Midlands at West Brom and he was in charge of Derby County. At that time, it seemed, he wanted to be on friendly terms. But everything changed, very dramatically too, when I took over at Manchester United. For no useful purpose, or any justifiable and good reason, Docherty became the most venomous enemy outside the Old Trafford walls. I do believe that since United sacked him in the late seventies, he has become insanely jealous of any incumbent of that managerial chair. In the first place it was his immediate successor, Dave Sexton, who was treated to abuse. Then it was me. Next, and particularly in the early years, Alex Ferguson suffered a bucketful as well. His continuous sniping took place from the shelter of the local radio station or certain hit-and-run newspapers. The day I figured he was completely off his trolley was after I bought Bryan Robson and Remi Moses. His weird and wonderful remark was: 'I don't understand Atkinson – he only buys good players.' If you can work that one out, let me know. I've been trying for years. But, in truth, it was one of his kinder comments.

Now we all have opinions and there is no harm in that, and some of us enjoy working for the media, and there is nothing wrong with that either. Most of us, however, don't vary our opinions almost like mood swings dictated by whatever the demands of other interested parties might be at the time. But Docherty, the supreme opportunist, was more than content to fill the role of rent-a-quote and that's what bugged me about him. If the media wanted to slaughter some poor individual in public, it was just a case of reaching for the phone to get the Doc. You always had the impression that Docherty didn't necessarily have to believe the message. It was merely an activity to earn money at the expense of others. When I was still at the Hawthorns, Docherty was responsible for attacks on Dave Sexton that I regarded as disgusting. This, remember, was a manager who achieved the distinction – never to be repeated, I'll wager – of taking Manchester United into the Second Division and Aston Villa into the Third. Several other clubs suffered histories of serious decline under his management, and he swiftly dismantled Derby County's championship-winning team, disposing of outstanding players like Archie Gemmill, Don Masson and Bruce Rioch and replacing them with nonentities. And yet he had the brass neck to be judgemental about his peers while waiting for the cheque to arrive. Now, I dismiss his contributions, and they have fortunately become rarer, as the ramblings of a pathetic old man.

Malcolm Allison, a coach I truly admired, is another household name who was a serious disappointment in the end. I had regarded him, initially at least, as one of the major constructive influences on the game. But then, in the seventies, the decline started dramatically during the time he was in charge at Crystal

Palace and Allison completely lost the plot. I'm not talking of all that Barnum and Bailey stuff with the famous fedora and the rocket-sized cigars. That was all good fun in establishing a close rapport with the fans. There were, beneath all the showbiz and razzamatazz, more worrying trends. About the same time, Allison revealed traits that, eventually, undermined his well-established reputation.

I recall when I was running Cambridge United being invited to an end-of-campaign dinner for managers, at which Allison was the guest speaker. He had just returned from a stint in Turkey and was by then beginning to believe in his own myth, rather than being the bottom-line football man. Almost as soon as he was on his feet, big Mal was pontificating about every coach in England being a frightened man. He spieled on, dropping a few jaws along the way, about how the only way to approach a home game was to attack and put the opposition under the cosh from the start. And he delivered that little pearl as if it was some great revelation. I sat there thinking the thoughts of everybody else in the audience, and knowing that that was the tactic adopted by all managers anyway. At the time I could boast the most successful home record of any club in the country over the previous eighteen months. I knew how to play and so did all the other managers gathered in that room and finally I couldn't keep quiet. 'What are you trying to say, Malcolm? This is just too ridiculous for words.' Immediately, he took umbrage, but I wasn't in the mood to be silenced. 'This is all complete rubbish, just a load of gibberish.' He started to get aggressive and I interrupted him again: 'Malcolm, that won't do you any good either, so forget all the macho stuff.'

Some years later, we crossed swords again. He was helping out at Bristol Rovers and I was manager of Villa when we faced each other in an FA Cup tie. Typically, he tried to create the hype, get some cheap publicity, and earn himself a few headlines. At one stage it plummeted to the sewer-level propaganda you often see surrounding a big-fight promotion. Certain of his comments were personally disparaging and unnecessary, like: 'I would never regard Ron Atkinson as a friend. I much prefer the company of people like Bobby Moore and Terry Venables.' Whenever a Cup Final that I was involved in came around, he would be begging tickets or bumming his way into a VIP reception, and, yes, I always made him very welcome. I felt sorry for the feller and tried to be of assistance. But I don't remember too many of his so-called preferred friends offering him serious help, like a job for instance, and that must speak volumes about Allison's sad decline. He had achieved something deserving of the highest praise in his first period at Manchester City. He relied on some good, developing players, a sound tactical system, and a dressing room motivated by great confidence. You just can't fault that. Yet Allison distanced himself from those basic beliefs, and his second coming at Maine Road was an unmitigated disaster. He began to consider himself more important than his players, or, at least, that's the way it appeared. Allison portrayed himself as some sort of coaching guru, whose methods couldn't be questioned or faulted. If it wasn't the way to the madhouse, it was certainly the route to the unemployment queue. In the last ten or fifteen years of his career, I maintain that Malcolm Allison talked complete and utter nonsense. He simply became a caricature of his former self.

Generally, I have had reasonably good relations with players at my many clubs. At West Brom, for instance, there were footballers of the late seventies who still remain extremely close friends. But, as in all walks of life, there is always the exception and the exception at the Hawthorns was a defender called Paddy Mulligan. From the first moment we clapped eyes on each other the feeling was mutual, I suppose. I simply loathed the feller. Very quickly, I brought in Brendan Batson to replace him. It didn't disturb the dressing room morale too much because Mulligan was scarce on friends inside there as well. What I considered to be cynical sniping was a source of disruption; Mulligan appeared to have turned disharmony into an art form. To such a degree that, as we flew back from a game with the Portuguese club Sporting Braga in September 1978, Bryan Robson and Len Cantello approached me and almost demanded: 'Gaffer, you have to get that Mulligan out of here. He's just bad news.' I told them: 'Don't you worry, lads. You just concentrate on being the best in the business and leave the rest to me.' Colin Addison, my assistant, also raised the Mulligan issue, explaining that the player himself felt dispirited and left out of team matters. We set up a meeting. In walked Mulligan and almost before he had reached his seat, he tossed in the grenade: 'Boss, I don't think you like me.' Reply: 'Paddy, I can't effing stand you.' He suggested that might mean he would have to leave the club in the very near future. Answer: 'You can bet money on it.' As he left, Addison raised his eyebrows at the dialogue. I told him: 'That's how I feel about the situation. Players expect the truth; well, he's just got it.'

Within seven or eight months of my arrival at West Brom, Mulligan was history. When you have to release young players from a club it is always done with a heavy heart, but seeing Mulligan leave just made my day. He was an embittered pro who also, subsequently, betrayed his great mentor and idol Johnny Giles over arrangements for Mulligan's testimonial in Dublin. He broadcast that Liam Brady, then at Juventus, was going to appear, even though Gilesy had long known that was impossible and had told Mulligan that. The Irish public were let down and, in Giles's opinion, that was unforgivable. Mulligan was expelled from the magic circle in Dublin and, thankfully, he's hardly raised his head since. Good player – bad news.

And then there was Peter Barnes. He was a player I protected and promoted for much of his career, invited him into my home and family in fact, but I feel much happier about him now. Because I haven't seen Barnes since he crawled back under his favourite stone. That might seem a brutally harsh dismissal of any footballer, but I can still barely believe the kind of act he stooped to a few years ago. It was at the height of the bungs hysteria when accusing fingers were being jabbed at many a top-name manager. Every time a player moved, or so it seemed, the inevitable slur followed and I was the victim of one such unfortunate innuendo. Barnes was the culprit. He claimed that an underhand cheque was part of the arrangement when he left Coventry for Manchester United in the early eighties. It developed into an issue for public discussion when Barnes decided to go to the newspapers and sell his story. For a week, he made life very embarrassing for me, despite my closest associates begging the question: 'If there was something illegal, why has it taken Barnes ten years or more to reveal it?' Naturally, I took the obvious steps to protect my name and an FA Commission eventually cleared me of any wrongdoing. Later, an out-of-court settlement was paid to me after legal action against certain newspapers. But no amount of financial compensation could ever erase what I saw as a despicable betrayal by Barnes.

I had resurrected his career any number of times. I did feel seriously let down by Barnes. Docherty, Allison and Mulligan occupy a different category, but Barnes, for all his frailties, was someone I had considered close to me. I had raised and helped him throughout much of his football life, even when other people had questioned my support of what they saw as a seriously lost cause. Some of his closest friends, part of the same playing group, have told me since they now despise him for what he did to me. I can well understand their reaction. The way Barnes behaved was typical of a weakness in his character, the same root flaw that stopped him realizing his full potential as a player. He had an abundance of skill, but no strength of mind. That's what prevented him being a great footballer. He would always blame others, repeatedly offering the lamest excuse, for his own shortcomings. I always recognized that, yet still tried to help him as much as I could. Now, if I saw Barnes lying sprawled in the gutter, I wouldn't grant him a second glance. I would drive straight past. That's sad, isn't it?

The last name in this inglorious gallery is Harry Gregg, the former Northern Ireland and Manchester United goalkeeper and, in truth, a very accomplished performer on a football field. That, I'm afraid, is the only concession I could ever make for Gregg. In every other way, he had to be treated with a very wary eye. No, I'm being too polite here, what I mean really is he had to be treated with contempt. Certainly, that was my opinion when, what shall we say, our lack of mutual respect first developed during the mid-seventies. It all started when he was manager of Swansea and I was in my final hours in charge of non-League Kettering Town. We had drawn with the Welshmen at their place in the FA Cup and now we had them on home territory. For me there was added significance; it was to be my last game before my move into management at Cambridge. I was desperate for a farewell victory and the team delivered it perfectly with a 3–1 scoreline. But a wonderful night was tragically scarred by Gregg's touchline behaviour and a broken-leg incident that ended the career of my brother Graham, who was playing for Kettering. A fired-up Robbie James, then just a seventeen-year-old football rookie, made the most horrendous tackle and, as soon as Graham crumpled in agony, you instinctively knew it was all over for him. With such a complicated and serious injury he couldn't possibly recover to play again.

While he was rushed by ambulance to hospital, I had plenty of time to brood and reflect on Gregg's unsavoury contribution to what had happened. As I left the ground, Gregg just happened to be in the car park. The altercation couldn't be avoided and, amid the heated words and a few insulting curses, we almost came to blows. The situation was saved by the intervention of others. Everybody has different ideas on how the game should be played. I wouldn't like one of my sides to play the way Swansea did that night because at times the challenges went beyond what I felt were the normal and acceptable limits of tackling in the game. To this day, and Graham never did play again, he must have that weighing on his conscience. I admit I was emotionally charged when all this happened. Consider the factors. It was my last day at Kettering, a great Cup tie had been won, and there was my brother with his leg in bits. When I arrived at the hospital Graham, still in his full football kit, repeatedly kept saying: 'It's terrible, just terrible.' I tried to reassure him, telling him he would be back in business within a few months. By the time he complained 'it's terrible' for a tenth time, I lost patience. 'For Chrissakes, don't worry, the docs will sort you out and it will be okay,' I said. 'It's all right for you,' he answered back. 'I have been here for two hours now and nobody has even offered me a bloody fag. I'm dying for a smoke.' In even the darkest moments, Graham always possessed the depth of character to look on the bright side of life.

Gregg was funny, too, but in a very different way. Funny peculiar, if you know what I mean. And he never had the best of luck, did he? At least not when I landed the Manchester United job and he was already on the staff. To be fair to him, he didn't need much telling; he understood immediately he was Old

Trafford history. I understood then, that he had been critical of Dave Sexton, my predecessor. Throughout my career, I have always come down hard on what I call the backbiters in any club. Within the camp, words, hard words and even harder actions, have always been acceptable; outside that inner sanctum, the moaning and niggling could never be tolerated. That has always been my policy and, whatever Gregg's previous problems with me, on that score alone he had to go. I never wanted to be associated with him in any way, shape or form. Even the good times can be bad, as with my brother Graham's experience, but I've never been convinced the people I see as the bad guys could ever be good guys for me again.

CHAPTER TWELVE

Maestros, Mentors And Movers

In my managerial career, I have been very fortunate to have shared a fair bit of football history with some of the most famous and accomplished men ever to hold down the job. Sure, I was a little late arriving on the scene for the likes of Stan Cullis, Sir Matt Busby and, of course, the great Bill Nick – the wise and wonderful Mr Nicholson of Spurs. Two other legends, Bill Shankly and Don Revie, were also just about winding-up their time in the big league when, wet behind the ears but ready for any kind of action, I was moving in. But for all those illustrious names, I still consider that I came into competition, and occasional conflict, with the manager I can only judge as the greatest of all time. That class of one known as Brian Clough. I suspect more than a few people might raise a questioning eyebrow at this opinion and they are entitled to do exactly that. But if you consider Clough's achievements and, just as significantly, the places where he achieved them, I think my argument is sound. Two European Cups, numerous domestic trophies, plus League championships with both Derby and Nottingham Forest, clubs that are hardly among the most recognized of football's greatest institutions, are surely of the highest merit. It is an outstanding record, proof for all time of Clough's pure majesty as a manager, even if he behaved on occasions like the biggest screwball you ever met.

As anybody who ever got close to him will agree, Cloughie was always a very complex, often bizarre, individual. I don't mind admitting that I never really figured him out. For instance, when I first took control at West Brom, he was firmly established at the City Ground as the big shot of the Midlands football plain. At the time, though, the old Baggies had a pretty decent team, full of flair players, and we were very much part of the European scene. Forest, as well, were predictably enjoying life and, consequently, the two clubs were often thrown together. For some reason, Cloughie and his sidekick, Peter Taylor, took a bit of a shine to me, the upstart young manager now stalking their patch. Maybe they saw in me someone with a similar view of football and its over-pompous establishment. Anyway, whatever the reasons, we all got on famously well. Until Manchester United made me their manager in 1981. It was as if I had been beamed to another planet overnight. Cloughie simply cast me aside. Unless it was a business conversation that couldn't be avoided, he never spoke to me once and, as for the social scene, forget it. I was shunned, an outcast, and for a while I was baffled and a little miffed at the unexpected treatment. I had been declared a non-person by the great man within his immediate circle of friends and associates. The exclusion zone lasted for roughly five years. Then, within a month of my sacking at United, I had to go to Forest on a TV assignment. As soon as I poked my nose through the front door, I was welcomed like Cloughie's longest-lost pal. He ushered me into his office for a drink and I couldn't shut him up. We talked for almost two hours. That was life with Brian, a wonderful, charming, unfathomable oddball.

The fact that I didn't exist for him during half a decade

probably confirms the view that Cloughie had a fixation, amounting almost to a grudge buried deep inside his soul, about United. People much closer to him than me have suggested Brian always felt that, once Sir Matt's time with the club was over, he should have been given the job. And maybe he should, at least on his stature and record at the time. My other theory about Cloughie, though, is that if he had been installed at one of the major city clubs, a Liverpool, an Arsenal or even a United, his peculiarly individual management style might perhaps not have been half as successful. He could not have ridden roughshod, a bit like a blacksmith with attitude, over certain areas and factions within such differently structured places. He always ruled his players by enforcement and fear and, no problems there, Cloughie might have got away with that whichever dressing room he dominated. But the methods and manner of approach he adopted with directors, for instance, wouldn't have been accepted by men of great stature in boardrooms, where toleration levels were not as relaxed.

Leeds, for instance, was a disaster just waiting for Clough to arrive. It could never work for him; that job, any contemporary would tell you, was mission impossible for him. It lasted just forty-four days and that's about forty three longer than I would have given him. Before he arrived at Elland Road, Clough hadn't just been critical of Leeds, he had been downright abusively insulting. He had slaughtered their top players publicly with sneering judgements and remarks they would never be able to forget. Typically, Cloughie ignored all that and took the job on. Mind you, he had good reason. At the time he was working at Brighton. Nice place, shame about the football! He just felt out of the game's mainstream, he needed the buzz again, and that's what fatally tempted him back to his native Yorkshire and Leeds.

With other equally media-conscious clubs, there would also

have been ambushes waiting to happen. While Clough could, at a time of his own choosing, be an extremely valuable source of stories for journalists, he rationed them to suit his own moods and purpose. He would stubbornly go for weeks without uttering a syllable to the press, even at the traditional after-match press conferences. Now, anybody who has operated in football at Old Trafford, Newcastle, Merseyside and some of the London clubs, must accept that wouldn't work. You have to be aware of media responsibilities on an almost daily basis. The newspapers and local radio stations have a big audience to feed and they are highly demanding of a regular news supply. Cloughie, doing his own thing, would soon be under the cosh as, I have got to say, rapidly happened in that ill-fated stay at Leeds. That's the nature of the man, though, a complete, twenty-four-carat oddball. For all my admiration of his success, I would never recommend a soul to copy his management approach. You might look at any number of other managers and suggest there is something for the learning curve within their particular style. With Brian, just forget it. I know one or two of his ex-players have fallen into the trap and clambered out, just, when they realize their terrible mistake. While management is, in the final analysis, about being your own man, there will only ever be one Brian Clough. Nobody else should attempt to do the job his way, unless they fancy seeing the white-coat visitors on a fairly regular basis.

This feller, may I remind you, had the mind games sorted out long before dear old Fergie had heard of the phrase. Let me provide you with one example that, in the long term, gave me some amusement and helped me settle a score with such a consummate wind-up merchant. At Forest, he had a snug-fit arrangement for his own dugout: smack, bang on the half-way line. The visitors were accommodated, for want of a better word, somewhere on the outer edge of the city limits. Or that's the way it felt at the time. Our dugout, in fact, was in the most inaccessible, damned awful place miles on the other side of Cloughie's tunnel, a lousy vantage point which gave the impression you were watching the game from behind the goalmouth. So when I first went there with West Brom, I challenged him. 'What's that all about, Brian? Why don't you give us all a decent dugout position to do our job?' He just looked at big Pete, a sneaky, knowing grin on his face, and left me standing there without an answer. Okay pal, I thought to myself, if that's the tune, we can both play it. Back at the Hawthorns, when Forest arrived for the corresponding League game that season, I dropped lucky. The ground was being redeveloped and half the main stand was incomplete. My dugout, a real state of the art affair, had been priority. There it was, finished, just the job, and right on the half-way line. The idea was to erect a temporary shelter for Cloughie's entourage just a few yards away. Oh yeah! That morning I grabbed the groundsman and gave him instructions. 'See that mudheap down there, with all the JCBs and wheelbarrows, and girders and planks on the ground, and the knee-deep sludge? Now that's where Mr Clough wants to be,' I told him. 'And another thing. When you get over there, nail down that bloody dugout so King Kong couldn't move it. Know what I am saying?' We won 2–1 and, even better, the rain gods were on my side and it bucketed down all afternoon. When it was all over, I waited at the top of the tunnel as Cloughie trudged from the farthest point of the ground, plastered in mud and soaked to the skin, Pete and him looking like two drowned rats, until they arrived back. I shook their hands and simply asked: 'You moved that dugout at Forest yet?' Then I turned on my heel, gave them that little sly smile, and left them to it. You couldn't allow Cloughie to win all the psychological battles, or you were doomed. For all of that, though, he was the greatest boss our game has ever known.

He was also a total contradiction: the extrovert who behaved like an introvert, and I have often wondered if he had allowed himself more outlets whether it all might have been very different for him. He committed himself to almost the self-isolation of a hermit. You couldn't even get him on the telephone, except via a go-between who vetted every call. Of course, Clough had his own coterie of close friends, but I always felt it might have been wiser for him to seek more involvement in football's social scene. His great hero was Frank Sinatra – I sometimes suspected he tried to behave like him, too. You know: the deliberately adopted appearance of being a little distant, a bit different from the rest of us, that air of mystery, if you like. The occasion of a Wembley Cup Final comes to mind when, just like Frank, he made a grand exit before anybody else. His Forest players were still climbing the ceremonial steps when Brian, regally waving to the crowd, took the acclaim on his way to the tunnel. When he beat Malmö in the European Cup Final, he couldn't resist another gesture either. His team did their lap of honour and then Cloughie, with Pete by his side, insisted on doing his own. Not, you must acknowledge, the behaviour of a normal, everyday manager. But, for all the oddities, one clear, unquestioned fact is that Clough had a brilliant grasp of the game not granted to most mortals. His secret was his ability to turn tactical complexities and instructions into a very simple message for his players. There is a myth that he never actually went near Forest's training ground. That I don't accept. In five minutes flat you could see that all his most famous sides were the most coached and rehearsed teams I have ever watched. Even if you clad them in the Bayern Munich strip they would have been instantly recognizable for what they were: a Cloughie side.

For example, he honed into an art form the gift he had of transforming into outstanding performers players most clubs shunned as lost causes. In that category Kenny Burns, a blessed player but at times a character you wanted to curse for his behavioural problems, is a prime case. For a while, Clough made sure Kenny was one of the finest defenders in the country and kept his maverick tendencies under control. Maybe he did it with the same kind of intimidation that saw Trevor Francis, within hours of becoming England's first £1 million player, ordered to make the tea and play for the A-team. Then, of course, there was the classic reinvention of John Robertson. At one time he might have been discarded as a down-and-out inside forward. Shrewdly, Clough nursed his development until he emerged as one of the most intelligent creators I have ever seen. The Forest system of play was shaped around his particular skills as the wide-left midfielder and link to Clough's front play-ers, the vital unit in their success story.

Once he finished, and when he was still far from being an old man, it was sad to see Cloughie suffering from health problems. The stories are legion in the game that it was all down to drink. Personally, I can't give an answer. All I can say is that in all my time with Clough, amid all the rumours about him being drunk at games, I never saw him under the influence.

In selecting Clough as my No. 1 manager, I have to concede that the most popular manager of all time has to be that other idiosyncratic genius, Bill Shankly. Nobody is immortal, but Shanks lives on down the decades, his legend increasing almost by the month. There isn't a single crust-earner on the after-dinner circuit who doesn't rely on at least one Shankly homily to get his act rolling. There are literally dozens of them, all of them hilarious, but none seems to be quite so funny when recalled by someone else as when they originally fell from the lips of the great man. My earliest experience of Shanks was when I was just kicking off at Cambridge and he had already slung the boots in the corner and finished at Liverpool. If ever I wanted some sound advice, or even an emotional lift on a rough day, I would reach for the phone and call Bill at his home. I always made sure that John Docherty, my first-team coach at the time, had the extension clamped to his ear as well. We would spend many an hour doing that, most of it with the pair of us in stitches listening in on Shanks's stories and experience-bred philosophy of the game. He would never hurry you impatiently off the blower and you always felt ten times better, like a man reborn, when the receiver was finally back resting in the cradle.

Another manager I was forever seeking advice and help from at that time was Billy Nicholson at White Hart Lane. He had this dour, grimly determined image but Bill was one of the most illuminating advisers you could run to. As a young hopeful in the management business, I was never too shy to seek out the people who had been there and done it. They were of enormous help, too, when I wanted to pick their brains to try to unearth all the trade secrets.

The last time I sought out a bit of professional back-up from Shanks was when I was embroiled in the transfer pursuit of Bryan Robson. I bumped into him while I was in charge at Old Trafford, where he was taking a look at John Toshack, one of his young management protégés, who was managing Swansea. Before the game, we plonked ourselves down for the usual cup of tea and talked and talked and talked. It was always like that with Bill. The issue of Robson inevitably cropped up in the conversation and, being totally honest, it was at a time when I half suspected we might be stymied in the signing attempt. I just threw Shanks a line, asking him: 'If it was you doing the buying, what would you pay for Robbo.' He didn't hesitate for a split second, replying: 'Whatever it takes, son, go get him. Just pay the money.' If I ever needed any words of advice to reinforce my opinion, Shanks provided them. Sadly, within ten days of our chat, he passed away. Eventually, we secured Robson's transfer and his performances, both for United and England, were clear testimony to Shankly's judgement.

Much earlier in my management, I would regularly extend an invitation to Bill to join West Brom on their football travels. He was great to have around, a wonderful influence on the players, and they would listen like grandkids at the fireside as he poured out his Liverpool stories. As I have already made plain, capturing that biting, home-truth humour of Shankly is very difficult if not impossible. On one trip, though, I found Willie Johnstone, the great Scottish winger, almost on the floor of the bus in a hysterical, laughing heap. He had just told Bill that Newcastle had fifty-four professionals on their books. Shanks, laconic as ever, had replied: 'Aye, son, that's right, but most of 'em cannae play. They are just helping to shrink the dole queues on Tyneside.' That was just typical of the man. You never quite knew whether he was being funny or deadly serious. And, on reflection, I'm not too sure Shanks did either.

His successor at Liverpool was Bob Paisley. This, believe me, was The Fox of football, as cunning and cute as any manager to walk the planet. He did everything simply based on experience and nobody, before or since, had more of that particular quality to draw on. Folklore grew around Bob, until he seemed to be enveloped in a certain air of mystique. He could, apparently, watch a racehorse – and that was his second abiding love – or a player, and tell you instantly if either was suffering from injury. Even, I have been assured, if something nasty might happen to them in the near future. It might sound spooky, but by carefully assessing a footballer's running style, Bob could detect if he had cartilage damage. That, though, was only part of Paisley's incredible breadth of knowledge. He knew football backwards, forwards and sideways. In terms of winning medals and collecting trophies, if not in personality, he was the Jack Nicklaus of football. I don't think his record of achievement and honours is ever likely to be equalled, only envied. Some have questioned whether, if Bob had left Liverpool at any time, he could have been as successful at another club. Who knows? The question doesn't arise, really, because his success at Anfield made certain they would never release him anyway.

I can't say I had too many dealings with Mr Paisley, except when I played against his teams with United. But I did have an input, a secret until now, in his great Wembley farewell in 1983. That was Bob's final season and, if you recall, Liverpool beat United in the Coca-Cola Cup Final. I nudged Graeme Souness and suggested: 'Let the boss go up for the Cup – it's his last big day, isn't it?' Souey took the hint and ushered a bashful Bob up the famous steps for the presentation. The papers got it slightly wrong, praising Souness for his noble action and rightly so, but I also like to think I played a proud, if relatively small part, on Bob Paisley's glorious retirement day.

The whole of football, certainly the management fraternity anyway, could not ever have wished for anything better, I suspect, than the spectacle of my big pal Jim Smith – the Bald Eagle himself – finishing his career with a Cup Final flourish. He is among the most popular guys ever to earn a crust in our business and there's arguably as many anecdotes doing the rounds about Smithy as there are about Shanks. He can tell a few himself, with relish and panache too, particularly late into the night and preferably with a glass of red wine in one hand and a ten-inch Havana in the other – while sweating buckets and appearing as though his forehead has sprung a leak. Believe me, Jim is a sight to behold and a real bloke's bloke. He it was who inspired me to return to the game after the frustration of that fiasco at Coventry. Just watching him revelling in everything at Derby stirred in me the yearning to have another crack. All that wheeler-dealing for foreign players, turning out a team playing good stuff, that swanky new stadium, well, it just triggered the old adrenalin rush again. Irresistible, don't you think? Smithy, mind you, has always been a great act to follow and nobody has been more worthy of his recognition and success. His football teams were never anything less than solid, dependable, attractive outfits, guaranteed to give value for money. A measure of the man who, in truth, genuinely deserved to be given an opportunity with one of the major clubs. Okay, I am aware he managed Newcastle United but that was long before they were launched back into orbit by Sir John Hall's financial clout.

Talking of which reminds me of a hilarious night with Jim at a country club dinner a few years back. It was a function in honour of Jim's achievement in raising little Oxford from the Third Division to the old First Division, a fine piece of stewardship that should never be disregarded. Smithy had a few words to say, but the main speaker was the late Brian Johnston, the legendary Jonners of fancy cakes and cricket fame. Next on the bill was an excellent comic called Roger de Courcy, better known for his TV ventriloquist act with Nookie Bear. Roger's first mistake was setting up for business right alongside Jim's position at the top table. The next was thinking he could get away with such a foolhardy notion. Because, very swiftly and fatally, Jim became engrossed in the behaviour of Nookie Bear, a fascination maybe encouraged by some very fine claret. The rest of us, ball-gowned ladies and dinner-jacketed men, could have packed in and gone home. Jim was oblivious to all of us. As far as he was concerned it was Nookie and him alone in that room, and Nookie was telling jokes. And Nookie, it seemed, had taken on a human scale. Every time Nookie told a joke, Jim just roared with laughter and punched it right in the face, almost lifting poor old Roger off his feet. With the rest of us almost crying on the floor, holding our aching ribs in laughter, this poor little puppet ended up looking as if it had done ten rounds with Tyson. And Rog was getting more than a little miffed. In the end, he turned to me and almost pleaded: 'Hey, for pity's sake, tell yer mate it's only a bloody doll and it's only made of papier mâché.' At which Smithy smacked Nookie once more. Maybe it was just for luck and if it was no manager has ever earned a helping hand more.

Lawrie McMenemy was someone who generously gave me all the advice I needed in my early days in the job. For years he had a huge input at Southampton, first as a manager and then in an administrator's role. Nobody has pioneered that relatively new concept better than he did at the Dell. In the early eighties he turned away from the obvious temptation of managing Manchester United because of his long-time attachment to the south coast club. When I was approached instead, he called me and urged me without hesitation: 'Don't worry about anything at Old Trafford – just focus on your football beliefs. Everything will come your way if you do just that.' It was a message I obeyed to the letter and it was always the philosophy I shared with anyone else moving into a new position with daunting responsibilities. You might say it's the one thing I got off the back of a Lawrie! But, joking apart, he was always the manager I would speak to before I sussed out and tackled any new, possibly difficult issue.

Another confidant in those far-off days was John Bond, a very different, more volatile type of character than Big Mac. But when I was at Cambridge and a day off cropped up, there was only one place to find me. Down at Norwich watching Bondy doing a training set-up; he was simply fantastic at it. I consider Dave Sexton the best coach I ever saw, but the boy John was not far behind in his technical and tactical knowledge. Sadly, he was probably the biggest under-achiever I have ever come across.

The trouble with Bondy was that he was just too erratic. No, he was worse than that – at times he was plain crackers. He wouldn't know his mind from one day to the next, and was capable of a complete mental somersault in his opinions of players, teams, transfers or anything else you cared to mention. He could be a charmer, but you never knew what was coming next. When I was at West Brom, I invited him up to see us play Leicester in a League Cup fixture. Naturally, the invitation extended to the boardroom after the match. Suddenly, I felt a tug of the sleeve and one of my directors urged me into a quiet corner. 'I can't really believe this,' he whispered. 'Is that John Bond supposed to be a friend of yours? Because he's just told the chairman, "Mr Millichip, if you are ever looking for a new manager, I would be very interested in the position." Thought you should know that.' I just laughed. 'That's Bondy – he can't help himself. When he opens his mouth anything can come out.' He proved that again when we shared the Manchester soccer scene for a little while. It was almost a war of the back-page headlines between City and United. His time at City was very brief, and it was very sad to see him go, because he had a lot more to offer at Maine Road than he ever achieved. He should never have walked out as impetuously as he did, particularly over a private matter that was unrelated to football. Even in his Norwich days, where he elevated a quiet backwater club to rare prominence, he used to tell me: 'I don't need this. I can do without it. I would be better off horse racing.' There was only one reply: 'John, you don't do anything better than what you are doing now. Think about it.'

As a manager he was very much a disciple of Ron Greenwood and had learned well the lessons of the West Ham preacherman. I always felt, in those impressive early years, that he would have made an excellent England coach. His technical knowledge was superb and, at least in the short-term, Bondy might have got away with his fundamental weakness – man management. He never learned the art of diplomacy, of dealing with individual players differently, or of engaging the brain before running off at the mouth. We could always have a laugh together, but some-times a slip of Bondy's lip would provoke a problem. He button-holed me at my daughter's wedding in September 1987 and berated me about all the mistakes I was supposed to have made at Manchester United. It was embarrassing for a start, and not the most sensitive moment to raise such a topic. Bryan Robson, in the end, really laced into Bondy and he walked off still muttering to himself. He didn't make contact for years after that. Then, while I was at Villa, a third party called and asked if I could find some scouting work for John. It wasn't a problem. I told Brian Whitehouse, my chief scout, to expect a call. None came. For the next five or six weeks, Brian informed me that he had attempted to track down Bondy at various telephone numbers without success. The latest info had been that he was running his son Kevin's sandwich stall down in Southampton. I thought nothing more of it. Next news, the local paper in Birmingham has Bondy slaughtering me: 'Ron let me down.' The claim, of course, was that I hadn't helped out an old mate with a job to give him access back into the game. It was untrue, but mud sticks. When I later challenged John about the story, he said it had all been distorted and taken out of context.

Big Lawrie, on the other hand, was superb at man manage-ment, and if these two had ever joined together they could have been the managerial dream team. Lawrie never had the same football background, or maybe it was an indoctrination, that Bond had. His start was at Bishop Auckland, and later his development continued under Alan Brown, that terrifying spectre of authority in north-east football. But if his upbringing was not quite the classical route of so many managers, Lawrie was blessed with the secret of handling big-time players and getting them to fulfil their potential. At Southampton, he once had a first team boasting six England captains, thus giving birth to an often-asked sports quiz question. Eventually, a fateful touch of sporting sentiment, and a longing for the homeland maybe tempted Lawrie to take over at Sunderland. It was hard to resist but, with hindsight, surely it was also a mistake. If he had remained at the Dell, I am convinced he would have finished up as chairman and maybe that's the direction he should have followed.

The perfect partnership is a matter of elusive chemistry, and many a club has been thrown into confusion and chaos down the years in search of it. But here I have an admission to make: I would have sacrificed a lot of other rewards if, at some time in the past, and much earlier than happened at Villa, I could have worked in tandem with Dave Sexton. For me he's the top man, an untouchable coach beyond any other, and I have cast an eye on many of the world's most renowned figures down the years. I have never seen anyone able to teach the game better than Dave. He had just one handicap: he was portrayed as a reclusive, dour and unapproachable man. Never has anybody been more unfortunately miscast. Dave's one of the nicest, funniest fellers I have ever met. I even had him crooning one of his favourite Old Kent Road songs to the Villa players and he went down a bomb. But whether he was showbiz, or just deadly serious, it did not matter. Dave was always a football man with an ability and enthusiasm second to none. He was an ideas man, not the airy-fairy type either, but a brass tacks operator with an amazing focus on inventive coaching and not just the functional stuff. In other words he was able to open the eyes of players. He didn't work them, he trained them to understand the precious secrets of how to really play. Dave's was always a morning's teach-in and never just a practice. I can't think of any better example than Dwight Yorke. Yorky was always a talent but Dave, as I said earlier, opened his eyes and made him aware of team-mates and other options out there on the park. Since then I have sometimes watched Dwight do something in a game and thought quietly to myself: 'Yes, I remember that session. That was pure Sexton.'

Long before he arrived on Villa's staff, Dave won trophies of his own. He also spent many years on the fringes of the England set-up. That was no less than a tragic waste. He should really have been the coach with our national squad and we might well have benefited from the technical renaissance in our game a lot earlier. He was unlucky not to be champion twice over, nudged into second place both at QPR and United. He was sacked at Old Trafford and I arrived. There again, on reflection, that was another error of judgement. They should have made me manager, kept Dave out of the media scrum as first-team coach, and United might have latched on to the winning formula a lot sooner. And, yes, that is a serious observation.

Very much of the same knowledgeable generation was John Lyall, another with an incisive football brain. His most significant years were spent with West Ham and even when John left for Ipswich, he didn't stop being the guy who kept blowing bubbles. A true Hammer, in fact. As rival managers we had a fairly close professional releationship, reinforced by a secret little ritual we both felt brought us a touch of luck. It started when I was at West Brom and John's mob knocked us out of the FA Cup in 1980. Every single round after that, I made sure I sent him a best-wishes telegram. They carried on all the way to Wembley, finishing off with Trevor Brooking's famous headed goal that beat Arsenal and won John his precious tin pot. A couple of years later, by which time I had reached Old Trafford, my United beat his United in the third round. It was John's turn to pay for the telegrams and, you've guessed it, we went all the way and lifted the FA Cup after a replay with Brighton.

I have always kept in touch with John even after he decided he had had enough of the game. It's sad when football orientated people like him distance themselves from the trade in which they are so proficient and so badly missed. I know John is a bit of a handyman, with a relish for doing all the jobs that cost me a fortune around his big pad. He loves fishing, too. But, really, he should still be involved. There is a well of information there which the game shouldn't allow to remain untapped. When we have these talking-head management courses, it's the likes of John who should be doing the talking. Point one is that he is a deep thinker on football. Points two, three, four and five, are that John Lyall has actually put his thoughts and philosophy into practice and succeeded. And that, end of argument, is the whole point.

As Dave Bassett so aptly phrased it, the game is now populated by the designer manager. You know who I am talking about. The big name who just steps off the pitch, takes off the sponsored boots, and walks straight into a high-profile manager's position. Most of them are independently wealthy and don't need the game any longer for their daily survival. This can be both good and bad in a manager. Firstly, I concede, it is a strength that they won't scare easily; or be pressured and panicked by a boardroom suddenly getting heavy. Why? Well, for the simple reason that they don't need to take Smart-money Bloggs's wages and his chairman's bluster. On the other hand, though, and for that very same reason they are more likely to pack their bags and walk away at the first hint of difficulty – simply because they don't need the job anyway. I don't want to sit on the fence, and I genuinely do see both sides of the proposition, but for me there is real merit in learning the management side at all levels. I soaked up more information, all of it very valuable later in my professional life, in my first six months as a manager than I did in fifteen years of playing. And most times at the small-fry, lower-league clubs cash is so scarce you need to do every job under the sun; and that constitutes the fastest learning curve I know.

Danny Wilson and Alan Curbishley have followed the old pattern and they are men I truly admire with, I hope, guaranteed futures. The new-route boys are, obviously, the breed of Kenny Dalglish, Kevin Keegan, Ray Wilkins and Bryan Robson, all of whom have enjoyed varying degrees of success from the sensational to the eminently satisfactory. In all honesty, I suspect the favoured candidate, in selecting from the tried-and-trusted or the celebrity name, depends on the club and the circumstances. Robbo, for instance, has given an incredible impetus to Middlesbrough in a very short time. There have been anxieties, disappointments, a rumpus or two with foreign imports, and three trips to Wembley, and the once disillusioned, driven-away Teeside public have come rolling back to the Riverside. With a lesser personality, a lower-profile manager, that probably wouldn't have happened. The starting point for the revolution was Robson himself.

No argument, though, the most successful of this generation, at least as we approach the millennium, is Dalglish. Nobody was more gobsmacked when the announcement was made in the mid-eighties that Liverpool had decided to place their faith in Kenny and he was appointed as player-manager. His record as a player bears any kind of scrutiny; in simple terms, he was one of the all-time greats. That reputation was determined by his own matchless temperament and skills, whereas his future in management relied on others. But here too he was fortunate. At Anfield he inherited a fabulous side and was blessed in having good people around him and a proven, ready-made establishment to cushion his progress in the early formative days. Then he quit, another bolt out of the blue for me. It was after that epic 4–4 Cup result with Everton in 1991 and, once again, it was an announcement that stunned the rest of football. But this was a man who had already endured the heartache of the Heysel disaster when he took it upon himself to make sure nobody walked alone in the aftermath of the mind-numbing tragedy of Hillsborough. He involved himself in counselling, carrying the burdens of others on his shoulders for a little while at least. How much the experience of such traumas, that most of us, mercifully, have never known, influenced his decision to step down at Anfield, only Kenny himself knows.

He might, with the wisdom of hindsight, have chosen to seek a breathing space, a period of recuperation and mental regeneration away from the club. Then, revitalized, Kenny could have returned and continued the Liverpool dynasty. When he opted to walk off the golf course and take on a much more demanding challenge at Blackburn Rovers, there was the inevitable question: Could Dalglish do it on his own without the formidable assistance of the Anfield machine? Well, he didn't take too long to deliver the answer. It came at Ewood Park, when he fulfilled Jack Walker's dream of turning a small-town, unfashionable club into the champions of England. The churlish claimed he had lottery-loads of money to work the miracle and, it's true, he did. But didn't Kenny spend the fortune well? Most of his signings were durable types who served their purpose and got him his money back when the time was right. More than anything, though, he sussed out the goalscorers he needed and, in all fairness, so he should. Not many ever surpassed Dalglish as a front player and his influence on Alan Shearer and Chris Sutton, not to mention Mike Newell in the early days, was evident for all to see. The rest of the team, a solid base of discipline and organization, was clearly the input of Ray Harford, Kenny's No. 2.

At Newcastle, another largely unexpected development following the sudden departure of Kevin Keegan, Kenny's story has been somewhat less than a football fairytale. But, in his first two years, it should not be dismissed that he twice led the club into European competition, even if both times it was a much shorter experience than he would have liked. He felt the transition had to be made from Keegan's all-singing, all-dancing regime to a more pragmatic approach, and, in that respect, one issue about Dalglish is beyond contradiction: his deep, well-founded football knowledge. He was always a soccer nut, you know, not just a player relying on the personality cult and his own legend. I'm told he has action-packed videos by the score and carefully studies players from across the world in his search to improve any team he manages. The only thing that bugs me about Dalglish is the sight of him on the box. I sometimes feel like screaming at the screen: 'Kenny, why don't you do us all a favour, including yourself, and lighten up?' He doesn't need to be so obstructive and evasive, even cussed, in his approach to an essential part of the job – public relations. This is, after all, an entertainment industry in which we are paid handsomely to work. Dalglish is known as a wind-up merchant and it's my view that he has always taken a perverse joy in being the media's most awkward customer. Keeps him happy, even if most of the time he looks downright miserable.

His long-time mate, and eventual successor at Anfield, was

Graeme Souness. And a wild, wild, impetuous boy, I might add. But whatever criticism was ever levelled at Souey, and at times it was delivered by the crane load, he was always a man prepared to stand alone. Remember, too, he was the single, immovable force that galvanized and revolutionized Scottish football. In his time as Rangers manager he had nothing less than a monumental impact. He was bold, courageous, ambitious and, yes, also impetuous because that has always been the nature of the beast. With all those qualities, he raised the status of Scotland's favourite pastime throughout the football world. Players who would never have dreamed of a trip to Jockland, except for a fleeting holiday, couldn't wait to join the Rangers squad. Who else, for example, but Graeme would have had the guts, the sheer bravado, to persuade Mo Johnson to join Rangers when Mo had already stage-managed a press conference, vowing a return from France to his old club, Celtic? Well, Souey did without a blush, a blink or a thought for the fanatics who wouldn't normally walk down the same side of the street as a Catholic. That, for me, was a quality in the man that made up for any of the minor faults in his nature. Souey said to hell with tradition and the bigoted, intransigent past, and always enjoyed modern-day life, preferably if it was in the fast lane.

Maybe on his return to Liverpool Souness moved just a little too fast. He was in a desperate hurry to turn his beloved club around. And when that happens, things fall off and get lost along the way. He had been shaken and saddened by what met his eyes when he walked through Anfield's doors. As a home-coming member of arguably the finest club side there's ever been, he found it particularly galling that, in his own fiery opin-ion, certain players didn't feel the same passion he had never lost for the Liverpool cause. The old impetuousness crept in and trapped him again. Maybe he alienated a few of the senior pros when, with a more cunning approach, he might have used them for the immediate benefit of the team. As John Bond once advised me: 'Use players until they are of no further use – then eliminate.' Not the nicest of sentiments, admittedly, and just a touch brutal for my taste, but I understood Bondy's cynical message. Maybe if Souey had adopted the same theory he would have survived longer and the likes of Bruce Grobbelaar and John Barnes wouldn't have been so upset by his methods. For individuals like that, strong-minded and opinionated themselves, he was just too, what shall we say, up-front in style. He did, though, perpetuate the grass roots development at Liverpool that had begun in Dalglish's era. The club did not have a reputation for producing their own young players and Kenny changed that, by launching a different approach. Souness displayed the courage to carry on his work and to give the likes of Robbie Fowler, Steve McManaman and, later of course, Michael Owen a platform for their talents. Now Liverpool can boast about their own kids as much as they do down the other end of the East Lancs Road.

Alex Ferguson, of course, has had them falling off a conveyor belt – almost at birth, some of his most loyal disciples would like you to believe. But, like Souness, Fergie was an impetuous tartan arrival when he took over my job at United. In his latter years at the club, although never completely eliminating the mood swings, he has taken a much mellower stance on the job. His appointment at Old Trafford inevitably proved something of an eye opener as he very rapidly discovered that simply because it was United, it didn't automatically come with the territory that they would to win all their League games. Not even against the likes of Norwich, Wimbledon and even humble Oxford. No, this was very definitely not comfort zone fixtures at, say, Arbroath or Falkirk. So we all heard about the verbal volleys, dressing-room rollockings and the christening of Fergie as the Hair Dryer. I suspect Alex considered himself fortunate to have survived those four or five rough years. Inside the boardroom, maybe because a successor wasn't to be seen on the horizon or, more praiseworthily, through an element of far-sighted wisdom, patience prevailed and it paid off. I think in those testing early days, Alex may also have reflected on some of the hasty and unnecessary comments he had made about my regime. They were scathing and, when it came to pointing fingers at the fitness and discipline of my players and they were ill-advised. If, indeed, a crackdown on fitness and discipline was necessary, and if one was applied, I must say it took some considerable time to have any impact. Let's just say we all had to wait until the nineties for it to have any discernible effect.

Compliments are more my style, not barbed, back-biting comments, and I have to confess that Fergie has had a huge influence on the United empire. The turnaround in their fortunes was massively rewarding, both financially and in terms of trophies, and his place in history has rightly been assured. His success is based on a number of managerial strengths including single-mindedness, dedication and a fearsome will to win. But, having conceded all of that, I also think that two other prime figures were a major factor in his achievements. One, of course, was Brian Kidd, an outstanding coach and organizer who willingly embarked on regular tours of the famous foreign clubs of Italy, Spain, Germany and Holland and returned with tips on technique, training and tactics to pass on to United's players. The other – could we ever forget him? – was Eric Cantona. His transfer had an element of fluke about it. The initial enquiry was from Leeds, who were interested in Denis Irwin. When that was swiftly knocked back, the dialogue swung to Eric and the deal was done. I suspect his signing effectively changed everything for United. You need a bit of fortune to be a long-time winner and that was Fergie's stroke of luck. As I recall, United weren't exactly the football experts' fancy for the championship when Eric arrived – a player who had hardly been rated at Leeds, but who found in Old Trafford the sporting domain that suited him perfectly. If there is such a thing in football, to use the tired cliché, he was a marriage made in heaven for United. And Ferguson. Cantona added a crucial extra dimension and his presence was massively influential on the likes of Ryan Giggs and the rest of the youngsters who responded to his guidance and inspiration, both in the Premiership and, equally important, on the training ground. Eric, above all things, was a dedicated athlete who treated his trade with the utmost professionalism. And the kids learned to do the same.

In his time at United, Fergie shaped and moulded several teams. All were impressive in their own way, but the one with so many talented young players in it rightly sticks in the mind. They were raised in the right manner, very much under Alex's stringent, no-nonsense code, but also benefiting from a valuable backroom guru called Eric Harrison. He was one of the best signings I made in my five years with the club. When I was shown the door, Eric stayed and subsequently had a masterful influence on the likes of David Beckham, Nicky Butt, Paul Scholes and the Neville brothers, Gary and Phil. He might never have figured in a back-page headline in his life, but Eric was a coach whose contribution to United's dominant seasons should not be underestimated. Yet, while an admirer of youthful ability, my own favourite United team were the Double-winners of 1994. The team with Andrei Kanchelskis and Ryan Giggs playing wide, Eric and Sparky down the middle, that hard-as-nails back four, and Keano and Paul Ince scaring the living daylights out of many a midfield. Wonderful they were, and Alex has a right to be proud of both their collective skills and their combative nature.

Fergie himself, as we all have learned, loved to be a little, er, combative when the mood took him. He picked on me once and picked on the wrong target. He accused me of letting a story out to the press about Gordon Strachan's impending transfer when, eventually, he finished up at Leeds United. I was innocent and I was angry. To this day I can remember the exact response I bawled down the phone: 'Alex, you can forget anything like that and if you don't shut up, I'll be across there to shut you up. You are not talking to one of your silly footballers, you know, so I suggest for your own safety you shut up.' Later that same day, to be fair to the feller, Alex rang back to apologize. The transfer leak, he had discovered, had nothing to do with me. The incident was dead and buried. That's Alex. He blows hot at times, and he is a very passionate man. It's what has made him the most successful and revered United manager since the unsurpassable Sir Matt Busby.

CHAPTER THIRTEEN

Dream Team

Now we arrive at that favourite national pastime for every football fan in the land: grabbing that pen and a scrap of paper and scrawling on it, slow as you like, the old Dream Team. We all have one, plucked from memory and a number of golden moments, and no two of them are ever remotely the same. Which helps considerably in generating the interest in the first place. Me? Well, given an hour or two of quiet contemplation – and another year or two of due debate and consideration – I reckon I could select three or four. And that's simply picking from the chosen few who have operated under my management at various clubs in the last three decades or so. No, it's not that easy, not for me anyway. Too many favourites, that's my trouble. And, naturally, squeezing so many talented candidates into a single, magnificent, all-time-greats eleven had me racking my brains and almost wasting a whole ruddy forest in team sheets. But, forced into a corner with the selection pistol pointed at the temple, I have finally come up with a 4-4-2 formation, a side of power and flair, that I believe could tangle with any of the legends in British football history and deliver a respectable result.

In the goalkeeper's jersey, there's only one for me, and that's

Mark Bosnich. When I first brought him in at Villa I wasn't too sure about him. Bozzy was a bit on the hefty side and an Aussie with attitude to boot. But, after only a brief period of assessment, I knew what I had on my hands: the most accomplished keeper I ever had the fortune to work with. Later, his form was so impressive, I was left with another conviction that never left me. For a long while I have felt Mark was blessed with the ability to be the greatest exponent of his particular trade throughout the world. On one proviso. And that is being able to tame his suspect, sometimes volatile, temperament and keep it under control. When he was with me, I have to acknowledge he wasn't perfect. Few footballers are, in truth. Like any young keeper, and like most others in the maturing years, Mark was prone to making errors of judgement. But he had been granted a natural ability that few of his breed ever possess. Some keepers can save you games, and I have had a few of them in my time. Bozzy's great gift was that he could actually win you matches by making saves that were beyond expectation. Correction, that were beyond belief. He enjoyed one fantastic spell on the way to Villa's League Cup Final win against Manchester United when he was stopping penalties at a phenomenal rate. He had an athleticism and spring that mere mortals couldn't even dream about. Okay, Boz has dropped some horrendous clangers down the seasons. I've never suggested he was invincible – more precisely, that he was simply incredible. Most modern-era keepers are placed under the kind of surveillance that would have had the Stasi drooling because television's all-seeing eye allows nothing to escape, even less to be forgiven. Legends such as Gordon Banks and Pat Jennings might have been less revered in the nineties because, like anybody else, they were guilty of mistakes and they, too, would have been subjected to life under the media microscope. And that's never been easy.

At right-back, I have scribbled down the name of Roland Nilsson without even a second thought or a backward glance down memory lane. Why? Well, because this talented Swedish chap is the most consummate professional I have ever met in my life. I don't want to embarrass him too much, but Roland was a man without a flaw, and so many gifts he even gave me an inferiority complex. One story from my first spell with Sheffield Wednesday epitomized Nilsson's presence as a very rare personality in football. We were on an away trip down in Ipswich, staying in a fairly comfortable hotel with a grand piano in the lounge. Some of our lads started clowning about, attempting to play it in their own inimitable, plink-plonk fashion. Honest, it was just like a Les Dawson concerto and cats from miles around were suddenly heading abroad. Suddenly, Roland appeared, immaculate and looking like somebody out of a Bond movie. Over he strolled to the piano, flexed the fingers through a few practice notes, and then, with the aplomb of a Hallé virtuoso, started playing some wonderful classical overture. One of the lads, peering from behind a pillar, said it all: 'Roland, tell me please, is there anything you can't do?' Well, he certainly could play tennis and, another sickener, he looked like Stefan Edberg doing it. The blessings of the gods have clearly been bestowed upon him throughout his life. I signed him from Gothenburg for just £350,000 and soon discovered him to be a footballer who lived his career according to a very strict professional code. His lifestyle was right, he kept to the proper foods and even weighed his breakfast portions to the ounce. You could easily describe him as Mr Perfection but he was never a goodie-two-shoes or a bore about it. His value as a footballer was based on maintaining a good fitness level, being a superb team player and having a knack for cleverly reading any defensive danger. He could pass and tackle with the best of them; just an all-round performer really.

The character I would have playing alongside him in my back-four would, I suppose, be considered an invader from a very different planet. Paul McGrath, of course. He constantly defied every rule, written down or just accepted practice, in the game of football. In the last ten years of his marvellous career Paul, in theory, should never have been allowed on the pitch. Manchester United tried to persuade him to accept an insurance pay-off in compensation for his long-standing knee damage in 1989, yet he survived close to the highest levels until the winter of early '98. He was, in anybody's language, a phenomenon whose great power, will to win, desire, coolness under the severest pressure, and athleticism put him in a very rare category. Paul wasn't just a centre-back, although in that role I have seen none better, but could operate as a fullback or as a holding player in midfield, where Jack Charlton preferred him in his years of outstanding achievements with the Republic of Ireland. His boozing exploits were a byword in the game, and his defiance of all medical laws beyond belief, until you just had to see him as Supermac.

For years, the other central defensive partner would have been Ally Robertson, a vastly underrated performer from my first period at West Brom. If Ally had played for a more renowned, big-city club he would have collected bundles of caps for Scotland. But in more recent times that long-held judgement had to be altered by a close-up assessment of Des Walker. Incidentally, his favourite player, he told me, had always been McGrath, and these two in tandem would be an almost impenetrable barrier. I am the first to admit that until my second spell at Sheffield Wednesday, where I inherited Walker as one of the team's bigger names, I had always considered him an overblown talent. That opinion rapidly altered within weeks of arriving at Hillsborough except, I have got to concede, in five-a-sides. In this particular area of training-ground preparation he must remain the worst player I have ever come across – an assessment that will always be like a stab to the heart for walkabout Walker. But that, sorry Des old son, is the reality. You were crap. And another thing about him. He was the most awkward, cussed, argumentative player I met in years; a complete pain in the butt. I doubt if I have ever known a player so contrary. He could cause a row in an empty house, particularly on the subject of defensive technique or tactics. If you wanted him to push up, he insisted he should be dropping off. This man, believe me, might have represented the world at nitpicking. But could he play. His only weakness was distribution, and that was never as poor as some people suggested, but it was always counter-balanced by Des's pace, agility, tackling success, and a competitive spirit that couldn't be surpassed. It puzzled me that Glenn Hoddle ignored him for England's squad for the '98 World Cup in France. Walker would have strolled it.

The final place in my bomb-proof back line does not even bear argument. Again from my West Brom days it has to be Derek Statham and, yet again, I maintain that with a higher-profile club he would have boasted seventy England caps instead of the single-figure recognition he received. He was a magnificent performer and that very handy Scottish winger, Willie Johnstone, always said: 'Statham's the only player in the country I would pay money to watch.' Now, coming from a Jock, that's got to be some compliment. The only thing Derek didn't have was an element of luck. It cost him a move to Liverpool that would have set him up for life and guaranteed him a wider appreciation society. He failed the medical and that was the toughest call for Derek to take because it was almost as if he had been born for Anfield's controlled passing game. In truth, he was a calibre of defender who could, without a shadow of a doubt, have played in any great team in the world.

Gordon Strachan is next on the list. When he arrived at Old Trafford, he was barely twenty-seven and yet Alex Ferguson allowed me to sign him on the basis that wee Gordon's legs had gone. Never has such a myth been more emphatically exploded. Think about it. He played another thirteen years of top-level football after that and, although he never collected the hero grams he deserved at United, he was lauded along the rest of his personal route to glory and lasting fame. I still recall the sight of Strachan, already past his thirty-ninth birthday, tearing the defensive heart out of Spurs in one of the finest displays from a wide midfield player I have ever witnessed. It's never been easy unearthing that type of creator who understood the job properly. Gordon knew it to the letter and also realized that it demanded a lot of sweat and graft to do it well. On the field, he never failed me.

Neither, I might add, did my next midfield selection, the awesome Norman Whiteside. Only injury, as with Statham, denied him a fully rewarded career at the highest level. According to Strach, big Norman was the best player he ever played alongside. That kind of credit rating might puzzle a few people who considered Whiteside only an archetypal hard man. It was a description that was a curse on his name and a thoroughly undeserved scar on his reputation. Norman, no question, was able to look after himself but he could never be placed in the category of football hatchet-men. He had great vision, an exceptional football brain, and a mental picture of what was happening, second by split-second, in every game in which he played. Apart from all of that, he was also a clinically smooth finisher. Remember that fabulous Wembley goal when he bent his shot around Neville Southall, using a defender to screen his true intent, to win the FA Cup for United against Everton in 1985? His knowledge of the game was without flaw, too, and he was a great lad who I made captain at just twenty without a shred of concern in my mind. As I have always insisted about Norman, if he had been born with just a yard more pace he would have been a genuine candidate as the world's best ever player. I don't jest, either.

His central midfield partner just has to be Bryan Robson. Everything that has ever been said, written, or whispered behind closed doors, remains a litany of his greatness. I need say no more.

Outside Robson, though, must stand a player who, for maybe a season at the Hawthorns, outshone even Bryan himself. Laurie Cunningham was a footballer of such poetic balance I used to say he could race across a snowfield without leaving a footprint. He also had an inner conviction that success depended on a strong work ethic and he wasn't going to make it purely on the basis of being an outstanding athlete. Laurie was a misunderstood character too. Outsiders suspected that he had a chip on his shoulder, but that was more the public impression of a shy man and a studiously reflective thinker. He had some fabulous years, including a period with Real Madrid, but injury overshadowed the season when he should have been reaching maturity. Then, with a dramatic and tragic suddenness that stunned us all, his life was ended in a car accident in Spain. But I'll never forget the golden months when Laurie achieved that sublime level of absolute control over his game; a plateau reached by a very exclusive few. But with his inclusion forging the last link in my two banks of four, across defence and midfield, I have a good shape, plus a launch pad where there is pace to burn, physical strength, class and invention, individual matchwinners, and a goalkeeper possessed of the potential for world status. Just imagine in front of such a combination the most powerful and dynamic front players of the last twenty-five years. Many a defender would retire on the spot and I drool at the very thought of it.

First of all there is Mark Hughes, the complete warrior-footballer. He was always such an excellent exponent in the art of holding the ball in vital attacking areas, linking the play and feeding team-mates in for crucial strikes at goal. No one mastered it better, in fact. He wasn't the quickest, mind you. But as his ally up the sharp end I have Cyrille Regis. He could hold the ball up, too. Regis could head it, Regis could win it, Regis could dribble, and, no argument, Regis was the quickest. Now that's a fearsome pairing that would have caused absolute terror among any defence, particularly when supplied with the high-calibre ammunition from the men behind them. I can think of only one word to describe such a force – unstoppable. On reflection, I have worked with two other front players who might have challenged big Cyrille and Sparky for their place in my Dream Team. I'm talking here of Andy Gray and Trevor Francis and they, too, would have represented a sensational partnership. Trouble is, when they landed up at my training grounds, both Andy and Trevor were well past their supreme best.

With the eleven picked and in place, the next major question to arise is filling the places on the subs bench. No problem here, either, except in the elimination of quite a few candidates who might have understandably expected better. The keeper is again an easy pick in Gary Bailey, another cut off in his prime by injury. When that happened, he swiftly headed back to his native South Africa, forging a lucrative career in television, but not before leaving a big impression in my mind. On joining United, I questioned Gary's ability and made moves to replace him with Peter Shilton. Inside a week or two I readily reversed that opinion.

Gary was a much, much better operator than some would have you believe. In fact, he was top drawer. Steve Staunton nails down the position of defensive sub because of his comfortable manner as either a left-back or central defender and, at a pinch, midfielder. Next in the selection line stands Arnie Muhren, a total-footballing Dutchman who must consider himself a mite unlucky not to make the first pick. He was one of the classiest performers you could ever wish to see. Frank Stapleton, one of Arnie's beneficiaries from that can-opening left foot, gets the nod, too. For a couple of his early United seasons, Frank was arguably the best target man in Britain. For the last ball in the bag, we go abroad to one of the most exciting players Europe has admired in recent decades. I didn't have much time with Paulo Futre because his ultimate boss and mine – the notorious Jesus Gil – hurried me off the premises at Atletico Madrid. But in my brief time in Spain, I saw in him the spark of genius. It must have been much like the experience Sir Matt Busby enjoyed when Besty was in his pomp at United.

So, there they are, not merely the good but in every measurable aspect truly the very greatest of my management years. And yet, and yet, there remains one serious regret. The one you could never get your hands on to place in your team, take on the world and bring home the trophy loot. In my case, that elusive star was Ian Rush. I shudder to think what I might have won with Rushy in the firing line for either Manchester United or West Brom. He would have provided me with such firepower it chills my blood to think of it even now. You only have to consider the composite parts from which are forged the great strikers. Alan Shearer and Gary Lineker are classic examples of an invaluable breed. Shearer, for instance, always relied on a hard-driving style and eventually wore down rivals to the point where they turned up their toes and he grabbed his great goals. Lineker was a lurker, always drifting on the last man's shoulder; a predator in the purest sense. So let's mix the potion and see what represents a combination of the two. Well, in my mind, there is an answer – Rushy himself. He was a grafter, the best defender in a No. 9 shirt there's ever been, while up the other end he was lethal. If he got the ball in the box when facing one of my teams, I suffered one reaction: I just looked away, hating the inevitable, and knowing that he wouldn't miss. Now if only I could have got him around a bargaining table at some time in my life … the stuff of the sweetest dreams. Still, I can't complain too much, not with only one real regret in all the millions I traded and the famous names I signed. It was a dream, but I still have my fireside Dream Team to keep me warm.

CHAPTER FOURTEEN

Dream On

Dreams, I reckon, constitute roughly seventy-five per cent of the make-up of any true football man. Or is it really just pure, undiluted fantasy? Maybe for most of us that is a little nearer the mark. Whatever your point of view on that particular subject, it was the distant, if generally unreachable, possibilities that lured me with such irresistible influence back to the game in the late autumn of 1997. Much, I must acknowledge, against the wishes of my wife Maggie. Now, throughout our marriage Maggie has never been anything less than fully supportive in any decision I have ever taken in relation to my job. She wondered, for instance, if it could ever work with Doug Ellis at Villa, but she never stamped her foot and said: Don't do it. Equally, her realistic position on the second-coming of Sheffield Wednesday in my football life was very similar. She thought it was maybe unwise and that after twenty-five years in football management, the best career move was finally to stay out of it. There I was, revelling in a bit of day-to-day freedom at last. Some TV stints, a round or two of golf, the odd commercial opportunity, sunshine breaks whenever we felt like it, the whole damn shooting match was, in fact, mine. In other words, a financially secure retirement dream-world. The uncomfortable, driven-out feeling that filled my mind in the final months at Coventry had started to fade. What the hell, you might ask, possessed me to take on another pretty dicey Premiership post when I had such a soft option in my late fifties? Think about it and you should get it in one. Dead right, it was that dream again. The magnetic, mesmeric attraction of turning a football possibility into a reality. It's the bug no self-respecting boss worth the name has ever been able to resist.

It was for that reason, and that reason alone, that I found myself back on the doorstep of Hillsborough – with the permission of the missus, of course. Actually, I am now hurrying ahead of myself. Because, in the immediate weeks before my return, I had been offered a tempting alternative. A few foreign offers had come my way via the grapevine of contacts and agents but, having taken stock of my new lifestyle, they were never too high on the agenda. But when some very nice people within the Northern Ireland FA started to make noises about leading their national team in the European championship qualifiers, I listened, and listened seriously. This was a part-time apppoint-ment and was really worthy of consideration. More and more, its appeal grew, and following several telephone conversations, I even arranged a face-to-face meeting with an Irish delegation one weekend in October. I never made it and, just maybe, it was the old hand of fate that intervened. For the first time in absolutely ages, I took Maggie to the local cinema. The film was that box-office smash, *The Full Monty*, set, of course, in Sheffield. We laughed until our ribs ached, partly at the film and partly at what Bert McGhee, the old Wednesday chairman, had once told us. He promised we would love Sheffield because it reminded him of Rome. Now I have heard of virtual reality, but the Eternal City and the Steel City being twinned? Apart from the similarity of a few hills scattered around the place, you just have to be joking. Must have been all that industrial haze that blocked out the view of the Tyke Coliseum and the granite-block Vatican, I guess! Seriously, back to the story. As we were leaving the cinema, the car phone clicked in and, immediately, there was a very significant message on the answer machine. It was a representative of Dave Richards, the present-day chairman at Wednesday, and the request was simple: Would I be interested in rejoining my old club? The next day, Dave travelled down to see me and, after a very brief dialogue, offered me the job. He urged me to take a three-year deal, but I resisted. I figured a wait-and-see arrangement was better for both parties. My argument was that I should go in as the fireman, try and douse the relegation flames, and then assess how the building stood. Eventually, it was accepted I should take over team responsibilities until the end of the 1997–98 season. One concern was the potential for adverse reaction from the Hillsborough fans, some of whom were unimpressed by my departure from the club a few years earlier. Dave Richards reassured me. He explained that in a recent radio phone-in, I had come in as the landslide candidate to replace David Pleat.

Another management contemporary, Jim Smith at Derby, was undeniably the inspiration for my return to the game. Before joining Wednesday, I regularly popped across to see Jim's team playing such enthusiastic and enjoyable football. I figured if that old sod was still up to it, then why not me? Mind you, when I think back and reflect now on exactly what I took on at Wednesday, it's enough to chill the blood. When I arrived, they weren't just stricken, they were stranded, well adrift in the Premiership with a paltry nine points from the first thirteen games. I have often thought since that, if I hadn't been stoked up with so much passion and appetite for a new challenge, I might have been more sensible turning my back and walking away. But it wasn't like that at the time. As I got to the ground on that first comeback Saturday, with eventual champions Arsenal the opposition, my driver turned and said: 'Ron, I haven't seen you this excited about anything in years.' He was absolutely right. The result was right, too, as we beat the Gunners on one of those fairytale days that have always made this football job so worthwhile. From that early, significant bridgehead of success, though, my whole focus was nothing less than survival. The huge lift was the reward of four back-to-back victories that hoisted us out of the problem zone. Apart from Arsenal, our home victims included Manchester United and a couple of fairly comprehensive defeats of Spurs and Newcastle. Away from home territory, admittedly, the form was far more worrying. But safety was assured, ironically on our travels, when we beat Everton 3–1 at Goodison Park on 25 April, two weeks before a gritty, transitional campaign was wrapped up. Had the start of Wednesday's season not been so bleak and unrewarding, we could have ended somewhere in the top seven.

Along the way we recruited a few players who, if my personal convictions are justified, should forge the strength of Wednesday in years to come. Mostly they were imports from abroad, including Niklas Alexandersson, Goce Sedloski, Emerson and a richly talented kid called Francesco Sanetti, the last two arriving, along with Earl Barrett from Everton, on free transfers. The first two – the Macedonian defender Sedloski and Alexandersson – were desperately unfortunate to suffer serious injuries that prevented them from completing the first season. But I always saw them as the base rock for the future. Alexandersson, in particular, was truly impressive before he needed the dreaded cruciate knee ligament operation. Big things can be expected of him. It was a former colleague, Mick Brown, later to be appointed Manchester United's chief scout, who tipped me off about the Swede. At the time, Mick was employed by Blackburn Rovers. He said they had the full hit of midfield players, otherwise he would have advised a bid for Alexandersson. You don't need a steer like that more than once. We watched him and immediately saw the quality. We also discovered that he had a clause in his contract at Gothenburg that allowed him to leave for just £750,000. Enough said, deal done.

Another pal, this time Phil Black, gave me the nod about Emerson. He said he had skill, a bit of fire and real enthusiasm, and was just my sort of player. And he was Brazilian. Couldn't resist it, really, could I? The lad had been at Benfica, playing there with a Portuguese passport, but because of that famous club's financial problems there had been complications. Put simply, he walked out to save his career. Emerson, like so many foreigners, wanted to play in England. At first, he tried Stoke and Huddersfield. Neither could afford him. When I saw him play money was never the issue. Honestly, I swore on that first day he could be another Paul McGrath. There was the same physical power and skill level and the rest is basically down to ambition. But, just remember, this was a gem found by the roadside – because his cost to Wednesday was no more than the wages. At first, I signed him for three months. Rapidly, that agreement was torn up and the new one was for two years. The last one to be thrashed out was a three-year package.

Another who sneaked under the wire as a totally free investment was the Italian teenager Sanetti. Once again, the network of friends able to influence events, enlisted over years in the game, paid off. Young Francesco was with Genoa and first emerged as a special talent when he was acclaimed player of the World youth tournament in Italy, in a competition which included, incidentally, the cream of Manchester United's kids. He was allowed to escape under a loophole in the Italian regulations which granted their footballers, if they had not been signed as full-time professionals, permission to leave the country on a free transfer. Their loss was undoubtedly Wednesday's gain. This lad, only nineteen when he arrived, is a real technician.

So, also, is one of his fellow countrymen, Benito Carbone. You know something, he might lack Juninho's stamina, but I see him as a cleverer footballer and certainly much better in the air. Then, excuse me, but we come to something completely different. That man Paolo di Canio. Only I never called him that. I had a different name for him – the Volcano. Believe me, he should have been born with a four-minute warning. Did I have problems with him? How long have you got? But, like Carbone, I would never describe him as anything less than an immense talent. Paolo never stops running the gauntlet, whether it be with the establishment or his manager, but he has such passion and enthusiasm it would be interesting to see how he performed with a real top-league team. My ambition, given an admittedly brief amount of time, was always to try and prove that very point with Wednesday.

By the end of the season, after a couple of informal chats with the chairman, I had decided to give it a go for another year. My future was apparently secure until at least the summer of 1999. Or so I thought. I have to accept, albeit with some reluctance, that time must eventually run out on my management days sooner or later. But when I talked to Dave Richards, with relegation avoided and more rebuilding plans in place, there were still more than a few embers of ambition glowing within my heart. I thought, and it was a smashing thought, what an adventure it would be to attempt to take Wednesday to Wembley again. Or launch them back into Europe. You see, more dreams. Can't live without them, can we? The other objective was grooming a successor and, no, the experience with Gordon Strachan at

Coventry was never remotely a factor in deterring me from taking that route again. But then, when everything seemed so serene and settled, my management life was devastated by a decision that can't really have a logical justification to this day. I was out of a job – once again. And I was, frankly, deeply perplexed by the whole affair. It was, I don't mind admitting, like an explosion ripping me apart. Maybe, just maybe, I helped detonate it myself. That I will truly never know, but I'll leave you to consider the facts and reach your own conclusion. The first time I left Wednesday, in the late summer of 1991, I was accused of being a Judas. On the second occasion, seven years down the football road, I was able to demand an answer to a very serious question: Who might they now finger as the true traitor of Hillsborough? It certainly couldn't be me, that's for sure. I was desperate to stay. My deep commitment was very much focused on developing the Wednesday revival and taking this major club on to greater achievements. I felt I could look on the bright side`of life once more. How wrong can you be?

On that FA Cup Final weekend in mid-May 1998, when Arsenal secured their second Double with an accomplished victory over Newcastle United, I was left feeling numb with betrayal. I had been let down, sadly and some might conclude savagely, by weak men I believe should have been stronger. It was as difficult a situation for me to come to terms with as I have ever known. Rarely in my career have I felt more disappointed with people I had long considered to be decent, straight-talking types. They kept telling me they were, anyway, and maybe I was mug enough to believe them. Now I know why they had to keep repeating it so often – perhaps they were trying to convince themselves it was true. Whatever these pinstripes in the board-room might think now, I can tell them my own emotions were captured by two words – sheer disgust. I had been sold out, and

I can't be persuaded otherwise, for a few pieces of silver.

The exact price, around £500,000, was the cost of goalkeeper Kevin Pressman's fumble at Crystal Palace on the final day of the '98 season. It allowed Palace's Clinton Morrison to score and, instead of finishing thirteenth in the Premiership we dropped down to sixteenth. In financial terms, the prize money also dropped from £1.3 million to a touch below £800,000. Within an hour of that match-turning incident – and, no, Kevin I don't hold you personally responsible because mistakes happen in football – I could hear the muttering classes going on about the implications. It was then that I began to wonder whether it was me, and not the unfortunate Pressman, who was destined to pay the heaviest price. I rapidly discovered the answer. What chairman Richards and his cohorts failed to take into account, of course, was a greater financial issue. I, just remember, had been head-hunted to save them from relegation, not to win the championship. And that's exactly what I managed to achieve. If Wednesday had dropped out of the big league, it would have cost them between £6 and £7 million pounds. In reality, they were in profit. So I kept my side of the bargain. I kept them up with, of course, the valued assistance of first-team coach Peter Shreeves and the players. To the best of my knowledge, the chairman and his directors never kicked a ball.

After the Selhurst Park result, I felt a considerable change in the boardroom mood and attitude towards me. It had all been so different seven months earlier, when Wednesday had made their approach, with Mr Richards prepared to go on bended knee in pleading for me to return to the club. 'Ron,' he begged, 'you just have to come back, and we have to stay up. We're all looking down the barrel.' With only nine points after thirteen games, they were dead meat. And they knew it. I agreed to take over and, with a swift rallying of the troops, combined with a bit of tinkering here and there, the Wednesday revival got under way. In October 1997, I politely rejected the chairman's offer of a three-year contract, though he insisted the deal was the bedrock of his club's future. I urged caution and advised him: 'Let's wait and see, take stock when it's all over and we are safe. That's the time to take the decision.' Wednesday, after all, surely wouldn't want me on such an extended agreement if I had taken them down into Division One. But I never considered, not for the life of me, the alternative scenario – that I would be sacked after keeping a seriously threatened team in the major league. They should have been more than satisfied with my contribution to the cause. Well, shouldn't they?

Towards the end of the season, with relegation avoided, the chairman asked me about my future plans. I indicated I wanted to stay. Also I intended recruiting Nigel Pearson, a former Wednesday player, as a manager-elect. For at least a year I would groom him to take control`in the longer term. Fine, said the chairman, although he tossed a few alternative names into the pot. After a further twelve months, I told him, I would reflect on my position once more. A couple of weeks after our conversation, the club made me an offer which I had to refuse. It was worth considerably less than my existing wage agreement. It was, in fact, plain ludicrous. The chairman, maybe feeling the boardroom pressure, bleated on about the lost half-million pounds. Finances were tight, he said. No money for players, blah, blah, blah. The vibes were extremely negative and it was then that I first wondered if I would be around much longer at Wednesday.

On the eve of the Cup Final, Nigel Pearson, just back from a short break in New York, called and asked if we could meet for a chat about his new role alongside me at Hillsborough. I told him: 'You had better hang fire, Nige. Something funny is going on here. You might get the job on your own.' He insisted his prime motive for returning to his former club from Middlesbrough was to work alongside me. Come Saturday night, after I returned from Wembley, I decided I had to nail the truth, so I rang the chairman. There was a lot of bluster from him, simply a discussion going nowhere, so eventually I laid down the challenge: 'If that's the way you see it, maybe we should call it a draw.' His answer put me in the dole queue. Well, not quite, but you know what I mean. I felt driven out, almost like a criminal, despite constructing the solid foundations for a second time for Wednesday to re-emerge as a significant football force. They now have, with one or two adjustments, the right side on the field. It's the one off it that really worries me.

As for myself, it's difficult to predict what is going to happen. All I will say is that when my football management days finish I won't leave the game completely. The attachment, whether through media work or some other involvement, will continue. Thanks for your time – and see you at the back post!